Better Homes and Gardens®

101
Best-Loved
DESIGNS
from
Cross Stitch &
Country Crafts™

Better Homes and Gardens®

101

Best-Loved

DESIGNS

from

Cross Stitch & Country Crafts®

BETTER HOMES AND GARDENS® BOOKS
Des Moines, Iowa

BETTER HOMES AND GARDENS® BOOKS
101 Best-Loved Designs from Cross Stitch & Country Crafts

Editor: Carol Field Dahlstrom
Project Editor: Susan Banker
Art Director: Gayle Schadendorf
Copy Chief: Eve Mahr
Senior Writer: Barbara Hickey
Senior Graphic Designer: Rebecca Lau
Technical Editor: Colleen Johnson
Administrative Assistant: Peggy Daugherty
Contributing Technical Illustrator: Chris Neubauer
Production Manager: Douglas Johnston

Editor-in-Chief, Book Group: James D. Blume
Director, New Product Development: Ray Wolf
Managing Editor: Christopher Cavanaugh

Meredith Publishing Group
President, Publishing Group: Christopher Little
Vice President and Publishing Director: John P. Loughlin
Vice President, Retail Marketing: Jamie L. Martin
Marketing and Ancillary Sales Director: Maureen Ruth

Meredith Corporation
Chairman of the Board and Chief Executive Officer: Jack D. Rehm
President and Chief Operating Officer: William T. Kerr

Chairman of the Executive Committee: E.T. Meredith III

All of us at Better Homes and Gardens® Books are dedicated to providing you with the information and ideas you need to create beautiful and useful projects. We guarantee your satisfaction with this book for as long as you own it. We welcome your questions, comments, or suggestions. Please write to us at: Cross Stitch & Country Crafts® magazine, Better Homes and Gardens® Books, RW 235, 1716 Locust Street, Des Moines, IA 50309-3023.

Cover: Photograph by Hopkins Associates

Our "Mark of Excellence" craft seal assures you that every project in this publication has been constructed and checked under the direction of the crafts experts at Better Homes and Gardens® Cross Stitch & Country Crafts® magazine.

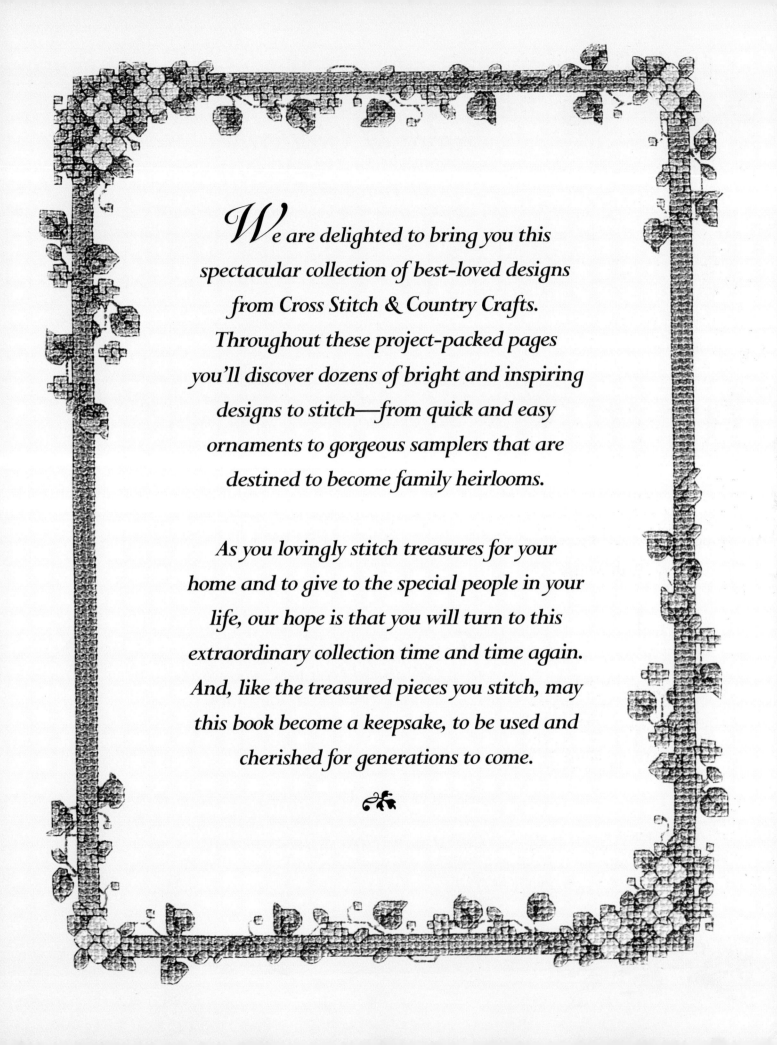

We are delighted to bring you this spectacular collection of best-loved designs from Cross Stitch & Country Crafts. Throughout these project-packed pages you'll discover dozens of bright and inspiring designs to stitch—from quick and easy ornaments to gorgeous samplers that are destined to become family heirlooms.

As you lovingly stitch treasures for your home and to give to the special people in your life, our hope is that you will turn to this extraordinary collection time and time again. And, like the treasured pieces you stitch, may this book become a keepsake, to be used and cherished for generations to come.

Table of Contents

Floral Fancies

Grace your walls and tea table with colorful blooms.

Holiday Treats

Add a special touch to every holiday gathering.

Sensational Samplers

Radiant samplers to stitch and give with love.

Needlework Necessities

Fun-to-stitch pieces to delight stitchers or seamstresses.

All-Time
FAVORITES

*F*rom busybody cats to the relaxing pastime of fly-fishing, all of the clever designs in this chapter have a personal meaning when stitched for someone special. Or, choose any of them to stitch for your own all-time favorite.

Cats, Baskets, and Quilts

Cats are extremely curious creatures and each one has its own personality. Our portraits, stitched on 14-count ivory Aida cloth, show three distinct felines against backgrounds of traditional quilts. One appears cute and innocent while bathing, one sly and mischievious getting ready to investigate, and the other is contently sleeping. Complete instructions and charts are on pages 15–17.

Antique Trains and Planes

Create a nostalgic duo by stitching these two handsome pieces on 14-count antique white Aida cloth. Metallic threads and attention to detail makes these wonderful old steam engines and war airplanes come to life. Complete instructions and charts begin on page 18.

Nature in her finest hour—
The kiss of life 'twixt
flight & flower

Hummingbird Sampler

These exquisite hummingbirds are all aflutter, stitched with brilliant shades of blending filament. Binoculars won't be needed to watch these beautifully colored birds, stitched on 28-count ivory Jobelan, as they float in the air around a cascade of pretty pink fuchsias. Complete instructions and chart begin on page 21.

Botanical Fruit

Reminiscent of historical textbook etchings, our botanical fruit series is stitched on classic 28-count antique white Jobelan fabric. Each fruit—the glorious pear, magnificent apple, and regal plum—features subtle shadings of color within the bounteous branches. For an added stitching challenge, the tiny backstitches of the line drawing and lettering are stitched over one thread of fabric. The complete instructions and charts begin on page 25.

Prunus domestica

Malus pumila

Pyrus communis

Prunus domestica

Flies and Lures

As a tribute to a favorite pastime, stitch this colorful piece that any angler would love. A variety of fly-fishing motifs were used to create this wonderful sampler stitched on 25-count oatmeal Floba fabric. As an extra reminder of the sport, stitch a paperweight to hold important messages. Instructions and chart begin on page 28.

14

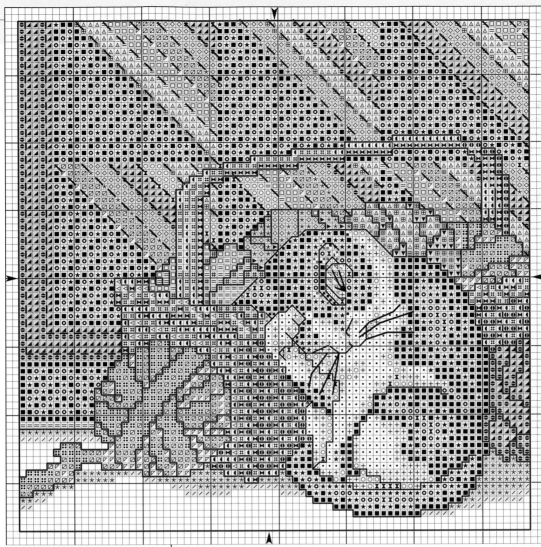

AMISH CAT

As shown on page 8.

MATERIALS

FABRIC

11x11-inch piece of 14-count ivory Aida cloth

FLOSS

Cotton embroidery floss in colors listed in key

SUPPLIES

Needle

Embroidery hoop

Desired frame and mat

INSTRUCTIONS

Tape or zigzag edges of fabric to prevent fraying. Find the center of chart and center of fabric; begin stitching there.

Use three plies of floss to work cross-stitches. Work all half cross-stitches using two plies of floss and stitching in direction of the symbol. Use two plies of floss to work the backstitches and straight stitches unless otherwise specified in the key. Press finished stitchery from the back. Frame and mat as desired.

AMISH CAT

ANCHOR		DMC	
002	•	000	White
897	◢	221	Shell pink
403	■	310	Black
979	▽	312	Light navy
399	○	318	Light steel
978	☑	322	Pale navy
100	▶	327	Deep antique violet
977	⊞	334	Dark baby blue
235	✕	414	Dark steel
398	+	415	Light pearl gray
358	⋈	433	Light chestnut
1046	◖	435	Dark chestnut
362	⊞	437	Medium tan
878	#	501	Dark blue green
877	=	502	Medium blue green
875	☐	503	True blue green
1041	⊙	535	Ash gray
885	◁	739	Pale tan
359	◐	801	Coffee brown
273	★	844	Beaver gray
045	⊜	902	Garnet
073	◺	963	Rose pink
871	✴	3041	Medium antique violet
870	◇	3042	Light antique violet

ANCHOR		DMC	
888	▼	3045	Dark yellow beige
887	⊞	3046	Medium yellow beige
886	△	3047	Light yellow beige

HALF CROSS-STITCH
(stitch in direction of symbol)

871	⟋	3041	Medium antique violet

BACKSTITCH

897	╱	221	Shell pink–border (3X)
403	╱	310	Black–cat
382	╱	3371	Black brown–basket weave
382	╱	3371	Black brown–basket outline and weave shadows, rag balls, edge of quilt

STRAIGHT STITCH

403	╱	310	Black– cat's eyes and nose (3X)
273	╱	844	Beaver gray–ear tuffs and whiskers, quilting lines

Stitch count: 75 high x 75 wide

Finished design sizes:
14-count fabric – 5 1/4 x 5 1/4 inches
11-count fabric – 6 3/4 x 6 3/4 inches
18-count fabric – 4 1/8 x 4 1/8 inches

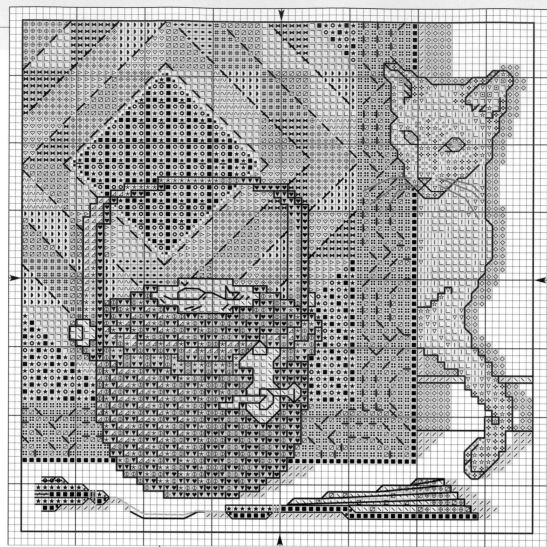

NANTUCKET CAT

ANCHOR		DMC	
403	■	310	Black
148	◗	311	True navy
978	◪	322	Pale navy
977	⊞	334	Dark baby blue
358	⋈	433	Light chestnut
878	#	501	Dark blue green
1042	∼	504	Pale blue green
1038	♡	519	Sky blue
1041	⊙	535	Ash gray
099	◆	552	Violet
900	◻	648	Light beaver gray
891	★	676	Light old gold
886	◿	677	Pale old gold
926	L	712	Cream
890	⏀	729	Medium old gold
1021	⌐	761	Salmon
023	▷	818	Pink
360	✺	839	Dark beige brown
379	☆	840	Medium beige brown
378	▽	841	True beige brown
388	▮	842	Light beige brown
273	★	844	Deep beaver gray
944	♥	869	Hazel
4146	▣	950	Rose beige
871	◢	3041	Medium antique violet
870	◇	3042	Light antique violet
888	▼	3045	Yellow beige
144	⊖	3325	True baby blue
036	◈	3326	Rose
068	⊕	3687	Mauve

ANCHOR		DMC	
BACKSTITCH			
403	╱	310	Black—part of cat's eyes (3X); cat's eyes, nose, left side of nose, mouth, fan frame, tassel (2X)
380	╱	838	Deep beige brown— basket weave (1X)
273	╱	844	Deep beaver gray—outline of fan, ivory attachments on basket, baseboard
871	╱	3041	Medium antique violet— tassel rope shadow
382	╱	3371	Black brown—cat, outline of basket, weave shadow
068	╱	3687	Mauve—border (3X)
STRAIGHT STITCH			
403	╱	310	Black—quilt lines in center diamond (1X)
926	╱	712	Cream—cat's whiskers (1X)
273	╱	844	Deep beaver gray—fan fold lines, quilt lines (1X)
382	╱	3371	Black brown—quilt lines
	╱	284	DMC gold metallic embroidery thread— wrap on fan and tassel
COUCHING			
	╱	284	DMC gold metallic embroidery thread—tassel string
FRENCH KNOT			
002	●	000	White—highlight in cat's eyes

Stitch count: 75 high x 75 wide
Finished design sizes:
14-count fabric – 5 1/4 x 5 1/4 inches
11-count fabric – 6 3/4 x 6 3/4 inches
18-count fabric – 4 1/8 x 4 1/8 inches

**NANTUCKET CAT

As shown on page 9.

MATERIALS

FABRIC

11x11-inch piece of 14-count ivory Aida cloth

THREADS

Cotton embroidery floss in colors listed in key

Metallic embroidery thread in color listed in key

SUPPLIES

Needle; embroidery hoop

Desired frame and mat

INSTRUCTIONS

Tape or zigzag the edges of fabric to prevent fraying. Find the center of the chart and the center of fabric; begin stitching there.

Use three plies of floss to work cross-stitches. Use two plies of floss

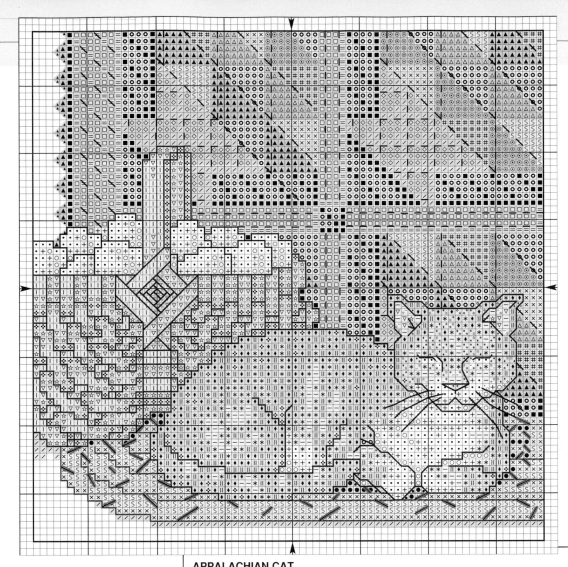

or two strands of the DMC gold metallic embroidery thread for the backstitches, straight stitches, French knots, and couching unless otherwise specified in key. Press the finished stitchery from the back. Frame and mat as desired.

★★APPALACHIAN CAT

As shown on page 8.

MATERIALS

FABRIC
11x11-inch piece of 14-count ivory Aida cloth

FLOSS
Cotton embroidery floss in colors listed in key

SUPPLIES
Needle
Embroidery hoop
Desired frame and mat

APPALACHIAN CAT

ANCHOR		DMC	
002	·	000	White
403	■	310	Black
399	○	318	Steel
038	▲	335	Medium rose
398	+	415	Pearl gray
1045	✳	436	Dark tan
878	#	501	Dark blue green
877	=	502	Medium blue green
875	□	503	True blue green
1041	◉	535	Ash gray
361	−	738	Light tan
024	◎	776	Pink
360	✤	839	Dark beige brown
379	☆	840	Medium beige brown
378	▽	841	True beige brown
388	I	842	Light beige brown
052	△	899	Light rose
1035	●	930	Dark antique blue
1034	×	931	Medium antique blue
1033	S	932	True antique blue
355	◆	975	Dark golden brown
1001	II	976	Medium golden brown

ANCHOR		DMC	
871	／	3041	Medium antique violet
870	◇	3042	Light antique violet

BACKSTITCH

038	／	335	Medium rose– border (3X)
273	／	844	Beaver gray–eggs
1035	／	930	Dark antique blue– rug
381	／	938	Coffee brown–cat's eyes (3X); cat, outline of basket, basket weave (2X)

STRAIGHT STITCH

403	／	310	Black–rug braid
388	／	842	Light beige brown– rug braid
273	／	844	Beaver gray–quilting lines; whiskers

Stitch count: 75 high x 75 wide
Finished design sizes:
14-count fabric – 5¼ x 5¼ inches
11-count fabric – 6¾ x 6¾ inches
18-count fabric – 4⅛ x 4⅛ inches

INSTRUCTIONS

Tape or zigzag edges of fabric to prevent fraying. Find the center of chart and the center of fabric; begin stitching there.

Use three plies of floss to work cross-stitches. Use two plies for backstitches and straight stitches unless otherwise specified in key. Press from back; frame as desired.

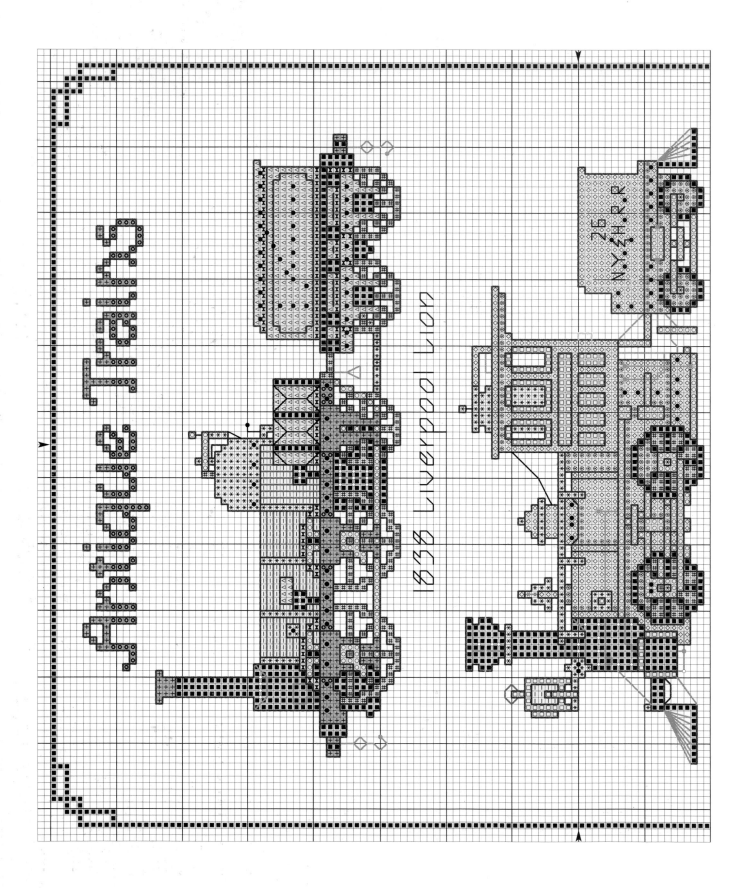

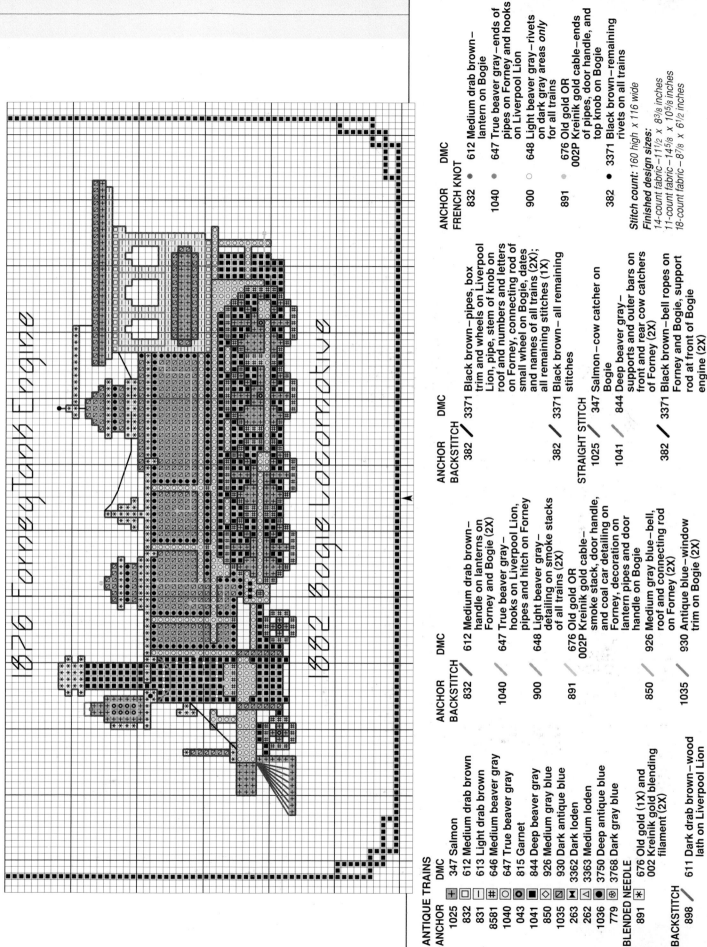

1876 Forney Tank Engine

1882 Bogie Locomotive

ANTIQUE TRAINS

ANCHOR		DMC	
1025	✚	347	Salmon
832	▫	612	Medium drab brown
831	❙	613	Light drab brown
8581	⌗	646	Medium beaver gray
1040	○	647	True beaver gray
043	◉	815	Garnet
1041	■	844	Deep beaver gray
850	◇	926	Medium gray blue
1035	▨	930	Dark antique blue
263	◤	3362	Dark loden
262	◿	3363	Medium loden
1036	●	3750	Deep antique blue
779	⊛	3768	Dark gray blue

BLENDED NEEDLE

891	✳	676	Old gold (1X) and
		002	Kreinik gold blending filament (2X)

BACKSTITCH

898	╱	611	Dark drab brown–wood lath on Liverpool Lion

ANCHOR	DMC	
BACKSTITCH		
832	612	Medium drab brown–handle on lanterns on Forney and Bogie (2X)
1040	647	True beaver gray–hooks on Liverpool Lion, pipes and hitch on Forney
900	648	Light beaver gray–detailing on smoke stacks of all trains (2X)
891	676	Old gold OR 002P Kreinik gold cable–smoke stack, door handle, and coal car detailing on Forney, decoration on lantern pipes and door handle on Bogie
850	926	Medium gray blue–bell, roof and connecting rod on Forney (2X)
1035	930	Antique blue–window trim on Bogie (2X)

ANCHOR	DMC	
BACKSTITCH		
382	3371	Black brown–pipes, box trim and wheels on Liverpool Lion, pipe, stem of knob on roof and numbers and letters on Forney, connecting rod of small wheel on Bogie, dates and names of all trains (2X); all remaining stitches (1X)
382	3371	Black brown–all remaining stitches
STRAIGHT STITCH		
1025	347	Salmon–cow catcher on Bogie
1041	844	Deep beaver gray–supports and outer bars on front and rear cow catchers of Forney (2X)
382	3371	Black brown–bell ropes on Forney and Bogie, support rod at front of Bogie engine (2X)

ANCHOR	DMC	
FRENCH KNOT		
832	●	612	Medium drab brown–lantern on Bogie
1040	●	647	True beaver gray–ends of pipes on Forney and hooks on Liverpool Lion
900	○	648	Light beaver gray–rivets on dark gray areas *only* for all trains
891	⬤	676	Old gold OR 002P Kreinik gold cable–ends of pipes, door handle, and top knob on Bogie
382	●	3371	Black brown–remaining rivets on all trains

Stitch count: 160 high x 116 wide

Finished design sizes:
14-count fabric–11½ x 8⅜ inches
11-count fabric–14⅝ x 10⅝ inches
18-count fabric–8⅞ x 6½ inches

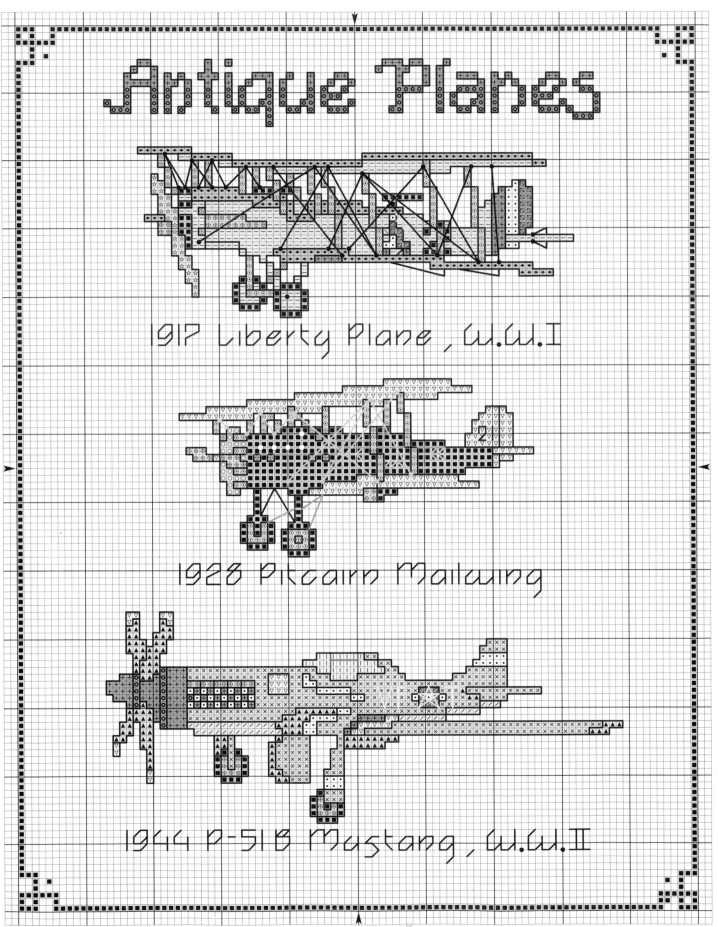

ANTIQUE PLANES

ANTIQUE PLANES

ANCHOR		DMC	
002	·	000	White
1025	+	347	Salmon
898	⊙	611	Dark drab brown
831	−	613	Light drab brown
1040	○	647	True beaver gray
900	╱	648	Light beaver gray
301	▽	744	Yellow
1012	╲	754	Peach
043	◎	815	Garnet
1041	■	844	Deep beaver gray
1035	◨	930	Dark antique blue
360	◆	3031	Mocha
888	☆	3045	Yellow beige
681	▲	3051	Dark gray green
262	✕	3052	Medium gray green
1031	▯	3753	Pale antique blue

BLENDED NEEDLE

| 234 | ⊕ | 762 | Pearl gray (1X) and |
| | | 001 | Kreinik silver blending filament (3X) |

BACKSTITCH

002	╱	000	White—trim on Liberty plane, "F" on Mustang (2X)
1025	╱	347	Salmon—detail on Liberty plane
301	╱	744	Yellow—decoration on Mailwing (2X)
397	╱	3024	Brown gray—decoration on Mailwing
360	╱	3031	Mocha—supports for wires on Liberty plane (2X)
681	╱	3051	Dark gray green—window frame of Mustang
403	╱	310	Black—numbers on Mailwing, dates and names of all planes(2X); all remaining stitches (1X)

STRAIGHT STITCH

002	╱	000	White—"V", "T" and star on Mustang (2X)
403	╱	310	Black—struts on Mailwing (2X)
403	╱	310	Black—struts on Mailwing (3X)
1040	╱	647	True beaver gray—wires on Mailwing
360	╱	3031	Mocha—wires on Liberty plane

FRENCH KNOT

403	●	310	Black—wheel hub of Liberty plane, lettering
1040	●	647	True beaver gray—ends of wires on Mailwing
397	○	3024	Brown gray—rivets on Mailwing
360	●	3031	Mocha—ends of wires on Liberty plane

Stitch count: 130 high x 100 wide
Finished design sizes:
14-count fabric—9³⁄₈ x 7¹⁄₄ inches
11-count fabric—11⁷⁄₈ x 9¹⁄₈ inches
18-count fabric—7¹⁄₄ x 5⁵⁄₈ inches

★★ANTIQUE TRAINS

As shown on page 10.

MATERIALS
FABRIC
18x14-inch piece of 14-count antique white Aida cloth
THREADS
Cotton embroidery floss in colors listed in key on page 19
One additional skein of deep beaver gray (DMC 844)
Metallic threads in colors listed in key on page 19
SUPPLIES
Needle
Embroidery hoop
Desired frame and mat

INSTRUCTIONS
Tape or zigzag the edges of the fabric to prevent fraying. Find the center of the chart and the center of the fabric; begin stitching there.

Use three plies of floss to work the cross-stitches. Work blended needle as specified in the key. Use one ply of floss to work all of the backstitches and the straight stitches unless otherwise specified in the key. Work all French knots using two plies of floss.

Press finished stitchery from the back. Frame and mat stitched piece as desired.

★★ANTIQUE PLANES

As shown on page 10.

MATERIALS
FABRIC
16x13-inch piece of 14-count antique white Aida cloth
THREADS
Cotton embroidery floss in colors listed in key
Blending filament in color listed in key
SUPPLIES
Needle; embroidery hoop
Desired frame and mat

INSTRUCTIONS
Tape or zigzag the edges of the fabric to prevent fraying. Find the center of the chart and the center of the fabric; begin stitching there.

Use three plies of floss to work the cross-stitches. Work blended needle as specified in the key. Use one ply of floss to work all the backstitches and the straight stitches unless otherwise specified in the key. Work all French knots using one ply of floss.

Press finished stitchery from the back. Frame and mat stitched piece as desired.

★★★HUMMINGBIRD SAMPLER

As shown on page 11.

MATERIALS
FABRIC
20x16-inch piece of 28-count ivory Jobelan fabric
THREADS
Cotton embroidery floss in colors listed in key on page 24
Blending filament in colors listed in key on page 24
SUPPLIES
Needle
Embroidery hoop
Desired frame and mat

INSTRUCTIONS
Tape or zigzag edges of fabric to prevent fraying. Find the center of chart and center of fabric; begin stitching there.

Use three plies of floss to work the cross-stitches over two threads of the fabric. Work the blended needle, the straight stitches, and the lazy daisy stitches as specified in the key. Work the backstitches using one ply of floss unless otherwise specified in the key.

Press finished stitchery from the back. Frame and mat stitched piece as desired.

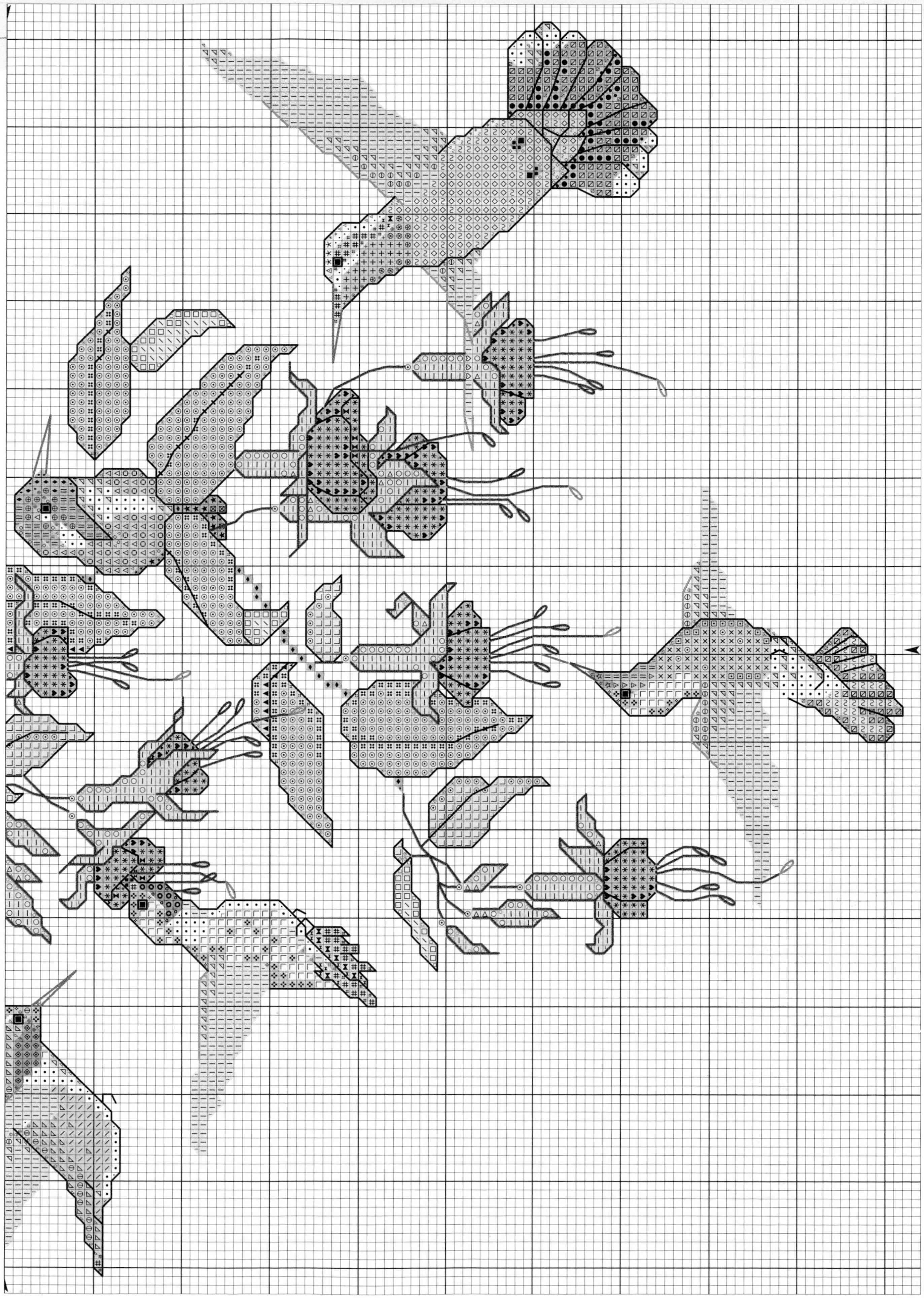

HUMMINGBIRD SAMPLER

ANCHOR		DMC	
002	•	000	White
1049	◣	301	Medium mahogany
1006	✶	304	Medium Christmas red
1019	✖	315	Dark antique mauve
399	⊘	318	Light steel
854	‖	371	Medium pecan
1047	◹	402	Pale mahogany
398	◺	415	Light pearl gray
860	◻	522	Dark olive drab
858	／	524	Light olive drab
050	△	605	Pale cranberry
273	#	645	Dark beaver gray
226	▷	702	Light Christmas green
234	—	762	Pale pearl gray
359	◆	801	Medium coffee brown
023	I	818	Pale pink
1041	✗	844	Deep beaver gray
1044	◀	895	Dark hunter green
1003	⊖	922	Light copper
1035	●	930	Dark antique blue
1034	◨	931	Medium antique blue
881	／	945	Dark ivory
360	★	3031	Deep mocha
903	✖	3032	Medium mocha
267	⊙	3346	Light hunter green
266	⊔	3347	Medium yellow green
264	■	3348	Light yellow green
382	▣	3371	Black brown
1028	◗	3685	Deep mauve
068	✶	3687	True mauve
049	◇	3689	Light mauve

ANCHOR DMC BLENDED NEEDLE

ANCHOR		DMC	
234	◿	762	Pale pearl gray (1X) and
049		3689	Light mauve (2X)
1006	◈	304	Medium Christmas red (1X) and
		003	Kreinik red blending filament (2X)
1006	◤	304	Medium Christmas red (1X) and
		012	Kreinik purple blending filament (2X)
013	◉	349	Dark coral (1X) and
		003	Kreinik red blending filament (2X)
267	✛	469	Dark avocado (1X) and
		006	Kreinik blue blending filament (2X)
266	⌐	471	Light avocado (1X) and
		045	Kreinik confetti gold blending filament (2X)
102	◆	550	Deep violet (1X) and
		012	Kreinik purple blending filament (2X)
098	⊕	553	Medium violet (1X) and
		012	Kreinik purple blending filament (2X)
096	‖	554	Light violet (1X) and
		012	Kreinik purple blending filament (2X)
226	✕	702	Light Christmas green (1X) and
		028	Kreinik citron blending filament (2X)
924	◁	731	Medium olive (1X) and
		045	Kreinik confetti gold blending filament (2X)
280	✳	733	Light olive (1X) and
		028	Kreinik citron blending filament (2X)
131	⊗	798	Dark Delft blue (1X) and
		033	Kreinik royal blue blending filament (2X)
130	+	809	True Delft blue (1X) and
		033	Kreinik royal blue blending filament (2X)
945	⬓	834	Pale bronze (1X) and
		028	Kreinik citron blending filament (2X)
229	▣	910	True emerald (1X) and
		008	Kreinik green filament (2X)
848	◇	927	Light gray blue (1X) and
		094	Kreinik star blue blending filament (2X)

ANCHOR DMC BLENDED NEEDLE

ANCHOR		DMC	
274	☑	928	Pale gray blue (1X) and
		094	Kreinik star blue blending filament (2X)
246	▣	986	Dark forest green (1X) and
		006	Kreinik blue blending filament (2X)
243	◁	988	Light forest green (1X) and
		015	Kreinik chartreuse blending filament (2X)
433	▽	996	Medium electric blue (1X) and
		094	Kreinik star blue blending filament (2X)

BACKSTITCH

399		318	Light steel–wings
1034		931	Medium antique blue–saying
360		3031	Deep mocha–parts of fuchsias
382		3371	Black brown–feet (2X); all remaining stitches (1X)

STRAIGHT STITCH

1006		304	Medium Christmas red–parts of white-eared and broad-billed hummingbirds (2X)
359		801	Medium coffee brown–stems (2X)
1041		844	Deep beaver gray–rest of bills (2X)
897		902	Deep garnet–pistils and stamens (2X)
382		3371	Black brown–centers of leaves (2X)

LAZY DAISY

380	𝟢	838	Deep beige brown–pistil ends (1X)
1003	𝟢	922	Dark copper–stamen ends (1X)

Stitch count: 204 high x 143 wide

Finished design sizes:
14-count fabric–14⅝ x 10¼ inches
11-count fabric–18⅝ x 13 inches
18-count fabric–11⅜ x 8 inches

BOTANICAL APPLE

Malus pumila

★★BOTANICAL APPLE

As shown on page 12.

MATERIALS

FABRIC
17x15-inch piece of 28-count antique white Jobelan fabric

FLOSS
Cotton embroidery floss in colors listed in key

SUPPLIES
Needle; embroidery hoop
Desired frame and mat

INSTRUCTIONS

Tape or zigzag edges of fabric to prevent fraying. Find the center of chart and the center of fabric; begin stitching there.

For colored apple motif, use three plies of floss to work cross-stitches over two threads of fabric. Use one ply of floss for backstitches.

Work the backstitches from the apple lettering chart over *one thread* of fabric, using one ply of floss.

Press finished stitchery from the back and frame as desired.

APPLE LETTERING CHART

Stitch count: 96 high x 70 wide
Finished design sizes:
14-count fabric – 6⁷/₈ x 5 inches
11-count fabric – 8³/₄ x 6³/₈ inches
18-count fabric – 5³/₈ x 3⁷/₈ inches

BOTANICAL APPLE		
ANCHOR		**DMC**
002	⌑	000 White
1006	◢	304 Medium Christmas red
9046	⊙	321 Light Christmas red
310	▨	434 Chestnut
1045	#	436 Tan
232	△	452 Shell gray
253	╱	472 Avocado
281	☆	580 Dark moss green
280	○	581 True moss green
314	＊	741 Medium tangerine
301	╲	744 Yellow
359	▲	801 Coffee brown
045	●	814 Dark garnet
218	■	890 Pistachio
050	◨	957 Geranium
244	▽	987 Forest green
1020	⊟	3713 Salmon
025	✕	3716 Rose pink
869	⊡	3743 Antique violet
1013	⊞	3778 Terra cotta
BACKSTITCH		
359	╱	801 Coffee brown– blossoms and name
382	╱	3371 Black brown– all remaining stitches

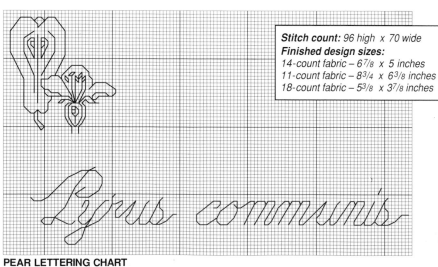

BOTANICAL PEAR

BOTANICAL PEAR
As shown on page 12.

MATERIALS
FABRIC
17x15-inch piece of 28-count antique white Jobelan fabric
FLOSS
Cotton embroidery floss in colors listed in key
SUPPLIES
Needle; embroidery hoop
Desired frame and mat

INSTRUCTIONS
Tape or zigzag edges of fabric to prevent fraying. Find the center of chart and the center of fabric; begin stitching there.

For colored pear motif, use three plies of floss to work cross-stitches over two threads of fabric. Use one ply of floss for all backstitches.

Work backstitches from pear lettering chart over *one thread* of fabric, using one ply of floss.

Press finished stitchery from the back and frame as desired.

Stitch count: 96 high x 70 wide
Finished design sizes:
14-count fabric – 6⅞ x 5 inches
11-count fabric – 8¾ x 6⅜ inches
18-count fabric – 5⅜ x 3⅞ inches

PEAR LETTERING CHART

BOTANICAL PEAR		
ANCHOR		**DMC**
002	•	000 White
1025	◆	347 Salmon
374	⊗	420 Hazel
232	+	452 Shell gray
267	#	469 Avocado
891	△	676 Light old gold
890	╱	729 Medium old gold
302	✕	743 True yellow
301	☆	744 Medium yellow
259	I	772 Loden
380	■	838 Deep beige brown
379	⊕	840 Medium beige brown
218	●	890 Pistachio
1003	✳	922 Copper
1002	▨	977 Golden brown
244	⊙	987 Forest green
292	−	3078 Lemon
268	▲	3345 Hunter green
266	◈	3347 Medium yellow green
264	◯	3348 Light yellow green
869	▽	3743 Antique violet
BACKSTITCH		
380	╱	838 Deep beige brown– most of pear, blossoms, cross-section and name
382	╱	3371 Dark brown– all remaining stitches

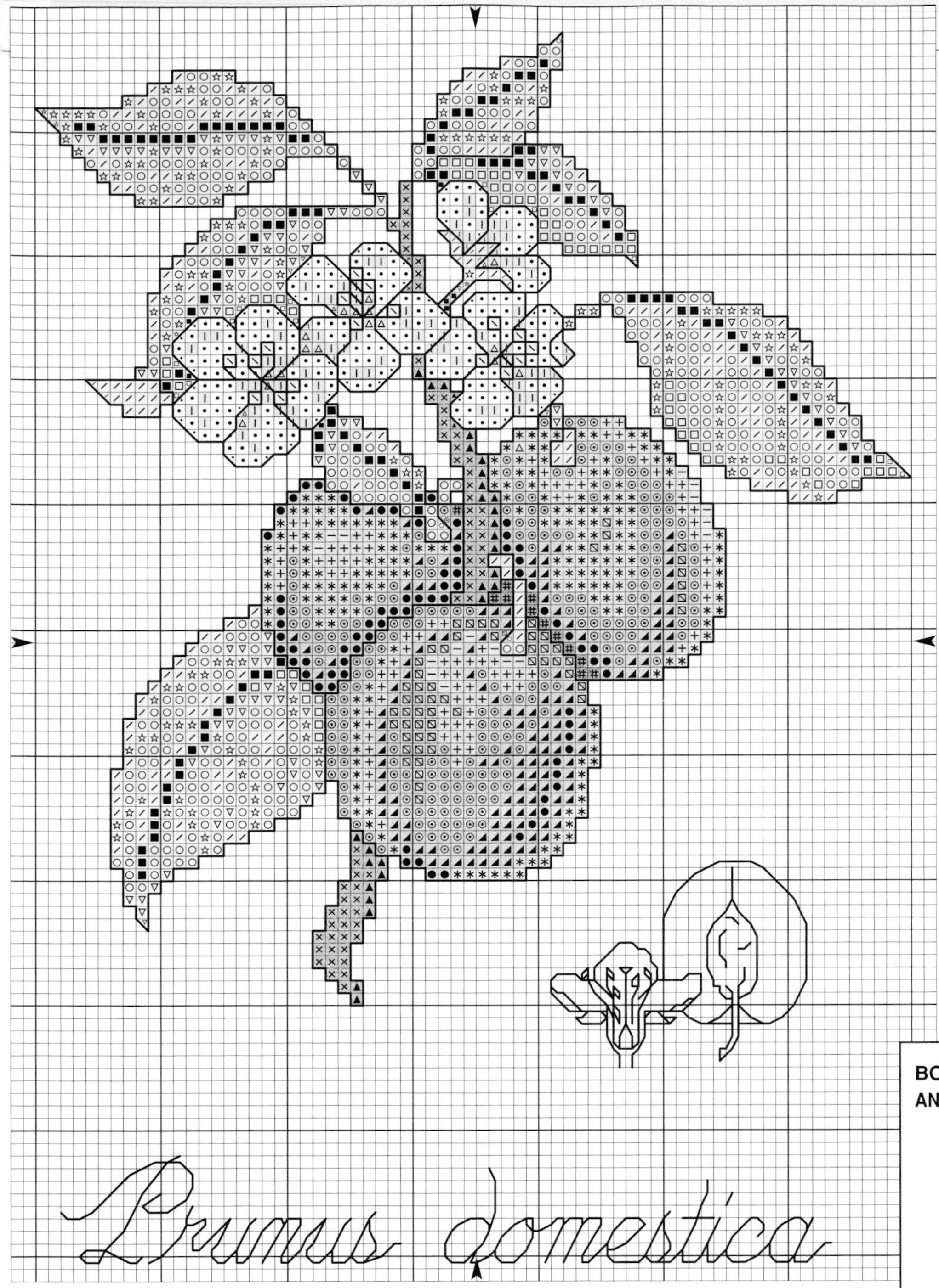

**BOTANICAL PLUM

As shown on page 13.

MATERIALS
FABRIC
17x15-inch piece of 28-count antique white Jobelan fabric
FLOSS
Cotton embroidery floss in colors listed in key
SUPPLIES
Needle; embroidery hoop
Desired frame and mat

INSTRUCTIONS
Tape or zigzag edges of fabric to prevent fraying. Find the center of chart and the center of fabric; begin stitching there.

For colored plum motif, use three plies of floss to work cross-stitches over two threads of fabric. Use one ply of floss for all backstitches.

Work the backstitches from the plum lettering chart over *one thread* of fabric, using one ply of floss.

Press finished stitchery from the back and frame as desired.

BOTANICAL PLUM

PLUM LETTERING CHART

Stitch count: 96 high x 70 wide
Finished design sizes:
14-count fabric – 6 7/8 x 5 inches
11-count fabric – 8 3/4 x 6 3/8 inches
18-count fabric – 5 3/8 x 3 7/8 inches

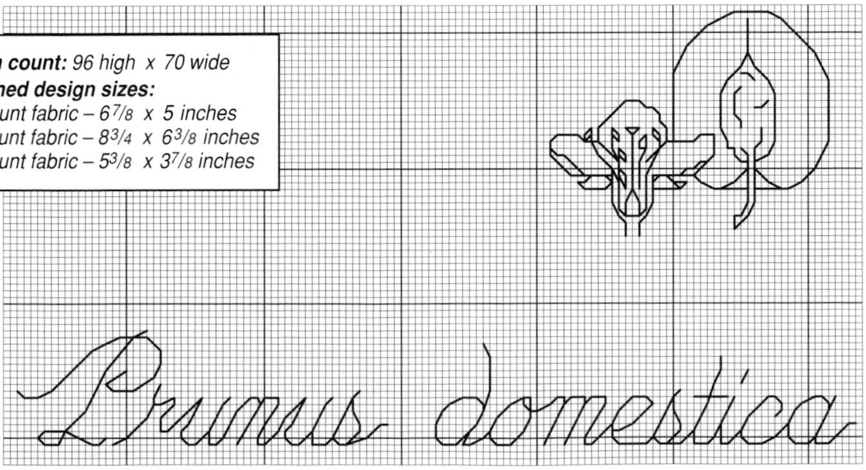

BOTANICAL PLUM		
ANCHOR		**DMC**
002	·	000 White
108	*	210 Light lavender
342	+	211 Pale lavender
100	◢	327 Antique violet
232	△	452 Shell gray
253	╱	472 Avocado
102	●	550 Deep violet
098	⊙	553 Medium violet
281	☆	580 Dark moss green
280	○	581 True moss green
300	◺	745 Yellow
045	▦	814 Garnet
379	✕	840 Beige brown
218	■	890 Pistachio
381	▲	938 Coffee brown
244	▽	987 Forest green
268	□	3345 Hunter green
060	◩	3688 Mauve
1020	—	3713 Salmon
869	I	3743 Antique violet
BACKSTITCH		
381	╱	938 Coffee brown— blossoms
382	╱	3371 Dark brown—plums, stems, leaves, cross-section and name

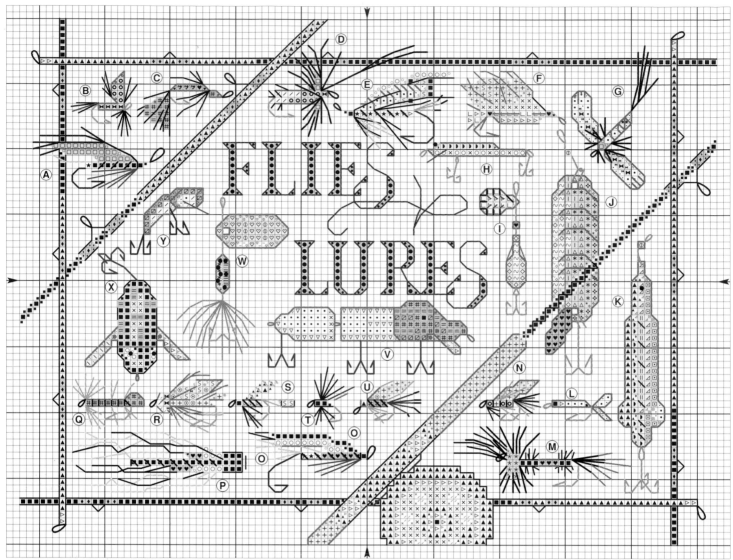

FLIES AND LURES

***FLIES AND LURES SAMPLER

As shown on page 14.

MATERIALS

FABRIC
14x16-inch piece of 25-count oatmeal Floba fabric

THREADS
Cotton embroidery floss in colors listed in key
Blending filament, metallic braid, and metallic cord in colors listed in key

SUPPLIES
Needle; embroidery hoop
Desired frame and mat

INSTRUCTIONS

Tape or zigzag edges of fabric to prevent fraying. Find the center of chart and center of fabric; begin stitching there.

Use three plies of floss to work the cross-stitches over two threads of the fabric. Work the blended needle as specified in key. Use two plies of floss to work all straight stitches and backstitches unless otherwise specified in the key. Work the French knots and the lazy daisy stitches using one ply of floss unless otherwise specified in the key.

Press the finished stitchery from the back. Frame and mat the stitched piece as desired.

**FLIES AND LURES PAPERWEIGHT

As shown on page 14.

MATERIALS

FABRIC
6x4-inch piece of 25-count oatmeal Floba fabric

THREADS
Cotton embroidery floss and blending filament in colors listed in key

SUPPLIES
Needle; embroidery hoop
4x2⅞-inch glass paperweight kit with self-stick insert and backing
Crafts glue

FLIES AND LURES

ANCHOR		DMC	
002	·	000	White
1049	□	301	Medium mahogany
403	■	310	Black
011	⊞	350	Medium coral
009	⊟	352	Pale coral
351	●	400	Dark mahogany
373	◇	422	Light hazel
310	✶	434	Chestnut
1045	S	436	Dark tan
253	I	472	Avocado
1041	▲	535	Ash gray
898	◎	611	Drab brown
8581	×	646	Medium beaver gray
900	▽	648	Light beaver gray
926	−	712	Cream
305	◯	725	True topaz
293	∿	727	Pale topaz
361	+	738	Light tan
359	⊙	801	Coffee brown
161	‖	813	Powder blue
045	◆	814	Garnet
013	♥	817	Deep coral
162	▢	825	Bright blue
218	✤	890	Pistachio
257	✳	905	Dark parrot green
255	△	907	Light parrot green
1033	▣	932	True antique blue
881	⧄	945	Ivory
1031	◣	3753	Pale antique blue
1013	▨	3778	Terra cotta
1050	⋈	3781	Mocha

BLENDED NEEDLE

ANCHOR		DMC	
002	⌐	000	White (2X) and
		032	Kreinik pearl blending filament (2X)
374	⟦	420	Medium hazel (2X) and
		002	Kreinik gold blending filament (2X)
373	♡	422	Light hazel (2X) and
		002	Kreinik gold blending filament (2X)
293	★	727	Pale topaz (2X) and
		028	Kreinik citron blending filament (2X)
274	▷	928	Gray blue (2X) and
		001	Kreinik silver blending filament (2X)
1033	◩	932	True antique blue (2X) and
		001	Kreinik silver blending filament (2X)

BACKSTITCH

ANCHOR		DMC	
002	╱	000	White–stripes on feather of S (1X)
403	╱	310	Black–leader guides on rods, stripes on tail of S (3X); most of rods, reel, part of body of M, head of P, bodies of T and X (1X)
351	╱	400	Dark mahogany–saying
1041	╱	535	Ash gray–stripes on K, head of P
305	╱	725	True topaz–head of H, eye of V, stripe on W, spots on X
045	╱	814	Garnet–zigzags on rod near handle
1050	╱	3781	Mocha–stripes on feather of E, stripes on wings and body of G, stripes on J and Y, rest of outlines of flies, lures, and rod handle (1X)
	╱	001	Kreinik silver blending filament–stripes on bodies of A, E, N, O, P, Q, S, and U; stripes on blade of I
	╱	005	Kreinik black blending filament–hooks of A, E, O, and Y (4X)
	╱	021	Kreinik copper #8 braid–rest of hooks, swivels on J & K, central stems of I & W (4X)
	╱	105C	Kreinik antique silver cord–body of F, hooks of F, V, and X; attachment of reel and rod

STRAIGHT STITCH

ANCHOR		DMC	
002	╱	000	White–highlights on body of C
1049	╱	301	Medium mahogany–wing of A, hackles of D, G, M; tails of G, M
403	╱	310	Black–tail tips of E, U; end of wing of O (3X); hackles of M, N, T (2X)
011	╱	350	Medium coral–hackles of C, E (1X)
374	╱	420	Medium hazel–body of I
310	╱	434	Chestnut–wing of F (1X)
1045	╱	436	Dark tan–tails of E and S, hackles and tails of N and Q, tips of hackles of R, hackle and wing of U
253	╱	472	Avocado–tail of W

STRAIGHT STITCH

ANCHOR		DMC	
898	╱	611	Drab brown–hackle of B, tails of B, D, and N
8581	╱	646	Medium beaver gray–lips on H and Y (3X)
926	╱	712	Cream–hackles of E and M
305	╱	725	True topaz–tails of A and O, hackles of E and P, wing of O
361	╱	738	Light tan–tails of B, N, T, and U
161	╱	813	Powder blue–holes on blade of I
013	╱	817	Deep coral–tail of C, hackle of P
162	╱	825	Bright blue–stripe on feather of E, hackle of S
433	╱	996	Electric blue–hackles of A and O
1050	╱	3781	Mocha–tail tips of M, hackles and tail of R, tail of T
	╱	001	Kreinik silver blending filament–base of wing of F (1X)
	╱	021	Kreinik copper #8 braid–split rings of J (1X)
	╱	105C	Kreinik antique silver cord–tail of F (1X)

FRENCH KNOT

ANCHOR		DMC	
403	●	310	Black–eyes of H and X (2X); spots on W (1X)
013	●	817	Deep coral–eyes of K (3X)
	·	021	Kreinik copper #8 braid–swivel of J
	●	105C	Kreinik antique silver cord–dots on V's mouth and X's wings

LAZY DAISY

ANCHOR		DMC	
	⸰	021	Kreinik copper #8 braid–loops of B, H, I, J, K, L, and W
	⸰	105C	Kreinik antique silver cord–loops of F, V, and X; connector on V
403	⸰	310	Black (1X) and
		005	Kreinik black blending filament (1X)–all other loops on flies, lures, and rods

Stitch count: 80 high x 106 wide
Finished design sizes:
12 1/2-count fabric–6 3/8 x 8 1/2 inches
14-count fabric–5 3/4 x 7 5/8 inches
18-count fabric–4 1/2 x 5 7/8 inches

INSTRUCTIONS

Tape or zigzag edges of fabric to prevent fraying. Find the "X" motif on the chart, *opposite*, and begin stitching it 1¾ inches from the left edge of the fabric, centering top to bottom. Stitch the "G" motif ⅛ inch from the wing tip of first motif.

Use three plies of embroidery floss to work the cross-stitches over two threads of the Floba fabric. Work blended needle as specified in key. Use two plies of embroidery floss to work all of the straight stitches and backstitches unless otherwise specified in key.

Work the French knots and the lazy daisy stitches using one ply of floss unless otherwise specified in the key.

Press the finished stitchery from the back. Assemble the paperweight according to instructions provided by the manufacturer.

*W*elcome to a blue-ribbon collection of exquisite cross-stitch designs. Each of the glorious pieces in this chapter is truly a work of art and will provide a challenge for even the most accomplished of stitchers.

Amid Amish Life

The Amish emphasize a life of goodness and spirituality. Our three vignettes, *Hanging the Quilts, Visiting the Neighbors,* and *Tending the Garden,* depict scenes from the life of the Amish community. These intricate designs may be worked individually as shown or all three designs can be stitched as one. Charts and the complete instructions begin on page 37.

Sunday Best

Dressed in her best attire, this demure young girl with her nosegay of spring blossoms is an endearing example of the folk-art style of the portrait painters of yesteryear. Petite cross-stitches define her eyes and brooch, while a smattering of specialty stitches add a lacy texture to her apron and pantaloons. Complete instructions and chart begin on page 42.

Young Man's Fancy

Designed to capture the uniquely American style of the mid-nineteenth century, this charming design is a perfect companion for Sunday Best, *opposite*. Our proper young gentleman with his pet squirrel is stitched over two threads on 28-count amber linen. His eyes and mouth are worked over just one thread. Complete instructions begin on page 42 and chart begins on page 46.

Christmas House

Our elegant holiday home is stitched in two layers on two different fabrics. The house interior is cross-stitched and accented with a rainbow of metallic threads. The house exterior is a glorious sampling of specialty stitches sure to make the most of your needlework expertise. When the two pieces are layered, they create a lovely treasure destined to become an heirloom. Complete instructions and charts are on pages 50–53.

Santa's List

This magnificent Victorian Santa is a masterpiece in needlework. The subtle shading and intricate details of the design provide realism to Santa and all of the carefully chosen toys waiting to be delivered to good boys and girls. Complete instructions and chart begin on page 54.

Spanish Sampler

An elegant mix of specialty stitches adds to the richness and intricacy of the design which incorporates many of the unique characteristics of historical Spanish samplers. Ornate geometric and floral borders surrounding a square central motif reflect the Spanish decorative style. Complete instructions and chart begin on page 57.

HANGING THE QUILTS

***HANGING THE QUILTS

As shown on page 30.

MATERIALS

FABRIC

15x11-inch piece of 25-count wedgwood Lugana fabric

FLOSS

Cotton embroidery floss in colors listed in key

One additional skein of white (DMC 000)

SUPPLIES

Needle

Embroidery hoop

Desired frame and mat

INSTRUCTIONS

Tape or zigzag edges of fabric to prevent fraying. Find center of chart and of fabric; begin stitching there.

Use three plies of floss to work cross-stitches over two threads of the fabric. Work half cross-stitches in the direction of the symbol using two plies of floss. Work straight stitches and French knots as specified in the key. Work satin stitches using two plies. Work backstitches using one ply of floss unless otherwise specified in key.

Press the finished stitchery from the back. Frame and mat stitched piece as desired.

***TENDING THE GARDEN

As shown on page 31.

MATERIALS

FABRIC

15x11-inch piece of 25-count wedgwood Lugana fabric

FLOSS

Cotton embroidery floss in colors listed in key

SUPPLIES

Needle

Embroidery hoop

Desired frame and mat

Continued on page 42

HANGING THE QUILTS AND TENDING THE GARDEN

ANCHOR		DMC	
002	·	000	White
110	◢	208	Dark lavender
108	◯	210	Light lavender
897	▲	221	Shell pink
403	■	310	Black
400	▶	317	True pewter
399	⊕	318	Light steel
100	◤	327	Deep antique violet
1025	✳	347	Salmon
010	◈	351	Coral
1014	◥	355	Dark terra cotta
5975	∟	356	Medium terra cotta
914	△	407	Cocoa
235	⊞	414	Dark steel
398	+	415	Pearl gray
358	◀	433	Light chestnut
310	⊙	434	Medium chestnut
1045	◗	436	Tan
878	◳	501	Dark blue green
875	◲	503	True blue green
860	−	522	Olive drab
1041	▼	535	Ash gray
098	☆	553	Violet
210	◨	562	Medium seafoam
208	♡	563	True seafoam
889	★	610	Deep drab brown
898	◖	611	Dark drab brown
832	◿	612	Medium drab brown
903	◘	640	Dark beige gray
392	S	642	Medium beige gray
830	▽	644	Light beige gray
891	◳	676	Light old gold
886	▣	677	Pale old gold
901	⊞	680	Dark old gold
293	◁	727	Topaz
890	=	729	Medium old gold
303	✶	742	Tangerine
177	▣	792	Dark cornflower blue
176	◨	793	Cornflower blue
169	♥	806	Dark peacock blue
168	∿	807	Medium peacock blue
164	⊞	824	Deep bright blue
161	◇	826	Medium bright blue
218	●	890	Pistachio
360	☒	898	Coffee brown
897	◑	902	Garnet
1035	◆	930	Dark antique blue
1034	‖	931	Medium antique blue
1033	◺	932	True antique blue
4146	▯	950	Rose beige
246	✤	986	Dark forest green
244	◱	987	Medium forest green
243	◹	988	Light forest green
242	✕	989	Pale forest green
189	◯	991	Aquamarine
186	▷	993	Light aquamarine
871	▽	3041	Medium antique violet
264	▢	3348	Yellow green
263	◆	3362	Dark loden
262	◍	3363	Medium loden
087	▦	3607	Dark fuchsia
086	⊖	3608	Medium fuchsia

HALF CROSS-STITCH
(stitch in direction of symbol)

002	◿	000	White

SATIN STITCH
(stitch in direction of symbol)

108	◥	210	Light lavender
243	◥	988	Light forest green

HANGING THE QUILT

BACKSTITCH

110	╱	208	Dark lavender–purple mountains
403	╱	310	Black–edge of bar quilt, lightning rod
401	╱	413	Dark pewter–clapboard lines on house, fence rails
235	╱	414	Dark steel–clouds, smoke
358	╱	433	Light chestnut–brown striped hill
1035	╱	930	Dark antique blue–blue mountains
861	╱	935	Dark pine green–cedar tree
246	╱	986	Dark forest green–apple trees, edge of lawn against road
263	╱	3362	Dark loden–green striped hill
382	╱	3371	Black brown–all remaining stitches

STRAIGHT STITCH

002	╱	000	White–woman's apron (2X)
403	╱	310	Black–clothes line, boy's suspenders (2X)
1025	╱	347	Deep salmon–chickens' wattle (2X)
401	╱	413	Dark pewter–fence posts (2X)
886	╱	677	Pale old gold–clothespins (3X)

FRENCH KNOT

403	●	310	Black–weather vane
382	●	3371	Black brown–chickens' eyes

TENDING THE GARDEN

BACKSTITCH

110	╱	208	Dark lavender–purple mountains
403	╱	310	Black–man's hat
401	╱	413	Dark pewter–distant farm
235	╱	414	Dark steel–clouds
310	╱	434	Chestnut–fence post highlight (2X)
218	╱	890	Pistachio–green hill above distant farm
360	╱	898	Coffee brown–gold striped hill
1035	╱	930	Dark antique blue–blue mountains
246	╱	986	Dark forest green–cabbage, gray green mounds
263	╱	3362	Dark loden–checked hill below distant farm
382	╱	3371	Black brown–all remaining stitches

STRAIGHT STITCH

002	╱	000	White–bonnet strap of woman dressed in purple (2X)
403	╱	310	Black–tops of silos and distant farm, man's suspenders (2X)
400	╱	317	True pewter–fence rails (2X)
398	╱	415	Pearl gray–hat band (3X)
382	╱	3371	Black brown–distant fence posts (3X)

FRENCH KNOT

1025	●	347	Salmon–apples (2X)
382	●	3371	Black brown–chicks' eyes (2X)

Stitch count: 126 high x 77 wide

Finished design sizes:
12$\frac{1}{2}$-count fabric – 10 x 6$\frac{1}{8}$ inches
14-count fabric – 9 x 5$\frac{1}{2}$ inches
18-count fabric – 7 x 4$\frac{3}{8}$ inches

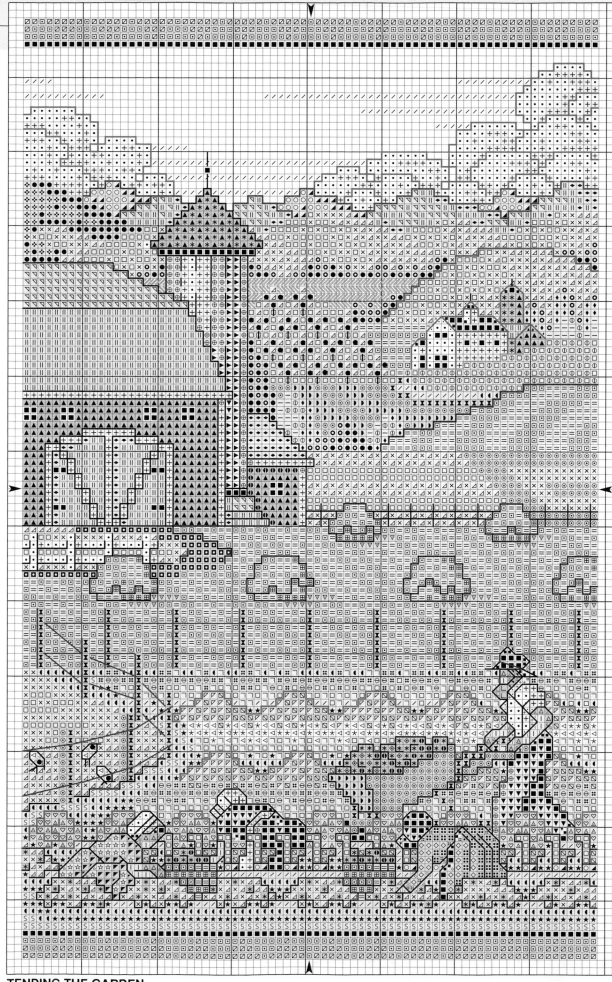

TENDING THE GARDEN

VISITING THE NEIGHBORS

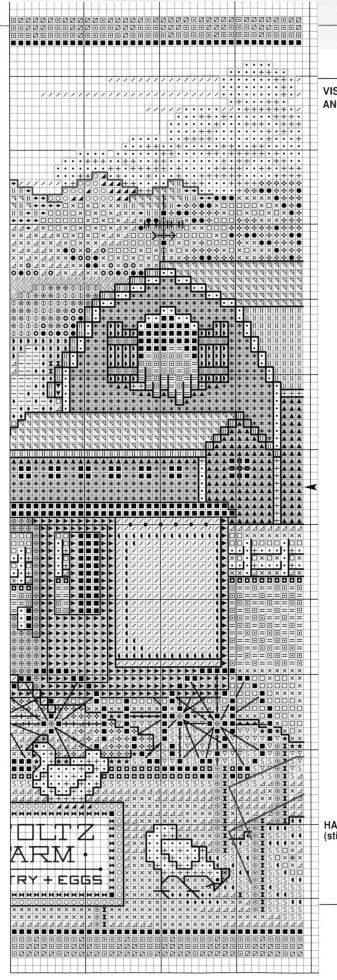

VISITING THE NEIGHBORS

ANCHOR		DMC	
002	·	000	White
110	◪	208	Dark lavender
108	○	210	Light lavender
897	▲	221	Shell pink
403	■	310	Black
400	▶	317	True pewter
399	⊕	318	Light steel
100	◩	327	Antique violet
1025	✳	347	Salmon
1014	◥	355	Dark terra cotta
5975	◣	356	Medium terra cotta
214	⊗	368	Light pistachio
914	△	407	Cocoa
235	⌗	414	Dark steel
398	+	415	Pearl gray
358	◀	433	Light chestnut
310	◉	434	Medium chestnut
1045	◐	436	Tan
860	–	522	Olive drab
1041	▼	535	Ash gray
098	☆	553	Violet
889	★	610	Deep drab brown
898	◖	611	Dark drab brown
832	⟋	612	Medium drab brown
903	▣	640	Dark beige gray
392	⑤	642	Medium beige gray
830	▽	644	Light beige gray
8581	⊠	646	Medium beaver gray
1040	◎	647	True beaver gray
886	▣	677	Pale old gold
901	⊞	680	Dark old gold
293	◁	727	Topaz
890	＝	729	Medium old gold
177	⋈	792	Dark cornflower blue
176	◨	793	Medium cornflower blue
164	⊞	824	Deep bright blue
161	◇	826	Medium bright blue
218	●	890	Deep pistachio
360	⊠	898	Coffee brown
1035	◆	930	Dark antique blue
1034	‖	931	Medium antique blue
1033	�	932	True antique blue
4146	▮	950	Rose beige
246	⊡	986	Dark forest green
244	◿	987	Medium forest green
243	⊓	988	Light forest green
242	✕	989	Pale forest green
189	◖	991	Aquamarine
264	▢	3348	Yellow green
263	◆	3362	Dark loden
262	⊕	3363	Medium loden
382	⬟	3371	Black brown
087	⊞	3607	Fuchsia

HALF CROSS-STITCH
(stitch in direction of symbol)

002	⟋	000	White

ANCHOR		DMC	

SATIN STITCH
(stitch in direction of symbol)

108	⟋	210	Light lavender
243	⟋	988	Light forest green

BACKSTITCH

110	⟋	208	Dark lavender – purple mountains
897	⟋	221	Shell pink – sign lettering
403	⟋	310	Black – sign line, carriage (1X); carriage lamps and mirror, lightning rod, weather vane (2X)
401	⟋	413	Dark pewter – clapboard lines on house
235	⟋	414	Dark steel – clouds
398	⟋	415	Pearl gray – girl's apron, barn window pane (2X)
218	⟋	890	Deep pistachio – large tree near house
1035	⟋	930	Dark antique blue – blue mountains
244	⟋	987	Medium forest green – edges of lawn and green field
263	⟋	3362	Dark loden – green striped hill, row of trees
382	⟋	3371	Black brown – house, barn, people, basket, carriage flap, horse, chickens, sign, road edge

STRAIGHT STITCH

403	⟋	310	Black – cellar door handle, horse's harness, man's suspenders (2X); horse's reins, wheel spokes (1X)
400	⟋	317	True pewter – fence wire (2X)
1025	⟋	347	Salmon – chickens' wattles (2X)
235	⟋	414	Dark steel – man's hat band (2X)
886	⟋	677	Pale old gold – basket handle (2X)
382	⟋	3371	Black brown – tree trunks (2X)

FRENCH KNOT

403	●	310	Black – lightning rods and sign (2X)
293		727	Topaz – horse's harness (2X)
382	●	3371	Black brown – carriage flap (2X), chickens' eyes (1X)

Stitch count: 126 high x 137 wide
Finished design sizes:
12 1/2-count fabric – 10 x 11 inches
14-count fabric – 9 x 9 7/8 inches
18-count fabric – 7 x 7 5/8 inches

INSTRUCTIONS

Tape or zigzag edges of fabric to prevent fraying. Find center of chart and of fabric; begin stitching there.

Use three plies of floss to work cross-stitches over two threads of fabric. Work half cross-stitches in direction of symbol using two plies. Work straight stitches and French knots as specified in key. Work satin stitches using two plies. Work back-stitches using one ply unless other-wise specified in key. Press stitchery from back; frame as desired.

★★★VISITING THE NEIGHBORS

As shown on page 31.

MATERIALS
FABRIC
15x16-inch piece of 25-count wedgwood Lugana fabric
FLOSS
Cotton embroidery floss in colors listed in key on page 41
One additional skein *each* of white (DMC 000), black (DMC 310), pearl gray (DMC 415), and pale forest green (DMC 989)
SUPPLIES
Needle; embroidery hoop
Desired frame and mat

INSTRUCTIONS

Tape or zigzag edges of fabric to prevent fraying. Find center of chart and of fabric; begin stitching there.

Use three plies of floss to work cross-stitches over two threads of fabric. Work half cross-stitches in direction of symbol using two plies. Work straight stitches and French knots as specified in key. Work satin stitches using two plies and back-stitches using one ply unless other-wise specified in key. Press stitchery from back and frame as desired.

To stitch all three designs as one, begin with a 15x28-inch piece of fabric. Starting about 2¼ inches

from edges, baste outline of design 126 stitches high x 291 stitches wide.

Count 77 stitches from one side of outlined area and baste from top to bottom of fabric. Repeat for opposite side of fabric.

Find center of *Visiting the Neighbors* chart and center of fabric; begin stitching there. Stitch design in same manner as for each individual por-tion of design, except, *do not* stitch borders yet. When central design is complete, continue stitching until both side charts are stitched.

Stitch blue and gold border, begin-ning at center of design and working outward across both side portions of design. Press and frame as desired.

★★★★SUNDAY BEST

As shown on page 32.

MATERIALS
FABRIC
23x15-inch piece of 28-count amber linen
FLOSS
Cotton embroidery floss in colors listed in key on page 46
One additional skein *each* of dark beige brown (DMC 839) and medium gray blue (DMC 926)
Two additional skeins *each* of white (DMC 000), medium beige brown (DMC 840), and light gray blue (DMC 927)
Five additional skeins of deep beige brown (DMC 838)
#8 braid in color listed in key on page 46
Metallic cord in color listed in key on page 46
#8 pearl cotton in color listed in key on page 46
SUPPLIES
Needle; embroidery hoop
Desired frame and mat

INSTRUCTIONS

Tape or zigzag edges of fabric to prevent fraying. Find center of chart and of fabric; begin stitching there.

For each section of design, work cross-stitches over two threads of fabric using three plies of floss, unless otherwise specified in key, before working specialty stitches. Work blended needle, French knots, and straight stitches as specified in key. Work half cross-stitches in direction of symbol using one ply. Work eye and pin charts in petite cross-stitches over *one thread* using one ply of floss. Work satin stitches over threads indicated on chart using plies specified in key. Work back-stitches using one ply unless other-wise specified in key.

Referring to diagrams, page 46, work Smyrna cross stitches, lazy daisy stitches, and Algerian eyelets as specified in key. For Algerian eyelets, give each stitch a gentle tug to open a small hole. Use one strand of cord to couch one strand of #8 braid. Press and frame as desired.

★★★★YOUNG MAN'S FANCY

As shown on page 33.

MATERIALS
FABRIC
23x15-inch piece of 28-count amber linen
FLOSS
Cotton embroidery floss in colors listed in key on page 49
One additional skein *each* of white (DMC 000), dark beaver gray (DMC 645), dark beige brown (DMC 839), deep beaver gray (DMC 844), medium gray blue (DMC 926), light gray blue (DMC 927), dark yellow beige (DMC 3045), medium yellow beige (DMC 3046), and dark gray blue (DMC 3768)
Five additional skeins of deep beige brown (DMC 838)
Metallic cable in color listed in key on page 49
SUPPLIES
Needle; embroidery hoop
Desired frame and mat

INSTRUCTIONS

Tape or zigzag edges of fabric to prevent fraying. Find the center of chart and the center of fabric; begin stitching there.

For each section of the design, work cross-stitches over two threads of fabric using three plies of floss, unless otherwise specified in key, before working specialty stitches. Work blended needle, French knots, and the straight stitches as specified in key. Work half cross-stitches in direction of symbol using one ply. Work eye and mouth charts in petite cross-stitches over *one thread* using one ply of floss. Work the back-stitches using one ply of floss unless otherwise specified in key.

Use one strand of cable to work chain stitches, referring to the diagram, *page 46.* Press finished stitchery from the back. Frame and mat as desired.

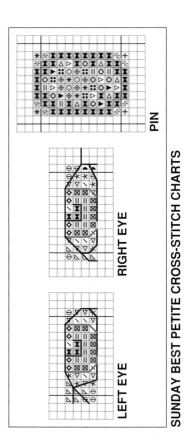

PIN

RIGHT EYE

LEFT EYE

SUNDAY BEST PETITE CROSS-STITCH CHARTS

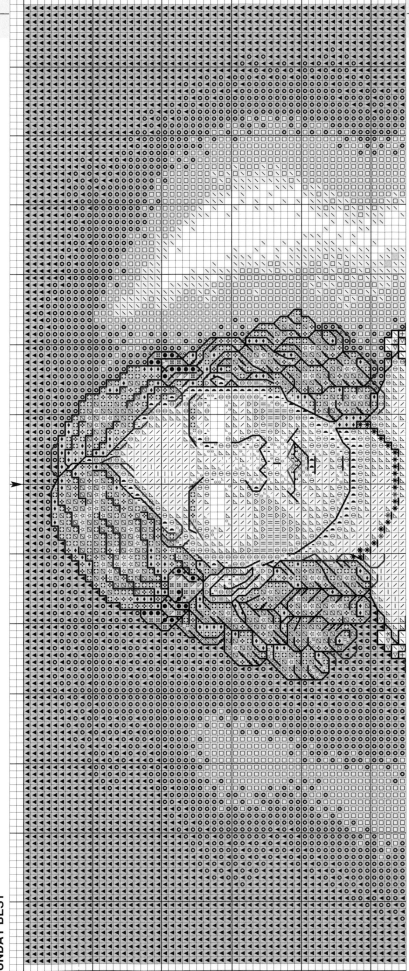

SUNDAY BEST

SUNDAY BEST

43

SUNDAY BEST

ANCHOR	DMC	
387		Ecru
002	000	White
002	000	White (1X)
002	000	White (2X)
215	320	True pistachio
118	340	Medium periwinkle
117	341	Light periwinkle
217	367	Medium pistachio
1010	951	Medium ivory
355	975	Deep golden brown
374	420	Hazel
358	433	Light chestnut
362	437	Tan
233	451	Dark shell gray
232	452	Medium shell gray
231	453	Light shell gray
266	471	Avocado
1039	518	Wedgwood blue
1038	519	Sky blue
168	597	Turquoise
273	645	Dark beaver gray
323	722	Light bittersweet
305	725	True topaz
293	727	Pale topaz
890	729	Old gold
300	745	Light yellow
1022	760	True salmon
1021	761	Light salmon
023	818	Pink
380	838	Deep beige brown (2X)
379	840	Medium beige brown (1X)
379	840	Medium beige brown
378	841	True beige brown
388	842	Light beige brown

ANCHOR	DMC	
1041	844	Deep beaver gray
1044	895	Dark hunter green
360	898	Coffee brown
851	924	Deep gray blue
850	926	Medium gray blue
848	927	Light gray blue
274	928	Pale gray blue
1010	951	Medium ivory
355	975	Deep golden brown
888	3045	Dark yellow beige
887	3046	Medium yellow beige
886	3047	Light yellow beige
1024	3328	Dark salmon
267	3346	Light hunter green
382	3371	Black brown
1028	3685	Deep mauve
068	3687	True mauve
060	3688	Medium mauve
1023	3712	Medium salmon
896	3721	Shell pink
075	3733	Medium dusty rose
1030	3746	Dark periwinkle
779	3768	Dark gray blue
1009	3770	True ivory
1007	3772	Cocoa

BLENDED NEEDLE

ANCHOR	DMC	
1046	435	Dark chestnut (2X) and
1001	976	Medium golden brown (1X)
882	758	Light terra cotta (2X) and
1008	3773	Rose beige (1X)
360	839	Dark beige brown (1X) and
379	840	Medium beige brown (1X)
850	926	Medium gray blue (2X) and
168	807	Medium peacock blue (1X)

ANCHOR	DMC	
BLENDED NEEDLE		
779	3768	Dark gray blue (2X) and
169	806	Dark peacock blue (1X)
868	3779	Pale terra cotta (2X) and
881	945	Dark ivory (1X)

HALF CROSS-STITCH
(stitch in direction of symbol)

379	840	Medium beige brown (1X)

BACKSTITCH

ANCHOR	DMC	
002	000	White—apron, pantaloons (2X)
358	433	Light chestnut—parts of eyebrows
324	721	Medium bittersweet—daffodils (2X)
1022	760	True salmon—lip highlights
1044	895	Dark hunter green—irises (2X)
382	3371	Black brown—part of eyelashes, pupils, center of mouth
896	3721	Shell pink—part of lips
380	838	Deep beige brown—some rose stems, rabbit's nose (2X); all remaining stitches

BLENDED BACKSTITCH

380	838	Deep beige brown (1X) and
358	433	Light chestnut (1X)—hair strands

STRAIGHT STITCH

233	451	Dark shell gray—centers of lazy daisies on apron and pantaloons (2X)
382	3371	Black brown—rest of eyelashes (2X)
1028	3685	Deep mauve—decoration on dress
068	3687	True mauve—decoration on dress

ANCHOR	DMC	
STRAIGHT STITCH		White #8 pearl cotton—nosegay (1X)

FRENCH KNOT

233	451	Dark shell gray—apron, pantaloons (3X)
266	471	Avocado—daffodil centers (2X)
293	727	Pale topaz—forget-me-not centers (2X)
380	838	Deep beige brown—primrose centers (2X)

LAZY DAISY

White #8 pearl cotton—apron, pantaloons (1X)

COUCHING

002HL Kreinik gold #8 braid and
002C Kreinik gold cord

SATIN STITCH

002	000	White—apron, pantaloons (4X)
232	452	Medium shell gray—apron, pantaloons (3X)

SMYRNA CROSS

002	000	White—nosegay (4X)
043	815	Garnet—necklace (3X)
059	3350	Deep dusty rose—necklace (3X)
1028	3685	Deep mauve—necklace (3X)

ALGERIAN EYELET

002	000	White—apron (4X)

Stitch count: 240 high x 138 wide
Finished design sizes:
14-count fabric — 17 1/8 x 9 7/8 inches
11-count fabric — 21 7/8 x 12 5/8 inches
18-count fabric — 13 3/8 x 7 3/4 inches

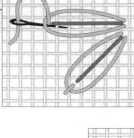

Lazy Daisy

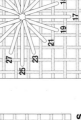

Slanted Satin

Algerian Eyelet

Smyrna Cross Variation

Upright Satin

Smyrna Cross Stitch

Chain Stitch

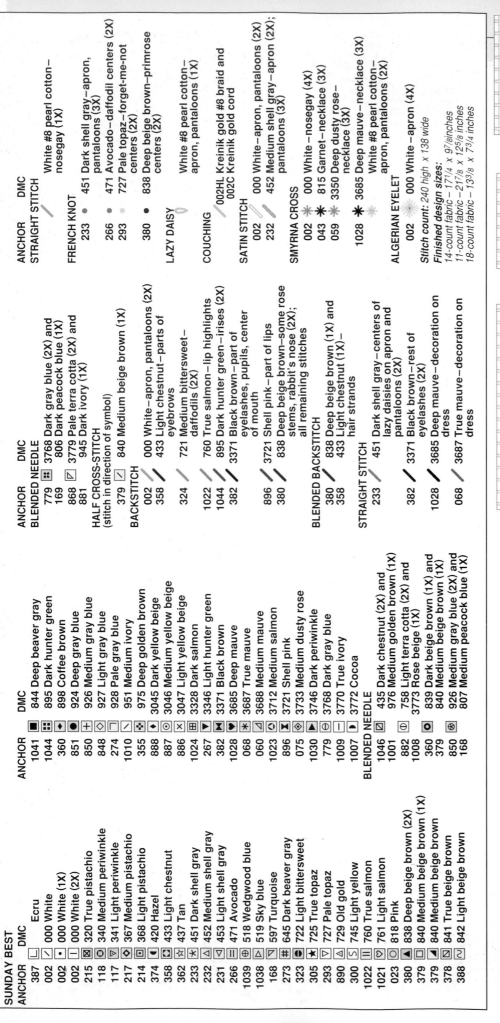

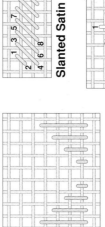

LEFT EYE

RIGHT EYE

MOUTH

YOUNG MAN'S FANCY
PETITE CROSS STITCH CHARTS

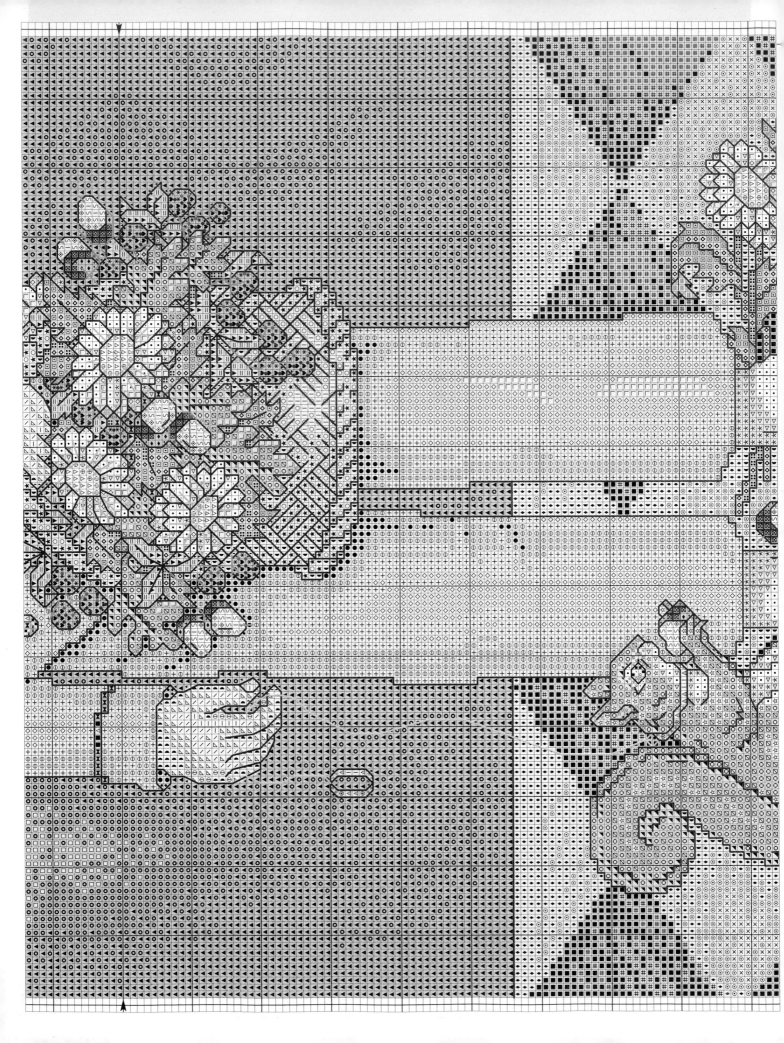

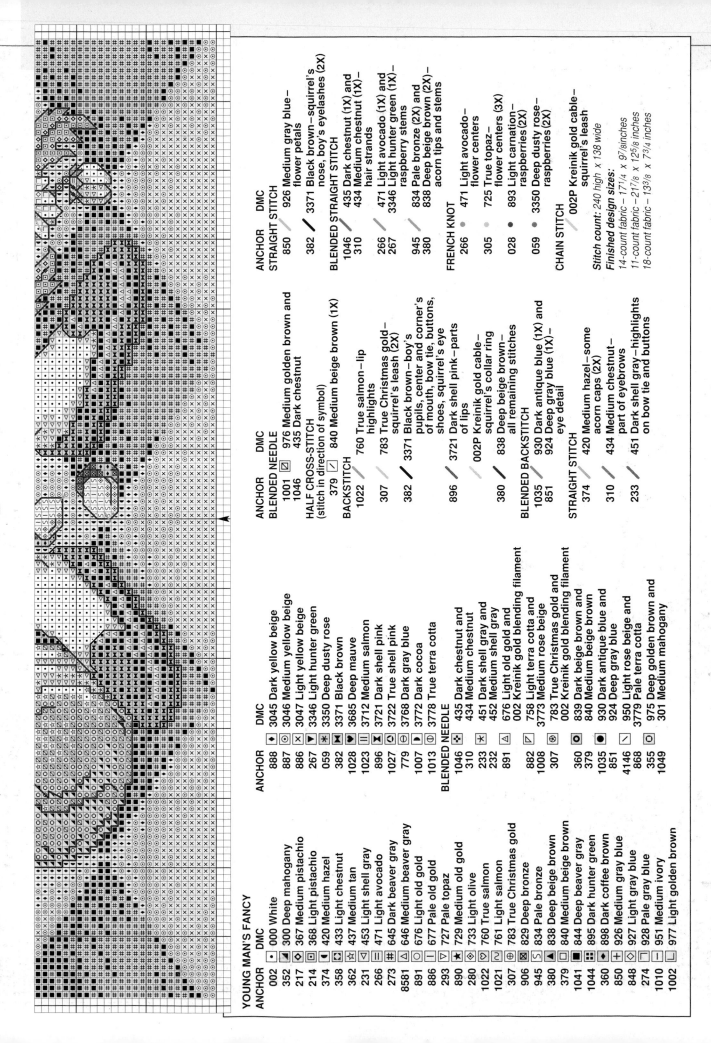

YOUNG MAN'S FANCY

ANCHOR		DMC	
002	•	000	White
352	◣	300	Deep mahogany
217	◆	367	Medium pistachio
214	▶	368	Light pistachio
374	▼	420	Medium hazel
358	◈	433	Light chestnut
362	✭	437	Medium tan
231	▽	453	Light shell gray
266	‖	471	Light avocado
273	#	645	Dark beaver gray
8581	◪	646	Medium beaver gray
891	○	676	Light old gold
886	◹	677	Pale old gold
293	▷	727	Pale topaz
890	★	729	Medium old gold
280	◈	733	Light olive
1022	◿	760	True salmon
1021	~	761	Light salmon
307	⊕	783	True Christmas gold
906	⊠	829	Deep bronze
945	S	834	Pale bronze
380	◀	838	Deep beige brown
379	□	840	Medium beige brown
1041	■	844	Deep beaver gray
1044	▦	895	Dark hunter green
360	◘	898	Dark coffee brown
850	+	926	Medium gray blue
848	◇	927	Light gray blue
274	⌐	928	Pale gray blue
1010	∣	951	Medium ivory
1002	∟	977	Light golden brown

ANCHOR		DMC	
888	◆	3045	Dark yellow beige
887	⊙	3046	Medium yellow beige
886	✕	3047	Light yellow beige
267	▶	3346	Light hunter green
059	✴	3350	Deep dusty rose
382	◪	3371	Black brown
1028	▶	3685	Deep mauve
1023	=	3712	Medium salmon
896	◪	3721	Dark shell pink
1027	◁	3722	True shell pink
779	⊕	3768	Dark gray blue
1007	◣	3772	Dark cocoa
1013	⊖	3778	True terra cotta

BLENDED NEEDLE

ANCHOR		DMC	
1046	✣	435	Dark chestnut and
310		434	Medium chestnut
233	✳	451	Dark shell gray and
232		452	Medium shell gray
891	◁	676	Light old gold and
		002	Kreinik gold blending filament
882	▷	758	Light terra cotta and
1008		3773	Medium rose beige
307	⊛	783	True Christmas gold and
		002	Kreinik gold blending filament
360	◘	839	Dark beige brown and
379		840	Medium beige brown
1035	●	930	Dark antique blue and
851		924	Deep gray blue
4146	/	950	Light rose beige and
868		3779	Pale terra cotta
355	◇	975	Deep golden brown and
1049		301	Medium mahogany

BLENDED NEEDLE

ANCHOR		DMC	
1001	☑	976	Medium golden brown and
1046		435	Dark chestnut

HALF CROSS-STITCH
(stitch in direction of symbol)

379	╱	840	Medium beige brown (1X)

BACKSTITCH

ANCHOR	DMC	
1022	760	True salmon—lip highlights
307	783	True Christmas gold—squirrel's leash (2X)
382	3371	Black brown—boy's pupils, center and corner's of mouth, bow tie, buttons, shoes, squirrel's eye
896	3721	Dark shell pink—parts of lips
	002P	Kreinik gold cable—squirrel's collar ring
380	838	Deep beige brown—all remaining stitches

BLENDED BACKSTITCH

1035	930	Dark antique blue (1X) and
851	924	Deep gray blue (1X)—eye detail

STRAIGHT STITCH

374	420	Medium hazel—some acorn caps (2X)
310	434	Medium chestnut—part of eyebrows
233	451	Dark shell gray—highlights on bow tie and buttons

STRAIGHT STITCH

ANCHOR	DMC	
850	926	Medium gray blue—flower petals
382	3371	Black brown—squirrel's nose, boy's eyelashes (2X)

BLENDED STRAIGHT STITCH

1046	435	Dark chestnut (1X) and
310	434	Medium chestnut (1X)—hair strands
266	471	Light avocado (1X) and
267	3346	Light hunter green (1X)—raspberry stems
945	834	Pale bronze (2X) and
380	838	Deep beige brown (2X)—acorn tips and stems

FRENCH KNOT

266	•	471	Light avocado—flower centers
305	•	725	True topaz—flower centers (3X)
028	●	893	Light carnation—raspberries (2X)
059	●	3350	Deep dusty rose—raspberries (2X)

CHAIN STITCH

	002P	Kreinik gold cable—squirrel's leash

Stitch count: 240 high x 138 wide

Finished design sizes:
14-count fabric – 17 1/4 x 9 7/8 inches
11-count fabric – 21 7/8 x 12 5/8 inches
18-count fabric – 13 3/8 x 7 3/4 inches

★★★★CHRISTMAS HOUSE

As shown on page 34.

MATERIALS

FABRICS
21x18-inch piece of 25-count platinum Dublin linen
21x18-inch piece of 36-count antique white Edinborough linen

THREADS
Cotton embroidery floss in colors listed in keys on pages 51 and 53
Blending filament in colors listed in keys on pages 51 and 53
Pearl cotton in sizes and colors listed in key on page 53
Metallic threads in colors listed in keys on pages 51 and 53

SUPPLIES
Needle; embroidery hoop
Red seed beads
Desired frame and mat

INSTRUCTIONS

For house exterior, tape or zigzag edges of 25-count Dublin to prevent fraying. Find the center of the top row of chart and vertical center of the fabric. Measure 4 inches from the top of the fabric; begin stitching the peak of the roof there.

Work all floss stitches *except* rice stitch and blended needle using two plies of floss. Work rice stitch and blended needle as specified in key. Work all pearl cotton stitches using one strand of thread.

For each section of the design, work all cross-stitches over two threads of fabric before working specialty stitches. Work satin stitches over threads as indicated on chart. Referring to diagrams, *right,* work rice stitches, oblong cross-stitches, four-sided backstitches, large, medium, and small Algerian eyelets, long-armed cross-stitches, crossed corner stitches, diamond satin stitches, twill stitches, octagonal Rhodes stitches, and queen stitches. For Algerian eyelets, give each stitch a gentle tug to open a small hole.

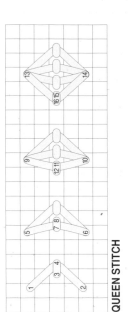

QUEEN STITCH

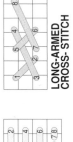

LONG-ARMED CROSS-STITCH

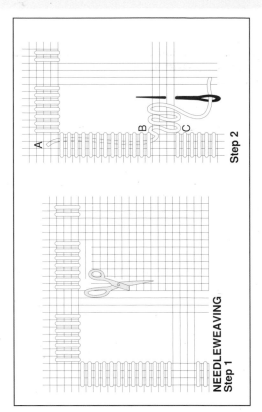

Step 2

NEEDLEWEAVING
Step 1

TWILL STITCH

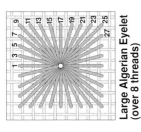

Large Algerian Eyelet (over 8 threads)

Medium Algerian Eyelet (over 6 threads)

Small Algerian Eyelet (over 4 threads)

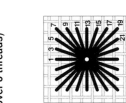

RICE STITCH

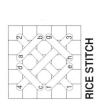

Top left quarter

CROSSED CORNERS STITCH

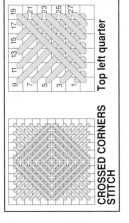

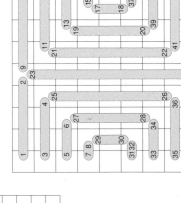

DIAMOND SATIN STITCH

FOUR-SIDED BACKSTITCH

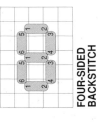

OCTAGONAL RHODES STITCH

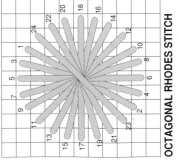

OBLONG CROSS-STITCH

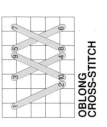

HALF CROSS-STITCH

50

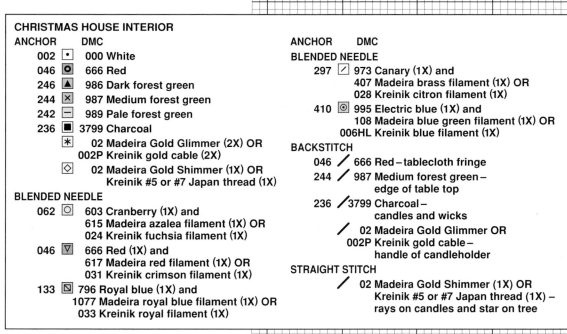

CHRISTMAS HOUSE INTERIOR
Stitch count: 111 high x 59 wide
Finished design size:
18-count fabric – 6¹⁄₈ x 3¹⁄₄ inches

CHRISTMAS HOUSE INTERIOR

ANCHOR		DMC	
002	•	000	White
046	⊙	666	Red
246	▲	986	Dark forest green
244	✕	987	Medium forest green
242	−	989	Pale forest green
236	■	3799	Charcoal
	✳	02	Madeira Gold Glimmer (2X) OR
		002P	Kreinik gold cable (2X)
	◇	02	Madeira Gold Shimmer (1X) OR
			Kreinik #5 or #7 Japan thread (1X)

BLENDED NEEDLE

062	⊚	603	Cranberry (1X) and
		615	Madeira azalea filament (1X) OR
		024	Kreinik fuchsia filament (1X)
046	▽	666	Red (1X) and
		617	Madeira red filament (1X) OR
		031	Kreinik crimson filament (1X)
133	◨	796	Royal blue (1X) and
		1077	Madeira royal blue filament (1X) OR
		033	Kreinik royal filament (1X)

ANCHOR		DMC	
BLENDED NEEDLE			
297	⊘	973	Canary (1X) and
		407	Madeira brass filament (1X) OR
		028	Kreinik citron filament (1X)
410	◉	995	Electric blue (1X) and
		108	Madeira blue green filament (1X) OR
		006HL	Kreinik blue filament (1X)

BACKSTITCH

046	╱	666	Red – tablecloth fringe
244	╱	987	Medium forest green – edge of table top
236	╱	3799	Charcoal – candles and wicks
	╱	02	Madeira Gold Glimmer OR
		002P	Kreinik gold cable – handle of candleholder

STRAIGHT STITCH

| | ╱ | 02 | Madeira Gold Shimmer (1X) OR |
| | | | Kreinik #5 or #7 Japan thread (1X) – rays on candles and star on tree |

For window frames, after working satin stitch blocks around the edges of each window, cut and remove threads inside the window areas, referring to needleweaving Step 1 diagram, *opposite.* Thread a needle with a 30-inch length of pearl cotton. Work needleweaving referring to Step 2 diagram. Use one ply of red floss to sew beads randomly to wreath on the door and garland on the fence.

For house interior, tape or zigzag edges of 36-count linen to prevent fraying. Find vertical center of chart and fabric. Measure 7 inches from top; begin cross-stitching top of white table candle (not wick) there.

Use two plies of floss or metallic thread as specified in key to work cross-stitches over two threads of fabric. Work the blended needle as specified in key. Work all of the backstitches and straight stitches using one ply of floss or one strand of metallic thread.

Press both pieces. Position house exterior atop house interior so Christmas tree and candle motifs show through window openings; baste at sides of fabric pieces to hold in place. Frame and mat as desired.

CHRISTMAS HOUSE INTERIOR

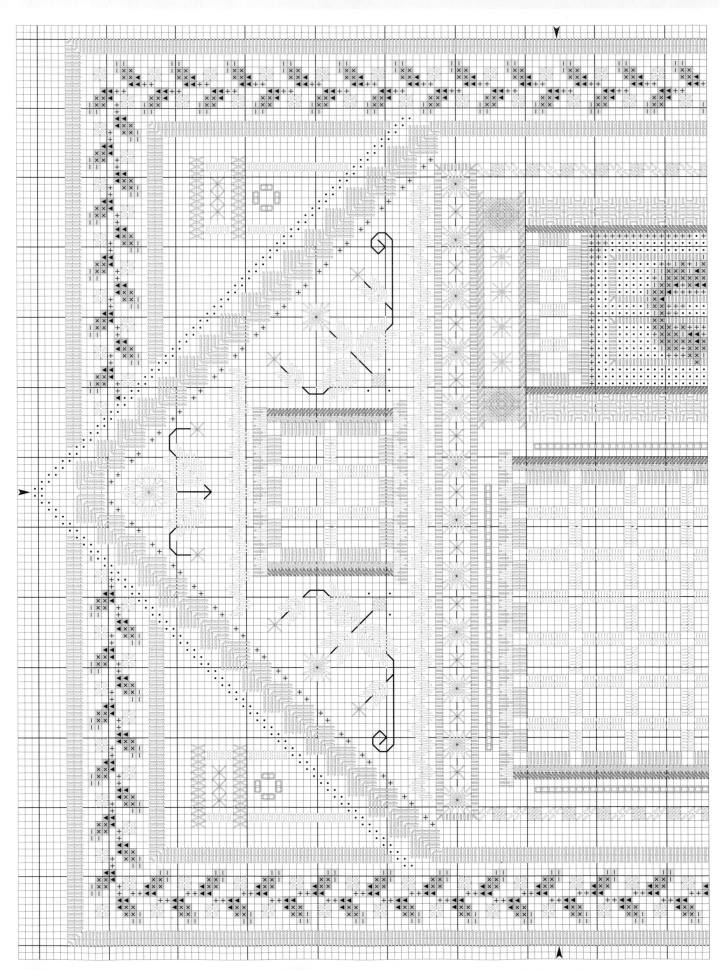

CHRISTMAS HOUSE EXTERIOR

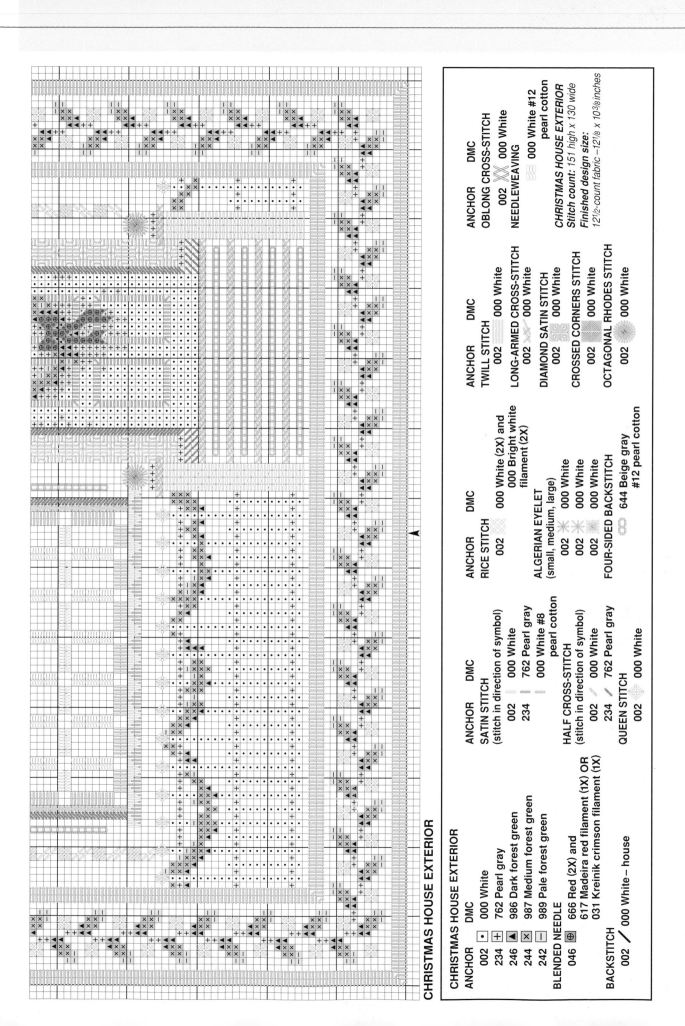

CHRISTMAS HOUSE EXTERIOR

ANCHOR	DMC
002	000 White
234	762 Pearl gray
246	986 Dark forest green
244	987 Medium forest green
242	989 Pale forest green

BLENDED NEEDLE

046	666 Red (2X) and
	617 Madeira red filament (1X) OR
	031 Kreinik crimson filament (1X)

BACKSTITCH

002	000 White – house

SATIN STITCH
(stitch in direction of symbol)

ANCHOR	DMC
002	000 White
234	762 Pearl gray
	000 White #8 pearl cotton

HALF CROSS-STITCH
(stitch in direction of symbol)

002	000 White
234	762 Pearl gray

QUEEN STITCH

002	000 White

RICE STITCH

ANCHOR	DMC
002	000 White (2X) and
	000 Bright white filament (2X)

ALGERIAN EYELET
(small, medium, large)

002	000 White
002	000 White
002	000 White

FOUR-SIDED BACKSTITCH

	644 Beige gray #12 pearl cotton

TWILL STITCH

ANCHOR	DMC
002	000 White

LONG-ARMED CROSS-STITCH

002	000 White

DIAMOND SATIN STITCH

002	000 White

CROSSED CORNERS STITCH

002	000 White

OCTAGONAL RHODES STITCH

002	000 White

OBLONG CROSS-STITCH

ANCHOR	DMC
002	000 White

NEEDLEWEAVING

	000 White #12 pearl cotton

CHRISTMAS HOUSE EXTERIOR
Stitch count: 151 high x 130 wide
Finished design size:
12½-count fabric – 12⅛ x 10⅜ inches

★★★★ SANTA'S LIST

As shown on page 35.

MATERIALS

FABRIC
24x18-inch piece of 27-count dirty
linen Linda fabric

FLOSS
Cotton embroidery floss in colors
listed in key on page 57

One additional skein *each* of deep
salmon (DMC 347), medium
chestnut (DMC 434), light shell
gray (DMC 453), deep garnet
(DMC 902), and light antique
violet (DMC 3042)

Two additional skeins *each* of
medium pistachio (DMC 367),
pearl gray (DMC 762), medium
garnet (DMC 815), deep coffee
brown (DMC 938), and black
brown (DMC 3371)

Three additional skeins *each* of
dark beige brown (DMC 839)
and medium beige brown
(DMC 840)

SUPPLIES
Needle
Embroidery hoop
Desired frame and mat

INSTRUCTIONS

Tape or zigzag the edges of the
Linda fabric to prevent fraying.
Find the center of the chart and
the center of the fabric; begin
stitching there.

Use three plies of floss to work
cross-stitches over two threads of
the fabric. Work the straight stitches, the French knots, and the lazy
daisy stitches as specified in the
key. Work backstitches using one
ply of floss unless otherwise
specified in the key.

Press the finished stitchery from
the back. Frame and mat stitchery
as desired.

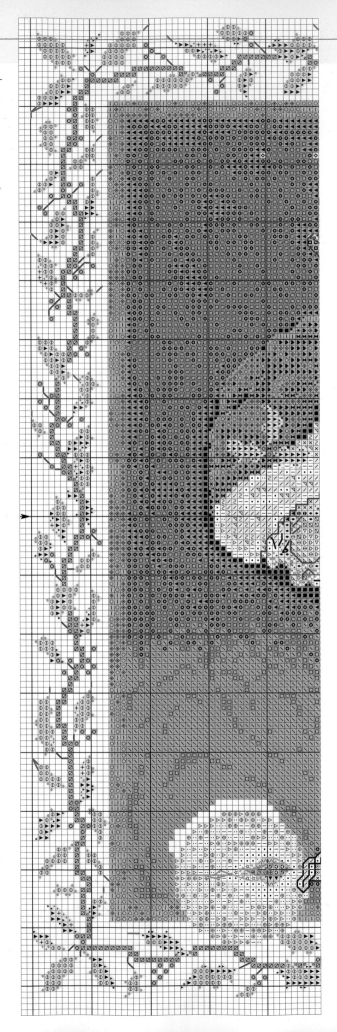

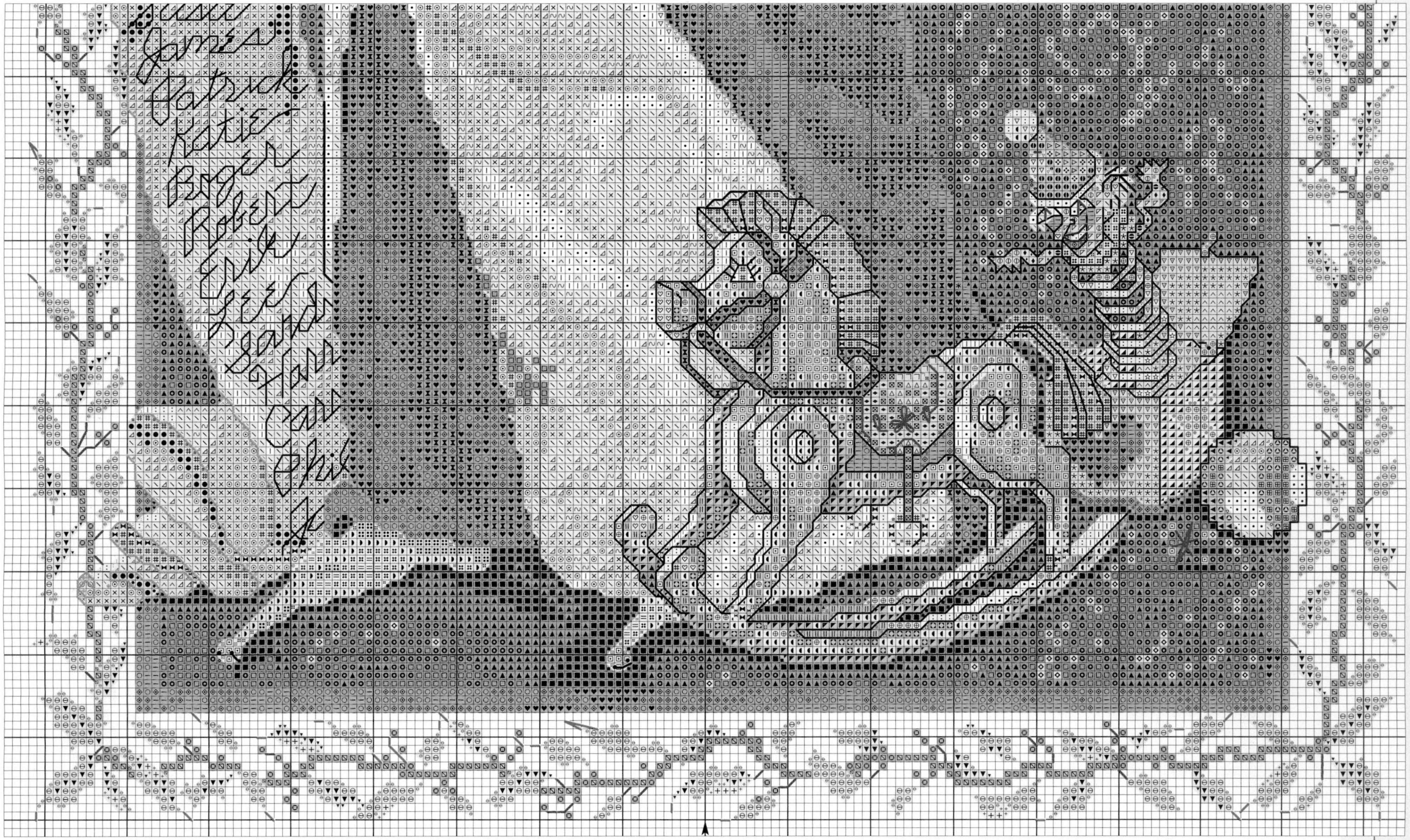

SANTA'S LIST

SANTA'S LIST

ANCHOR	DMC			ANCHOR	DMC			ANCHOR	DMC	
002	000	White		1022	760	True salmon		872	3740	Dark antique violet
1019	315	Dark antique mauve		234	762	Pearl gray		1036	3750	Deep antique blue
1017	316	Medium antique mauve		307	783	Christmas gold		169	3760	Wedgwood blue
400	317	True pewter		132	797	Royal blue		1007	3772	Dark cocoa
9046	321	True Christmas red		136	799	Medium Delft blue		393	3790	Beige gray
1025	347	Deep salmon		144	800	Pale Delft blue				
217	367	Medium pistachio		043	815	Medium garnet				
855	370	Dark pecan		271	819	Pink				
854	371	Medium pecan		945	834	Bronze				
401	413	Dark pewter		360	839	Dark beige brown				
374	420	Hazel		379	840	Medium beige brown				
358	433	Light chestnut		379	840	Medium beige brown (1X)				
310	434	Medium chestnut		218	890	Deep pistachio				
1045	436	Dark tan		897	902	Deep garnet				
233	451	Dark shell gray		340	920	Copper				
231	453	Light shell gray		1034	931	Medium antique blue				
266	471	Avocado		1033	932	True antique blue				
1005	498	Dark Christmas red		381	938	Deep coffee brown				
1042	504	Blue green		1011	948	Peach				
1038	519	Sky blue		076	961	Rose pink				
212	561	Seafoam		185	964	Aqua				
889	610	Drab brown		244	987	Medium forest green				
936	632	Deep cocoa		243	988	Light forest green				
891	676	Light old gold		187	992	Aquamarine				
886	677	Pale old gold		870	3042	Light antique violet				
926	712	Cream		681	3051	Dark gray green				
324	720	Dark bittersweet		261	3053	Light gray green				
326	721	Medium bittersweet		883	3064	Light cocoa				
305	725	Topaz		1024	3328	Dark salmon				
890	729	Old gold		382	3371	Black brown				
361	738	Light tan		068	3687	True mauve				
314	741	Tangerine		060	3688	Medium mauve				
1012	754	Medium peach		1023	3712	Medium salmon				
882	758	Terra cotta		1016	3727	Light antique mauve				

BACKSTITCH

ANCHOR	DMC	
002	000	White—part of list, Santa's mustache
400	317	True pewter—candle, rest of list, Santa's hair, beard and eyebrows, white present, jack-in-the box's hair, part of horse's mane
217	367	Medium pistachio—leaf tips in border (2X)
401	413	Dark pewter—white parts of suit
266	471	Avocado—bottom of candle wick (2X)
1005	498	Dark Christmas red—jack-in-the box's mouth
1038	519	Sky blue—yo-yo string (2X)
314	741	Tangerine—middle of candle flame
360	839	Dark beige brown—Santa's face and hands, doll, teddy bear, nutcracker's face, part of sack, saddle decoration
897	902	Deep garnet—nutcracker's mustache
340	920	Copper—bottom of candle flame
244	987	Medium forest green—top of candle wick (2X); croquet mallet (1X)
393	3790	Beige gray—stems in border (2X)
236	3799	Charcoal—names on list (2X)
382	3371	Black brown—all remaining stitches

STRAIGHT STITCH

ANCHOR	DMC	
400	317	True pewter—jingle bells (2X)
305	725	Topaz—book cover, lollipop stick (3X); top of candle flame, wagon decoration, nutcracker's hat (1X)
945	834	Bronze—jack (2X)
169	3760	Wedgwood blue—jack-in-the box's eyes (2X)

FRENCH KNOT

ANCHOR	DMC	
400	317	True pewter—jingle bells (2X)
305	725	Topaz—wagon decoration (2X)
382	3371	Black brown—teddy bear's nose (4X); teddy bear's eyes, hinge on box of jack-in-the box (2X)
236	3799	Charcoal—names on list (2X)

LAZY DAISY

ANCHOR	DMC	
360	839	Dark beige brown—saddle decoration (1X)

★★★★ SPANISH SAMPLER

As shown on page 36.

MATERIALS

FABRIC
19x19-inch piece of 28-count ivory Jubilee fabric

THREADS
Cotton embroidery floss in colors listed in key on pages 58–59

One additional skein *each* of ecru, deep gray blue (DMC 924), medium gray blue (DMC 926), and medium antique violet (DMC 3041)

Gold blending filament as listed in key on pages 58–59

SUPPLIES
Needle
Embroidery hoop
Red seed beads
Desired frame and mat

Stitch count: 250 high x 166 wide
Finished design sizes:
13½-count fabric – 18½ x 12¼ inches
14-count fabric – 17⅞ x 11⅞ inches
18-count fabric – 13⅞ x 9¼ inches

INSTRUCTIONS

Tape or zigzag edges of fabric to prevent fraying. Find the center of the chart and the center of the fabric; begin stitching there.

For each section of the design, work all cross-stitches over two threads of fabric using three plies of floss or two strands of blending filament, before working specialty stitches. Using three plies of floss, work all satin stitches over threads as indicated on chart.

Referring to the diagrams, pages 60–61, work the four-sided back-stitches, overcast backstitches, French knots, bullion knots, diamond eyelets and large, medium, and small Algerian eyelets. For Algerian eyelets, give each stitch a gentle tug to open a small hole in center. For four-sided backstitches, give each stitch a gentle tug to open a small hole at each corner. Work straight stitches and backstitches as specified in key. Attach beads using one ply of red floss.

Press finished stitchery from the back. Frame and mat as desired.

SPANISH SAMPLER

ANCHOR		DMC	
387	·		Ecru
897	▲	221	Deep shell pink
895	+	223	Medium shell pink
893	=	224	Light shell pink
168	×	597	Light turquoise
167	○	598	Medium turquoise
898	●	611	Dark drab brown
832	⊙	612	Medium drab brown
851	■	924	Deep gray blue
850	✳	926	Medium gray blue
871	◆	3041	Medium antique violet
870	△	3042	Light antique violet
262	□	3363	Medium loden
260	I	3364	Light loden

ANCHOR		DMC	
1027	⊠	3722	True shell pink
779	#	3768	Dark gray blue
	✶	002	Kreinik gold blending filament

SATIN STITCH
(stitch in direction of symbol)

387	╱		Ecru
897	╱	221	Deep shell pink
895	╱	223	Medium shell pink
893	╱	224	Light shell pink
167	╱	598	Medium turquoise
832	╱	612	Medium drab brown
851	╱	924	Deep gray blue
850	╱	926	Medium gray blue

ANCHOR		DMC	
848	╱	927	Light gray blue
871	╱	3041	Medium antique violet
262	╱	3363	Medium loden
260	╱	3364	Light loden
1027	╱	3722	True shell pink
779	╱	3768	Dark gray blue
	╱	002	Kreinik gold blending filament

LARGE ALGERIAN EYELET

893	✳	224	Light shell pink

MEDIUM ALGERIAN EYELET

897	✳	221	Deep shell pink
895	✳	223	Medium shell pink

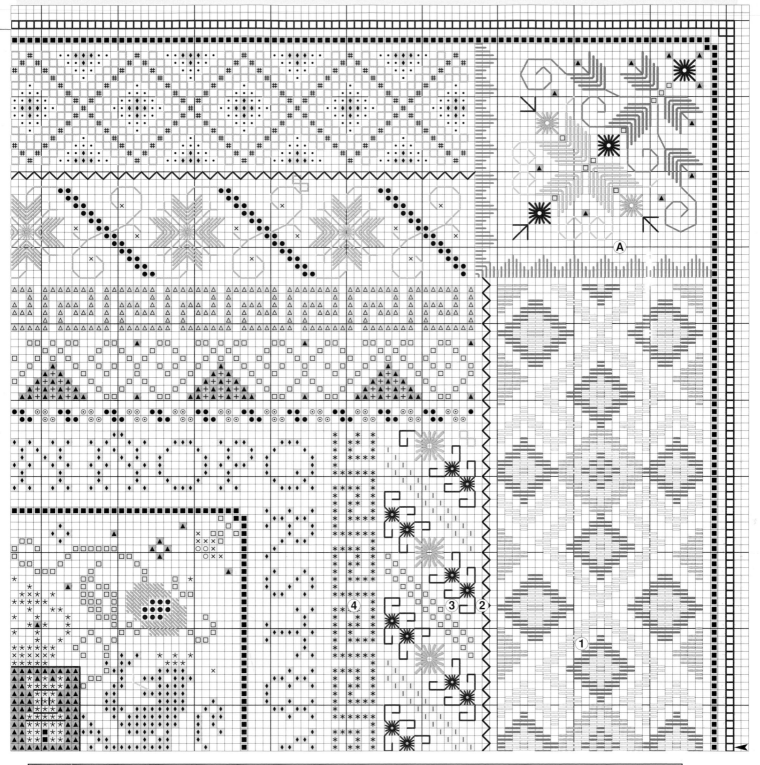

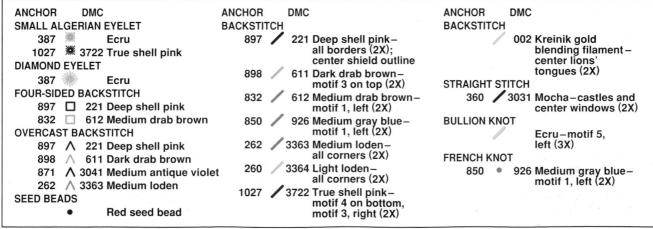

ANCHOR		DMC	
SMALL ALGERIAN EYELET			
387	✳		Ecru
1027	✳	3722	True shell pink
DIAMOND EYELET			
387	✳		Ecru
FOUR-SIDED BACKSTITCH			
897	☐	221	Deep shell pink
832	☐	612	Medium drab brown
OVERCAST BACKSTITCH			
897	∧	221	Deep shell pink
898	∧	611	Dark drab brown
871	∧	3041	Medium antique violet
262	∧	3363	Medium loden
SEED BEADS			
	●		Red seed bead

ANCHOR		DMC	
BACKSTITCH			
897	╱	221	Deep shell pink– all borders (2X); center shield outline
898	╱	611	Dark drab brown– motif 3 on top (2X)
832	╱	612	Medium drab brown– motif 1, left (2X)
850	╱	926	Medium gray blue– motif 1, left (2X)
262	╱	3363	Medium loden– all corners (2X)
260	╱	3364	Light loden– all corners (2X)
1027	╱	3722	True shell pink– motif 4 on bottom, motif 3, right (2X)

ANCHOR		DMC	
BACKSTITCH			
	╱	002	Kreinik gold blending filament– center lions' tongues (2X)
STRAIGHT STITCH			
360	╱	3031	Mocha–castles and center windows (2X)
BULLION KNOT			
	╱		Ecru–motif 5, left (3X)
FRENCH KNOT			
850	●	926	Medium gray blue– motif 1, left (2X)

SPANISH SAMPLER

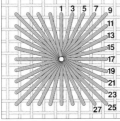

**Large Algerian Eyelet
(over 8 threads)**

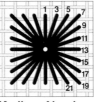

**Medium Algerian
Eyelet
(over 6 threads)**

**Small Algerian
Eyelet
(over 4 threads)**

Diamond Eyelet Stitch

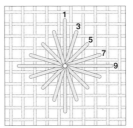

**Four-sided
Backstitch**

Overcast Backstitch

Four-sided Stitch Diagonal Variation

Attaching a Bead

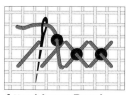

Bullion Knot

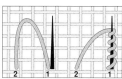

French Knot

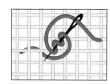

Stitch count: *191 high x 191 wide*
Finished design sizes:
14-count fabric – 13 3/4 x 13 3/4 inches
11-count fabric – 17 3/8 x 17 3/8 inches
18-count fabric – 10 5/8 x 10 5/8 inches

62

Country
COLLECTIBLES

*W*hat a spectacular assortment of homespun designs for country lovers everywhere. From hens nestled in their baskets to a quaint alphabet sampler surrounded by old-fashioned motifs, we have a country collectible for everyone!

Nesting Hens

This barnyard trio will provide a warm welcome in any room in your home. The hens, stitched on 18-count gray Aida cloth, will work up rather quickly because there are no fractional or specialty stitches. The complete instructions and charts are on pages 69–71.

Monday Meddler

Our young country lass has her hands full, bringing in the laundry. With aid from her impish friend, the goose, her chore is taking twice as long. The homestead scene is stitched on a separate piece of 27-count Linda fabric as the mat to create added dimension. Complete instructions and charts begin on page 72.

Harvest Helper

With pet pig at side, this charming country lad is eager to bring home the day's goodies from the vegetable patch. The welcoming sky was created with half cross-stitches using powder blue floss. The mat is created by stitching a farm on an additional piece of 27-count Linda fabric. Complete instructions and charts begin on page 73.

Country Cousins

These sunbonnet characters and the squawky geese will bring a smile to any child's face. Stitch them on 18-count Aida to make a sweet framed piece or over two threads on 18-count daffodil Tabby cloth fabric to create an afghan anyone would love to cuddle up in. Complete instructions and charts begin on page 76.

Country Alphabet

Apples, eggs, and teddy bears—just a few symbols that remind us of the quiet country life. All these motifs and letters combined form a wonderfully old-fashioned country alphabet sampler stitched on 14-count Aida cloth. Complete instructions are on page 77 and the chart is on page 78.

Country Delicious

This colorful homespun design is stitched on 28-count bone Jobelan. The bowl of crisp apples rests nicely upon a gingham-bordered tablecloth. Half cross-stitches worked with one ply of floss are used to create special highlights. Complete instructions are on page 77 and the chart is on page 79.

68

Stitch count: 75 high x 73 wide
Finished design sizes:
18-count fabric – 4⅛ x 4 inches
11-count fabric – 6⅞ x 6⅝ inches
14-count fabric – 5⅜ x 5¼ inches

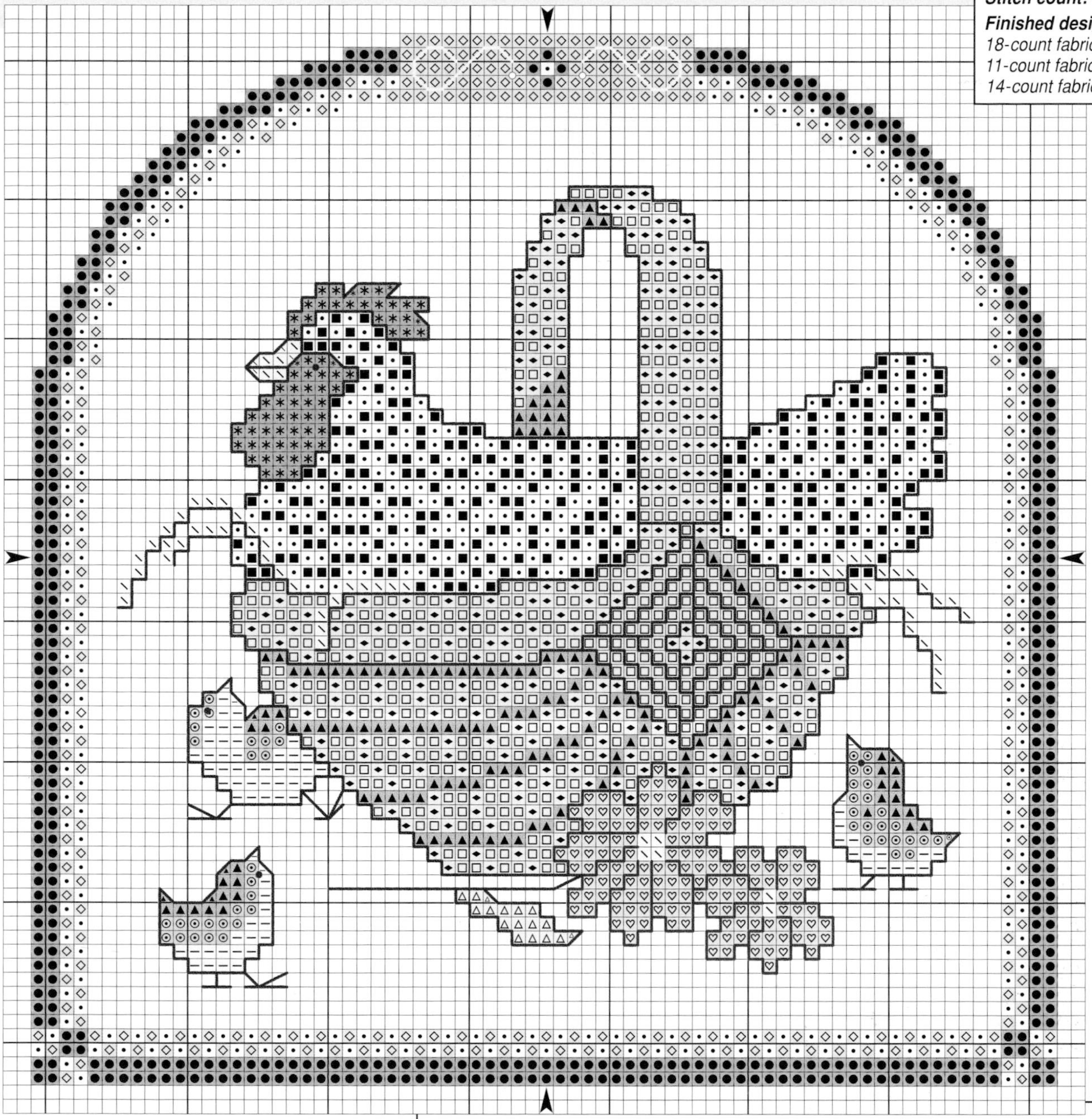

BARRED PLYMOUTH ROCK HEN

**BARRED PLYMOUTH ROCK HEN

As shown on page 62.

MATERIALS

FABRIC
8x8-inch piece of 18-count gray Aida cloth

FLOSS
Cotton embroidery floss in colors listed in key

SUPPLIES
Needle; embroidery hoop
Desired frame and mat

BARRED PLYMOUTH ROCK HEN

ANCHOR		DMC	
002	•	000	White
1049	◎	301	Medium mahogany
403	■	310	Black
1025	✳	347	Salmon
266	△	471	Avocado
891	＼	676	Light old gold
360	◆	839	Dark beige brown
378	□	841	True beige brown
897	●	902	Deep garnet
850	◇	926	Gray blue
381	▲	938	Coffee brown

ANCHOR		DMC	
886	─	3047	Yellow beige
049	♡	3689	Mauve
BACKSTITCH			
301		744	Yellow–border
897	╱	902	Deep garnet–flowers
381	╱	938	Coffee brown–stem, chick's legs (2X); all remaining stitches (1X)
FRENCH KNOT			
002	○	000	White–border
381	●	938	Coffee brown–eyes

INSTRUCTIONS

Tape or zigzag edges of fabric to prevent fraying. Find center of the chart and of fabric; begin stitching there. Use two plies of floss to work cross-stitches. Work backstitches and French knots using two plies unless otherwise specified in key. Press the finished stitchery from back. Frame and mat as desired.

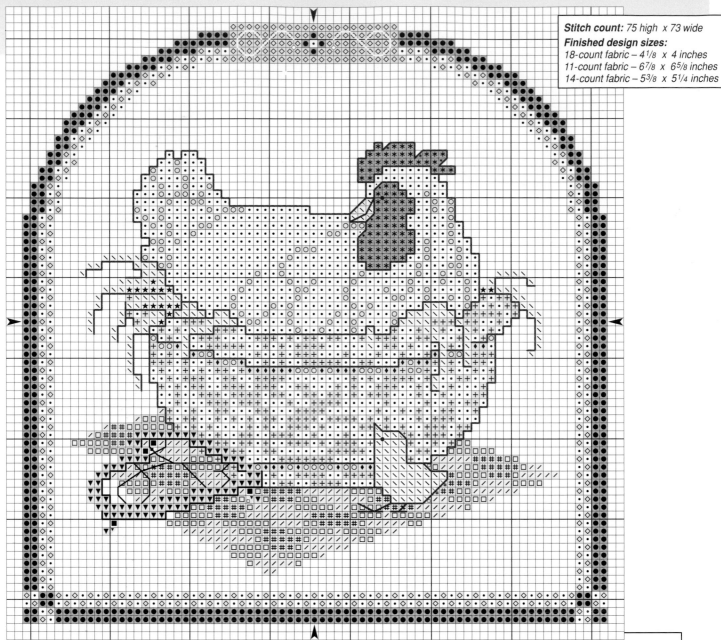

WHITE LEGHORN HEN

WHITE LEGHORN HEN				
ANCHOR		DMC		
002	·	000 White		
403	■	310 Black		
979	♦	312 Navy		
977	+	334 Dark baby blue		
1025	✳	347 Salmon		
398	○	415 Pearl gray		
891	◣	676 Light old gold		
901	★	680 Dark old gold		
379	⊞	840 Medium beige brown		
378	▢	841 True beige brown		
388	╱	842 Light beige brown		
1041	▼	844 Beaver gray		

ANCHOR		DMC
897	●	902 Deep garnet
850	◇	926 Gray blue

BACKSTITCH

403	╱	310 Black–outline of heart (1X); heart interior
301		744 Yellow–border
381	╱	938 Coffee brown– chick's legs (2X); all remaining stitches (1X)

FRENCH KNOT

002	○	000 White–border
381	●	938 Coffee brown–eyes

★★WHITE LEGHORN HEN

As shown on page 62.

MATERIALS

FABRIC
8x8-inch piece of 18-count gray Aida cloth

FLOSS
Cotton embroidery floss in colors listed in key

SUPPLIES
Needle; embroidery hoop
Desired frame and mat

INSTRUCTIONS

Tape or zigzag the edges of the gray Aida cloth to prevent it from fraying. Find the center of the chart and the center of the Aida cloth; begin stitching the design there.

Use two plies of the cotton embroidery floss to work all the cross-stitches. Work the backstitches and French knots using two plies of embroidery floss unless otherwise specified in key.

Press the finished stitchery from the back. Frame and mat the design as desired.

Stitch count: 75 high x 73 wide
Finished design sizes:
18-count fabric – 4 1/8 x 4 inches
11-count fabric – 6 7/8 x 6 5/8 inches
14-count fabric – 5 3/8 x 5 1/4 inches

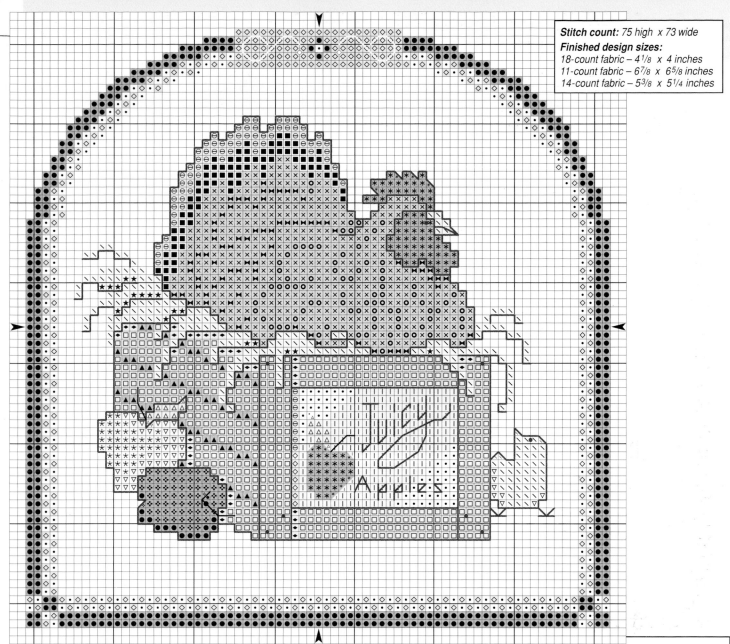

RHODE ISLAND RED HEN

RHODE ISLAND RED HEN				
ANCHOR	DMC		ANCHOR	DMC
002 ·	000 White		378 ▫	841 True beige brown
352 ⋈	300 Deep mahogany		897 ●	902 Deep garnet
403 ■	310 Black		1015 ◉	918 Red copper
1025 ✳	347 Salmon		340 ✕	920 Copper
266 △	471 Avocado		850 ◇	926 Gray blue
392 ⊖	642 Beige gray		381 ▲	938 Coffee brown
891 ⟍	676 Light old gold		BACKSTITCH	
901 ★	680 Dark old gold		403 ╱	310 Black–apple stems
890 ▽	729 Medium old gold		301	744 Yellow–border
301 ✴	744 Yellow		381 ╱	938 Coffee brown–chick's legs (2X); all remaining stitches (1X)
128 ⏐	775 Light baby blue		FRENCH KNOT	
1005 ❖	816 Light garnet		002 ○	000 White–border
360 ◆	839 Dark beige brown		381 ●	938 Coffee brown–eyes, nails in box

RHODE ISLAND RED HEN

As shown on page 63.

MATERIALS

FABRIC
8x8-inch piece of 18-count gray Aida cloth

FLOSS
Cotton embroidery floss in colors listed in key

SUPPLIES
Needle; embroidery hoop
Desired frame and mat

INSTRUCTIONS

Tape or zigzag edges of gray Aida cloth to prevent fraying. Find the center of the chart and the center of the fabric; begin stitching design there.

Use two plies of embroidery floss to work cross-stitches. Work the backstitches and French knots using two plies of floss unless otherwise specified in the key. Press finished stitchery from back. Frame and mat as desired.

Stitch count: 75 high x 73 wide
Finished design sizes:
18-count fabric – 4 1/8 x 4 inches
11-count fabric – 6 7/8 x 6 5/8 inches
14-count fabric – 5 3/8 x 5 1/4 inches

★★★MONDAY MEDDLER

As shown on page 64.

MATERIALS

FABRIC

Two 18x21-inch pieces of 27-count ivory Linda fabric

FLOSS

Cotton embroidery floss in colors listed in key

One additional skein of powder blue (DMC 828) floss

SUPPLIES

Needle; embroidery hoop

Erasable fabric marker

Ivory sewing thread

Mat with an 8½x10½-inch opening

18x21-inch piece of polyester fleece; crafts glue

Desired frame and additional mat

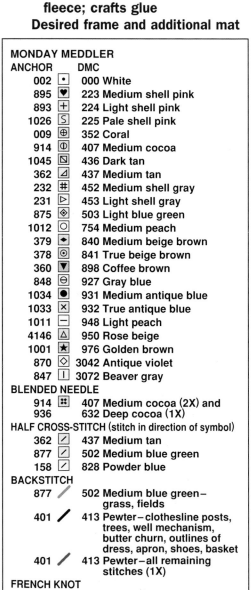

MONDAY MEDDLER		
ANCHOR	DMC	
002	·	000 White
895	♥	223 Medium shell pink
893	+	224 Light shell pink
1026	S	225 Pale shell pink
009	⊕	352 Coral
914	◫	407 Medium cocoa
1045	◩	436 Dark tan
362	◿	437 Medium tan
232	⊞	452 Medium shell gray
231	▷	453 Light shell gray
875	◈	503 Light blue green
1012	○	754 Medium peach
379	◆	840 Medium beige brown
378	◉	841 True beige brown
360	▼	898 Coffee brown
848	⊖	927 Gray blue
1034	●	931 Medium antique blue
1033	✕	932 True antique blue
1011	−	948 Light peach
4146	△	950 Rose beige
1001	★	976 Golden brown
870	◇	3042 Antique violet
847	⊺	3072 Beaver gray
BLENDED NEEDLE		
914	⊞	407 Medium cocoa (2X) and
936		632 Deep cocoa (1X)
HALF CROSS-STITCH (stitch in direction of symbol)		
362	⟋	437 Medium tan
877	⟋	502 Medium blue green
158	⟋	828 Powder blue
BACKSTITCH		
877	╱	502 Medium blue green– grass, fields
401	╱	413 Pewter–clothesline posts, trees, well mechanism, butter churn, outlines of dress, apron, shoes, basket
401	╱	413 Pewter–all remaining stitches (1X)
FRENCH KNOT		
401	●	413 Pewter–eyes, buttons

INSTRUCTIONS

Tape or zigzag edges of ivory Linda fabric to prevent fraying. For center stitchery, find the center of the chart and the center of one piece of fabric; begin stitching design there. For the mat, measure and mark a 10½x8½-inch rectangle in the center of remaining fabric. Machine-stitch along the marking. Begin stitching the mat motif in upper right-hand corner counting squares from dotted line on chart and machine stitching.

Use three plies of floss to work cross-stitches over two threads of fabric. Work half cross-stitches, in direction of symbol, using two plies of floss. Work blended needle as specified in the key. Work all the backstitches using two plies and French knots using four plies.

Glue fleece to front of mat; trim to match mat. Cut and remove

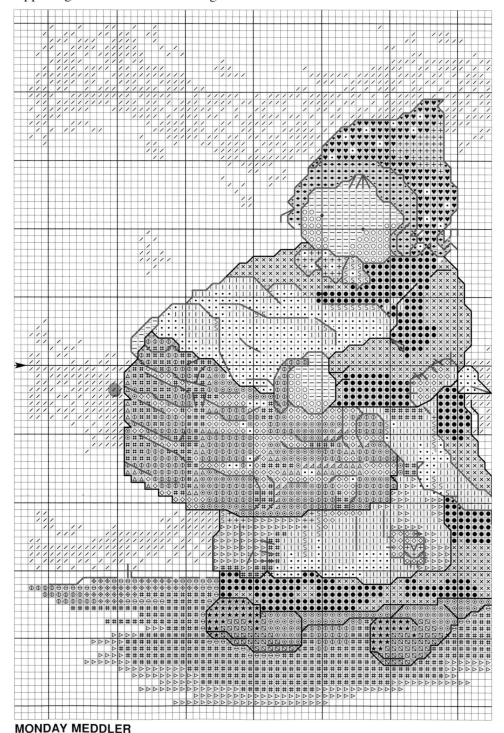

MONDAY MEDDLER

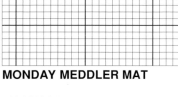

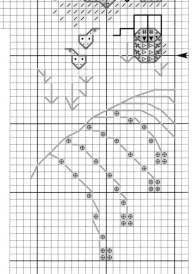

excess fabric 1 inch inside the machine stitching on stitched mat. Clip the corners carefully. Center fleece over the back of the mat design. Pull the edges to the back of the mat and glue, trimming outer edges as necessary. Position stitched mat on the design and frame as desired.

MONDAY MEDDLER MAT

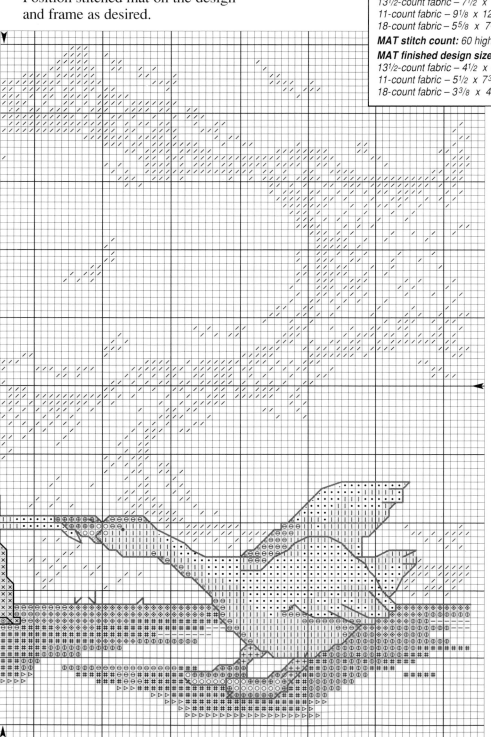

Stitch count: 100 high x 137 wide
Finished design sizes:
13½-count fabric – 7½ x 10⅛ inches
11-count fabric – 9⅛ x 12½ inches
18-count fabric – 5⅝ x 7⅝ inches
MAT stitch count: 60 high x 80 wide
MAT finished design sizes:
13½-count fabric – 4½ x 6 inches
11-count fabric – 5½ x 7⅜ inches
18-count fabric – 3⅜ x 4½ inches

***HARVEST HELPER
As shown on page 65.

MATERIALS
FABRIC
Two 18x21-inch pieces of 27-count ivory Linda fabric
FLOSS
Cotton embroidery floss in colors listed in key on page 75
One additional skein of powder blue (DMC 828) embroidery floss
SUPPLIES
Needle
Embroidery hoop
Erasable fabric marker
Ivory sewing thread
Mat with a 8½x10½-inch opening
18x21-inch piece of polyester fleece
Crafts glue
Desired frame and additional mat

INSTRUCTIONS
Tape or zigzag edges of fabric to prevent fraying. For center stitchery, find center of chart and center of one piece of fabric; begin stitching there. For mat, measure and mark a 10½x8½-inch rectangle in center of

remaining fabric. Machine-stitch along marking. Begin stitching the mat motif in lower left-hand corner, counting squares from dotted line on chart and machine stitching.

Use three plies of floss to work cross-stitches over two threads of fabric. Work half cross-stitches, in direction of symbol, using two plies of floss. Work backstitches using two plies of floss. Work French knots as specified in the key.

Glue fleece to front of mat; trim to match mat. Cut and remove excess fabric 1 inch inside machine stitching on stitched mat. Clip the corners carefully. Center the fleece over back of mat design and pull the edges to back of mat and glue, trimming outer edges as necessary. Position stitched mat on design and frame as desired.

Stitch count: 98 high x 137 wide
Finished design sizes:
13½-count fabric – 7¼ x 10⅛ inches
11-count fabric – 9 x 12½ inches
18-count fabric – 5½ x 7⅝ inches
MAT stitch count: 50 high x 84 wide
MAT finished design sizes:
13½-count fabric – 3⅝ x 6¼ inches
11-count fabric – 4½ x 7⅝ inches
18-count fabric – 2¾ x 4⅝ inches

HARVEST HELPER

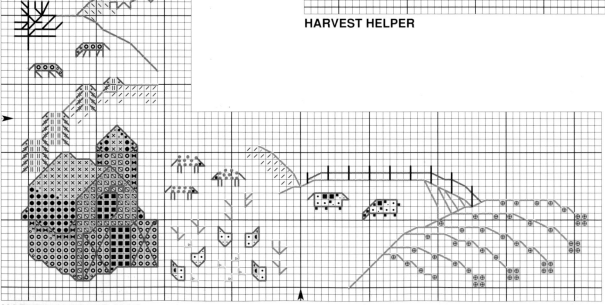

HARVEST HELPER MAT

HARVEST HELPER

ANCHOR		DMC	
002	⋅	000	White
893	⊞	224	Shell pink
215	⊡	320	True pistachio
011	◗	350	Medium coral
009	⊕	352	Pale coral
008	♡	353	Dark peach
217	▲	367	Medium pistachio
214	=	368	Light pistachio
914	⊕	407	Cocoa
401	■	413	Pewter
358	⋈	433	Deep golden brown
1046	◉	435	True golden brown
1045	◳	436	Dark tan
891	‖	676	Light old gold
886	▽	677	Pale old gold
890	✳	729	Medium old gold
361	☆	738	Light tan
302	▷	743	Yellow

ANCHOR		DMC	
1012	◯	754	Medium peach
144	~	800	Delft blue
378	⊙	841	True beige brown
388	▢	842	Light beige brown
1034	●	931	Medium antique blue
1033	✕	932	True antique blue
1011	−	948	Light peach
4146	△	950	Rose beige
1010	⌐	951	Ivory
393	♦	3022	Medium brown gray
899	✶	3023	Light brown gray
397	▨	3024	Pale brown gray

BLENDED NEEDLE

847	⊓	3072	Beaver gray (2X) and
1043		369	Pale pistachio (1X)

HALF CROSS-STITCH
(stitch in direction of symbol)

002	◳	000	White

ANCHOR		DMC	
362	⁄	437	Medium tan
158	⁄	828	Powder blue
871	◳	3041	Antique violet

BACKSTITCH

362	⁄	437	Medium tan−chicks
877	⁄	502	Blue green−hills, field grass in border (2X)
890	⁄	729	Medium old gold−corn silk
871	⁄	3041	Antique violet− hills in border
401	⁄	413	Pewter−pigs' eyelashes and tail, boy's cowlick, tree and posts, pumpkin tendrils (2X)
401	⁄	413	Pewter− all remaining stitches

FRENCH KNOT

401	•	413	Pewter−eyes, button (4X)
388	•	842	Light beige brown−sheep (3X)

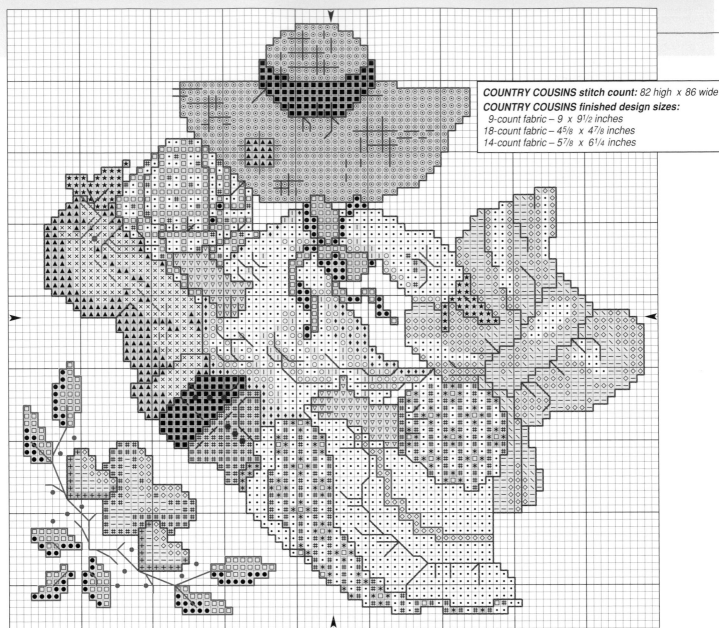

COUNTRY COUSINS

COUNTRY COUSINS stitch count: 82 high x 86 wide
COUNTRY COUSINS finished design sizes:
 9-count fabric – 9 x 9½ inches
 18-count fabric – 4⅝ x 4⅞ inches
 14-count fabric – 5⅞ x 6¼ inches

⋆⋆COUNTRY COUSINS

As shown on page 66.

MATERIALS
For framed piece
FABRIC
**10x10-inch piece of 18-count ivory
 Aida cloth**
FLOSS
**Cotton embroidery floss in colors
 listed in key**
SUPPLIES
**Needle; embroidery hoop
Desired frame and mat**

INSTRUCTIONS
Tape or zigzag edges of fabric to
prevent fraying. Find the center of
chart and the center of fabric; begin
stitching there.

Use two plies of floss to work
cross-stitches. Work blended needle
using one ply for each color of
floss. Work the backstitches for the
vines using two plies of floss and
the remaining backstitches and
French knots using one ply of floss.
Press finished stitchery from back.
Frame and mat as desired.

MATERIALS *for afghan*
FABRIC
**54x55-inch piece of 18-count
 daffodil Tabby cloth**
FLOSS
**Cotton embroidery floss in colors
 listed in key**

**Four additional skeins of white
 (DMC 000) embroidery floss
One additional skein of Nile green
 (DMC 954) embroidery floss**
SUPPLIES
**Needle; embroidery hoop
Tapestry needle
7 yards of ¼-inch-wide mint green
 satin ribbon**

INSTRUCTIONS
Measure 12¼ inches from edges
on one corner of fabric. Begin
stitching center of cousins motif as
indicated by arrows on chart.
Measure 10¼ inches from both
edges of each of the other three
corners; begin stitching center of
goose motif as indicated by arrows.

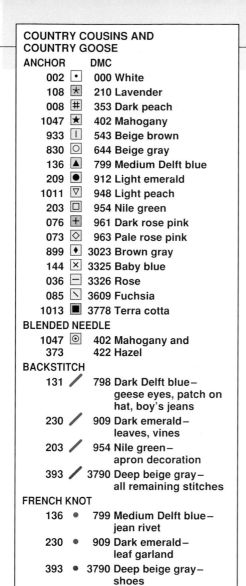

COUNTRY COUSINS AND COUNTRY GOOSE

ANCHOR		DMC	
002	·	000	White
108	⬚	210	Lavender
008	#	353	Dark peach
1047	★	402	Mahogany
933	I	543	Beige brown
830	O	644	Beige gray
136	▲	799	Medium Delft blue
209	●	912	Light emerald
1011	▽	948	Light peach
203	▢	954	Nile green
076	+	961	Dark rose pink
073	◇	963	Pale rose pink
899	◆	3023	Brown gray
144	✕	3325	Baby blue
036	−	3326	Rose
085	◤	3609	Fuchsia
1013	■	3778	Terra cotta

BLENDED NEEDLE

1047	◉	402	Mahogany and
373		422	Hazel

BACKSTITCH

131	/	798	Dark Delft blue— geese eyes, patch on hat, boy's jeans
230	/	909	Dark emerald— leaves, vines
203	/	954	Nile green— apron decoration
393	/	3790	Deep beige gray— all remaining stitches

FRENCH KNOT

136	●	799	Medium Delft blue— jean rivet
230	●	909	Dark emerald— leaf garland
393	●	3790	Deep beige gray— shoes

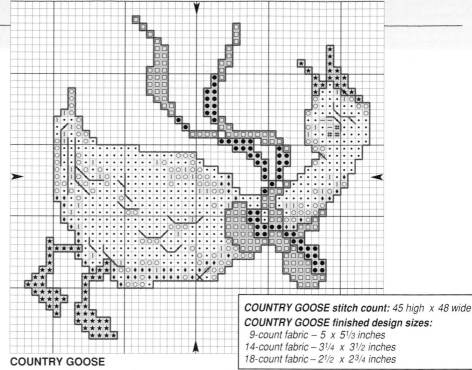

COUNTRY GOOSE

COUNTRY GOOSE stitch count: 45 high x 48 wide
COUNTRY GOOSE finished design sizes:
 9-count fabric – 5 x 5 1/3 inches
 14-count fabric – 3 1/4 x 3 1/2 inches
 18-count fabric – 2 1/2 x 2 3/4 inches

Use six plies of floss to work cross-stitches over two threads of fabric. Work blended needle using three plies of each color of floss. Work backstitches for vines using three plies and remaining backstitches using two plies. Work French knots using four plies.

Count 15 threads beyond stitching at each edge of fabric and remove one thread. Zigzag just inside thread that was removed on all four sides of fabric. Remove three more threads beyond first one on each side. Zigzag-stitch around fabric 1 inch beyond pulled-thread area. Trim fabric 4 inches beyond outermost zigzag stitches. Remove threads between cut edge and second row of zigzagging for fringe.

Cut mint green satin ribbon into four equal lengths. Using a tapestry needle, weave one length through pulled threads on one side, threading the ribbon under three threads and over six threads. Repeat for each edge. Center ribbons on respective sides; tie into bows where they meet at each corner. Weave ends of ribbon through pulled thread row in corner, weaving under three threads and over three threads. Trim ends of ribbon even with fringe.

★★ COUNTRY ALPHABET

As shown on page 67.

MATERIALS
FABRIC
11x12-inch piece of 14-count ivory Aida cloth
FLOSS
Cotton embroidery floss in colors listed in key on page 78
SUPPLIES
Needle; embroidery hoop
Desired frame and mat

INSTRUCTIONS
Tape or zigzag edges of fabric to prevent fraying. Find center of chart and center of fabric; begin stitching there.

Use two plies of floss to work cross-stitches. Work backstitches,

lazy daisy stitches, and French knots using two plies of floss unless otherwise specified in key. Work straight stitches using one ply. Press finished stitchery from back. Frame and mat as desired.

★★ COUNTRY DELICIOUS

As shown on page 68.

MATERIALS
FABRIC
12x14-inch piece of 28-count bone Jobelan fabric
FLOSS
Cotton embroidery floss in colors listed in key on page 79
SUPPLIES
Needle; embroidery hoop
Desired frame and mat

INSTRUCTIONS
Tape or zigzag edges of fabric to prevent fraying. Find center of chart and of fabric; begin stitching there.

Use three plies of floss to work cross-stitches over two threads of fabric. Work half cross-stitches, in direction of symbol, using two plies unless otherwise specified in key. Work backstitches using one ply. Press finished stitchery from the back. Frame and mat as desired.

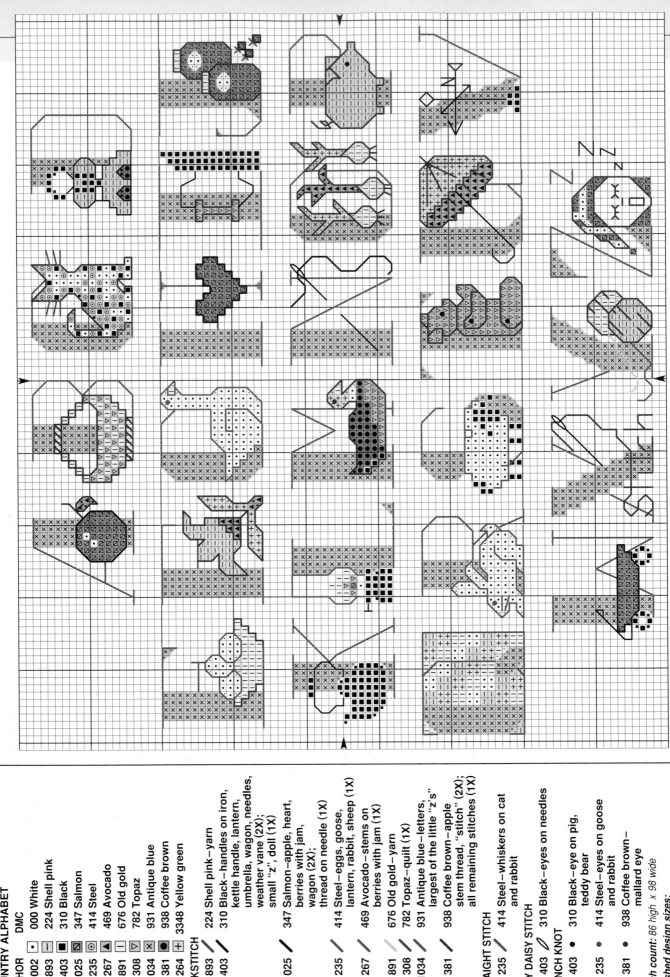

COUNTRY ALPHABET

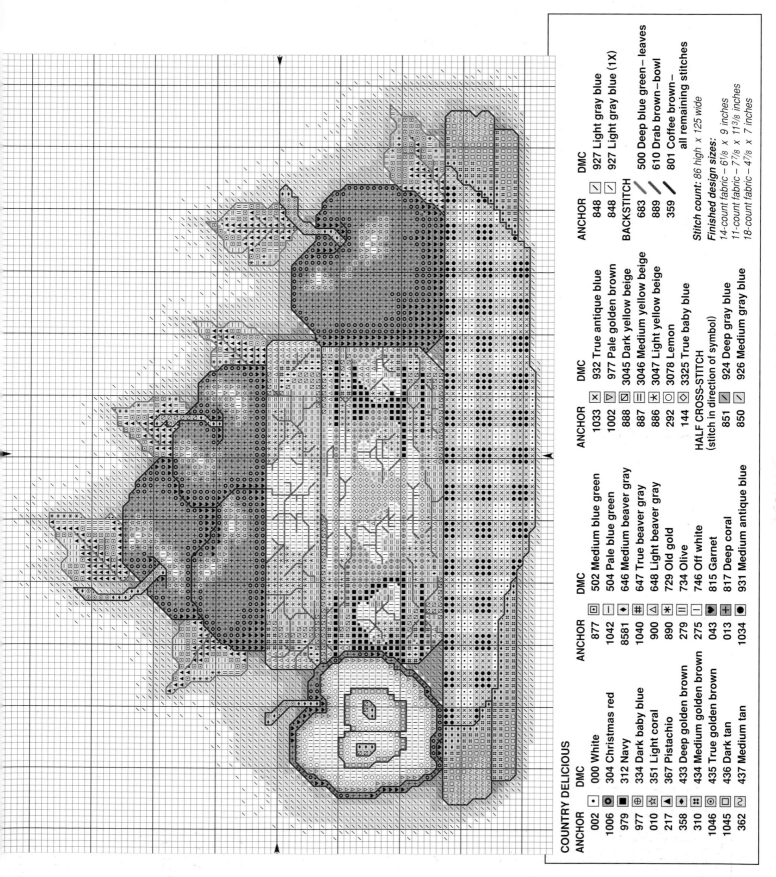

COUNTRY DELICIOUS

ANCHOR		DMC	
002	•	000	White
1006	◉	304	Christmas red
979	■	312	Navy
977	⊕	334	Dark baby blue
010	☆	351	Light coral
217	◄	367	Pistachio
358	◆	433	Deep golden brown
310	⊞	434	Medium golden brown
1046	⊙	435	True golden brown
1045	□	436	Dark tan
362	∽	437	Medium tan

ANCHOR		DMC	
877	⊡	502	Medium blue green
1042	—	504	Pale blue green
8581	◆	646	Medium beaver gray
1040	#	647	True beaver gray
900	△	648	Light beaver gray
890	✳	729	Old gold
279	‖	734	Olive
275	—	746	Off white
043	◖	815	Garnet
013	✚	817	Deep coral
1034	●	931	Medium antique blue

ANCHOR		DMC	
1033	✕	932	True antique blue
1002	▷	977	Pale golden brown
888	▨	3045	Dark yellow beige
887	‖	3046	Medium yellow beige
886	✴	3047	Light yellow beige
292	○	3078	Lemon
144	◇	3325	True baby blue

HALF CROSS-STITCH
(stitch in direction of symbol)

ANCHOR		DMC	
851	▷	924	Deep gray blue
850	⟋	926	Medium gray blue

ANCHOR		DMC	
848	⟋	927	Light gray blue
848	⟋	927	Light gray blue (1X)

BACKSTITCH

	DMC	
—	500	Deep blue green – leaves
—	610	Drab brown – bowl
—	801	Coffee brown – all remaining stitches

Stitch count: 86 high x 125 wide

Finished design sizes:
14-count fabric – 6 1/8 x 9 inches
11-count fabric – 7 7/8 x 11 3/8 inches
18-count fabric – 4 7/8 x 7 inches

Childhood
DELIGHTS

Bunnies and bears and babies, oh my! Proud moms and their precious little ones will be thrilled with these sweet designs. Motifs from many of these heirloom-quality projects can be used to create small keepsakes as well. With this adorable collection, it won't take long to find your favorite childhood delight.

Cottage Christening

All the bunnies are gathering to celebrate the birth of a precious child. Stitched on 28-count white Jubilee, this colorful sampler would make a cute addition to any child's room. One of the bunny motifs and a bear pal are stitched on soft baby sleepers to keep the wee one nice and warm on cool breezy nights. Instructions and charts begin on page 86.

81

Twins Sampler

There is something very special and unique about twins. To celebrate a double blessing, stitch our two little peas in a pod on 14-count white Aida cloth. Personalize this joyful sampler by changing the colors of the bow and the lettering to complement the colors of the twins' nursery. Complete instructions and charts begin on page 89.

Cool Penguin and Polar Bear

Kids of all ages will enjoy using these comical cozies on a picnic or at the beach. Stitched on 14-count vinyl weave, our cool Ms. Polar Bear soaks up the sun as proper Mr. Penguin enjoys a refreshing glass of lemonade while afloat. Once stitched, these adorable friends slip easily into plastic cup holders for cozies with real class. Complete instructions and charts begin on page 91.

Special Friends

What a great gift for a pal who is close to your heart! Stitch these cute bunnies as a sampler on 14-count ivory Aida cloth or on the inset of a pretty pillow. Either project can be completed in a weekend and is sure to be cherished for years to come. Complete instructions and charts begin on page 92.

Pencil Alphabet

Be sure to make the grade with teacher by stitching this quaint sampler on 14-count antique white Aida cloth. Using only eight colors and whole stitches, this eye-catching project can be stitched in a jiffy. Classmate name plates can also be created using the fun pencil letters. Instructions and chart are on page 93.

Bedtime Silhouette

What better way to capture the beautiful relationship between mother and child than with this touching silhouette. This bedtime scene is stitched on 30-count Murano fabric using just a handful of colors and will bless the walls of any child's or parent's bedroom. Complete instructions and chart begin on page 94.

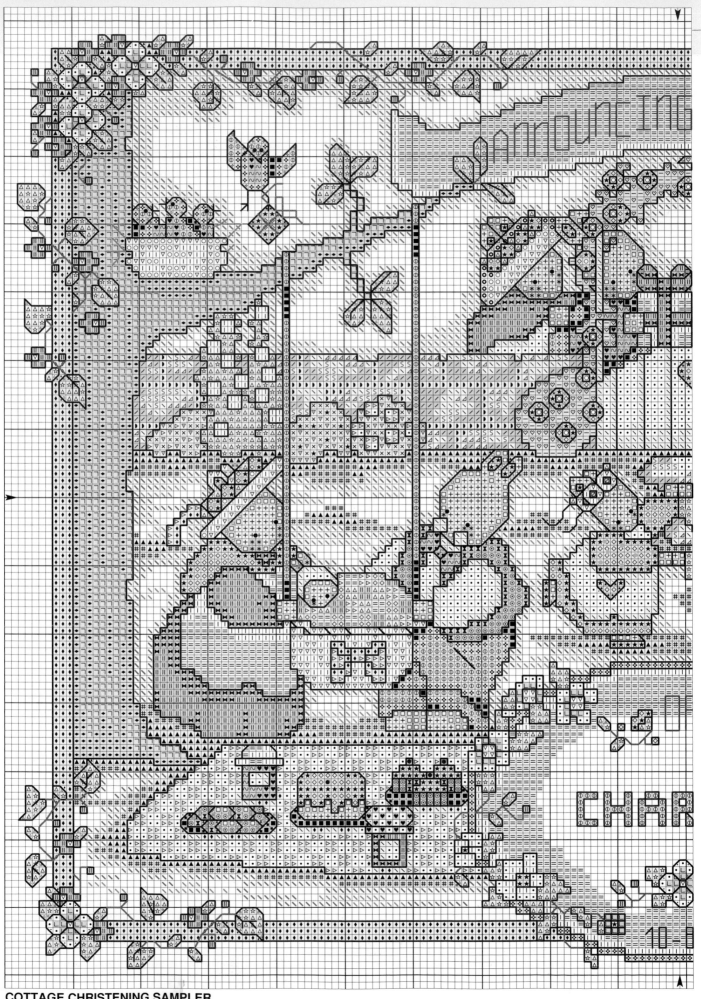

COTTAGE CHRISTENING SAMPLER

★★★COTTAGE CHRISTENING

As shown on page 80.

MATERIALS

FABRIC
14x16-inch piece of 28-count
   white Jubilee
THREADS
Cotton embroidery floss in colors
   listed in key
One additional skein each of white
   (DMC 000), dark baby blue
   (DMC 334), light pistachio
   (DMC 368), pale old gold (DMC
   677), cream (DMC 712), deep
   coffee brown (DMC 938), and
   light cocoa (DMC 3064)
SUPPLIES
Needle; embroidery hoop
Desired frame and mat

INSTRUCTIONS

Tape or zigzag edges of fabric to
prevent fraying. Find the center of
the chart and the center of the fabric; begin stitching there.

Use three plies of floss to work
cross-stitches and two plies of floss
to work half cross-stitches. Work all
backstitches, straight stitches, and
French knots using one ply of floss
unless otherwise specified in the
key. Press finished stitchery from
the back. Frame and mat as desired.

★★SLEEPERS

As shown on page 81.

MATERIALS *for each sleeper*
FABRICS
Purchased cotton baby sleeper
6x5-inch piece of 14-count waste
   canvas
4x3-inch piece of lightweight
   fusible interfacing
FLOSS
Cotton embroidery floss in colors
   listed in key
SUPPLIES
Needle; basting thread; tweezers

INSTRUCTIONS

Wash and dry sleepers. Tape or
zigzag edges of the waste canvas to
prevent fraying. Baste waste canvas
to front of sleeper, centering on left
or right side, with the top edge of
canvas at bottom of neckband. Find
center of chart and center of canvas;
begin stitching there.

Use three plies of floss to work
cross-stitches. Use one ply of floss
for backstitches unless otherwise
specified in the key. Remove basting threads and trim canvas close to
stitching. Wet the canvas. Use
tweezers to pull individual canvas
threads from under the cross-stitches. Fuse interfacing over the stitching on the inside of the sleeper following manufacturer's instructions.

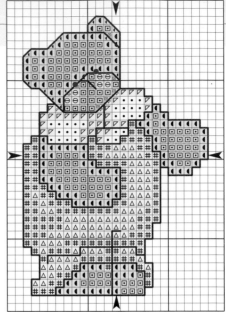

TEDDY BEAR SLEEPER

Teddy Bear Sleeper stitch count: 35 high x 23 wide
Teddy Bear Sleeper finished design sizes:
14-count fabric – 2¹/₂ x 1⁵/₈ inches
8¹/₂-count fabric – 4¹/₈ x 2³/₄ inches

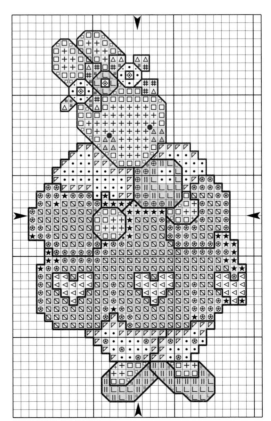

BUNNY SLEEPER

Bunny Sleeper stitch count: 46 high x 27 wide
Bunny Sleeper finished design sizes:
14-count fabric – 3¹/₄ x 2 inches
8¹/₂-count fabric – 5³/₈ x 3¹/₈ inches

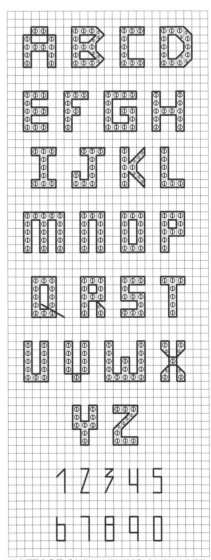

COTTAGE CHRISTENING ALPHABET

COTTAGE CHRISTENING SAMPLER AND BABY SLEEPERS

ANCHOR		DMC
002	•	000 White
110	⋈	208 Dark lavender
109	⊕	209 Medium lavender
108	‖	210 Light lavender
342	⌐	211 Pale lavender
979	■	312 Light navy
399	∕	318 Light steel
215	#	320 True pistachio
978	✛	322 Pale navy
977	♦	334 Dark baby blue
1025	♥	347 Deep salmon
008	△	353 Dark peach
5975	⊖	356 Medium terra cotta
217	☆	367 Medium pistachio
214	△	368 Light pistachio
235	▶	414 Dark steel
358	⊠	433 Light chestnut
1046	⊙	435 Dark chestnut
1045	◀	436 Dark tan
362	▣	437 Medium tan
208	−	563 Seafoam
936	◆	632 Deep cocoa
891	▽	676 Light old gold
886	⊔	677 Pale old gold
901	◯	680 Dark old gold
926	⊟	712 Cream
324	⊘	721 Medium bittersweet
323	✳	722 Light bittersweet

ANCHOR		DMC
890	◯	729 Medium old gold
361	▢	738 Light tan
885	+	739 Pale tan
302	◈	743 True yellow
300	◁	745 Light yellow
1022	✳	760 True salmon
234	◣	762 Pearl gray
128	▷	775 Light baby blue
024	◇	776 Pink
378	⌐	841 Beige brown
1033	⏄	932 Antique blue
206	♡	955 Nile green
075	★	962 Medium rose pink
073	◩	963 Pale rose pink
883	⍾	3064 Light cocoa
144	▷	3325 True baby blue
263	▲	3362 Dark loden
262	▽	3363 Medium loden
260	✕	3364 Light loden
1023	⍵	3712 Medium salmon
025	⊛	3716 Light rose pink
140	⏅	3755 Medium baby blue

HALF CROSS-STITCH
(stitch in direction of symbol)

215	╲	320 True pistachio
887	╲	3046 Yellow beige
140	╲	3755 Medium baby blue

ANCHOR		DMC
BACKSTITCH		
979	╱	312 Light navy–date (2X) and personalization (1X)
978	╱	322 Pale navy–"Announcing the Birth of" (2X)
217	╱	367 Medium pistacio–bird's package ribbon and vines (2X)
359	╱	801 Medium coffee brown– all stitches on the sleepers
075	╱	962 Medium rose pink–girl bunny's hair ribbons (2X)
381	╱	938 Deep coffee brown–all remaining stitches

STRAIGHT STITCH

890	╱	729 Medium old gold–nest (2X)

FRENCH KNOT

002	·	000 White–flower centers on hats, decoration on clothing
1025	●	347 Deep salmon–cherries on cakes (3X)
381	●	938 Deep coffee brown–bird's eyes (1X); all other eyes (2X)
382	●	3371 Black brown–eyes on the sleepers (1X)

Sampler stitch count: 140 high x 194 wide
Sampler finished design sizes:
14-count fabric –10 x 14 inches
11-count fabric –12 3/4 x 17 3/4 inches
18-count fabric – 8 x 11 inches

**TWINS SAMPLER

As shown on page 82.

MATERIALS

FABRIC
16x12-inch piece of 14-count white Aida cloth

FLOSS
Cotton embroidery floss in colors listed in key

One additional skein each of light avocado (DMC 471) and light hunter green (DMC 3346)

SUPPLIES
Needle
Embroidery hoop
Desired mat and frame

INSTRUCTIONS

Tape or zigzag edges of fabric to prevent fraying. Find the center of chart and the center of fabric; begin stitching there.

Use three plies of floss to work cross-stitches. Use one ply of floss to work backstitches unless otherwise specified in key. Press finished stitchery from the back. Frame and mat as desired.

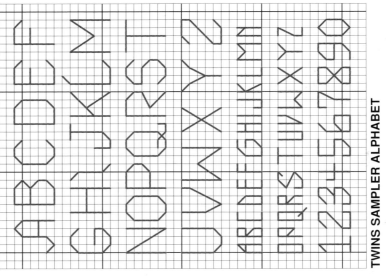

TWINS SAMPLER ALPHABET

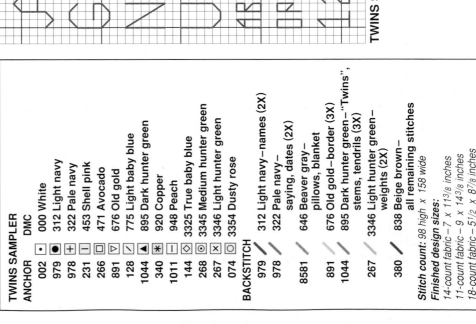

TWINS SAMPLER

ANCHOR		DMC
002	·	000 White
979	●	312 Light navy
978	+	322 Pale navy
231	−	453 Shell pink
266	▢	471 Avocado
891	▷	676 Old gold
128	◣	775 Light baby blue
1044	◀	895 Dark hunter green
340	✳	920 Copper
1011	▮	948 Peach
144	◇	3325 True baby blue
268	⊙	3345 Medium hunter green
267	✕	3346 Light hunter green
074	▢	3354 Dusty rose

BACKSTITCH		
979	╱	312 Light navy–names (2X)
978	╱	322 Pale navy– saying, dates (2X)
8581	╱	646 Beaver gray– pillows, blanket
891	╱	676 Old gold–border (3X)
1044	╱	895 Dark hunter green–"Twins", stems, tendrils (3X)
267	╱	3346 Light hunter green– weights (2X)
380	╱	838 Beige brown– all remaining stitches

Stitch count: 98 high x 158 wide
Finished design sizes:
14-count fabric – 7 x 11 3/8 inches
11-count fabric – 9 x 14 3/8 inches
18-count fabric – 5 1/2 x 8 7/8 inches

Lovebirds

Like two peas in a pod,
two gifts from God.

Michael Russell Harris
September 6, 1990

John Alexander Harris
September 6, 1990

TWINS SAMPLER

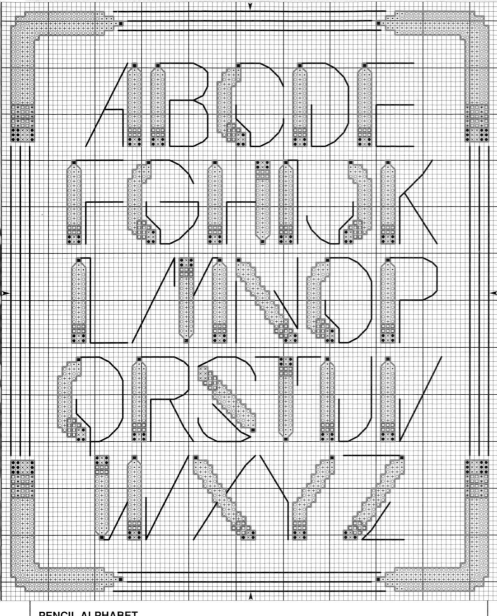

PENCIL ALPHABET

ANCHOR		DMC	
5975	●	356	Medium terra cotta
8581	✳	646	Medium beaver gray
900	□	648	Light beaver gray
303	＋	742	Light tangerine
882	✕	758	Light terra cotta
307	○	783	Christmas gold
1041	■	844	Deep beaver gray
4146	·	950	Rose beige

ANCHOR		DMC	
BACKSTITCH			
1041	／	844	Deep beaver gray – pencils (1X)
1041	／	844	Deep beaver gray – all remaining stitches (4X)

Stitch count: 124 high x 102 wide
Finished design sizes:
14-count fabric – 8⁷/₈ x 7³/₈ inches
11-count fabric – 11³/₈ x 9³/₈ inches
18-count fabric – 6⁷/₈ x 5³/₄ inches

facing and raw edges even. Sew a gathering thread through both layers, ¼ inch from raw edges. Pull to fit outside edge of pillow; pin with raw edges even. Adjust gathers evenly and sew to pillow along gathering line.

Sew back to front with raw edges even, leaving an opening for turning. Trim corners. Turn pillow right side out. Stuff firmly with fiberfill. Sew opening closed.

★★PENCIL ALPHABET

As shown on page 84.

MATERIALS
FABRIC
11x14-inch piece of 14-count antique white Aida
FLOSS
Cotton embroidery floss in colors listed in key

SUPPLIES
Needle; embroidery hoop
Desired frame and mat

INSTRUCTIONS
Tape or zigzag edges of fabric to prevent fraying. Find the center of the chart and the center of the fabric; begin stitching there.

Use three plies of floss to work all cross-stitches. Work backstitches using one ply of floss unless otherwise specified in the key. Press finished stitchery from the back. Frame and mat as desired.

★★NAME PLATE

As shown on page 84.

MATERIALS
FABRIC
12x4-inch piece of 14-count antique white Aida
12x4-inch piece of white fabric
FLOSS
Cotton embroidery floss in colors listed in key
SUPPLIES
Needle
Embroidery hoop
9⁷/₈x4-inch piece of medium-weight cardboard
9⁷/₈x2½ clear acrylic name plate
Crafts glue

INSTRUCTIONS
Tape or zigzag edges of fabric to prevent fraying. Center and stitch name, using alphabet and allowing two squares between letters. Use three plies of floss for all cross-stitches. Work backstitches using one ply of floss unless otherwise specified in the key.

Cut cardboard into two 9⁷/₈x2-inch pieces. Center design fabric atop one cardboard piece; pull edges to back and glue. Repeat for white fabric and remaining piece of cardboard. Glue wrong sides of cardboard pieces together; let dry. Slide stitched name into name plate.

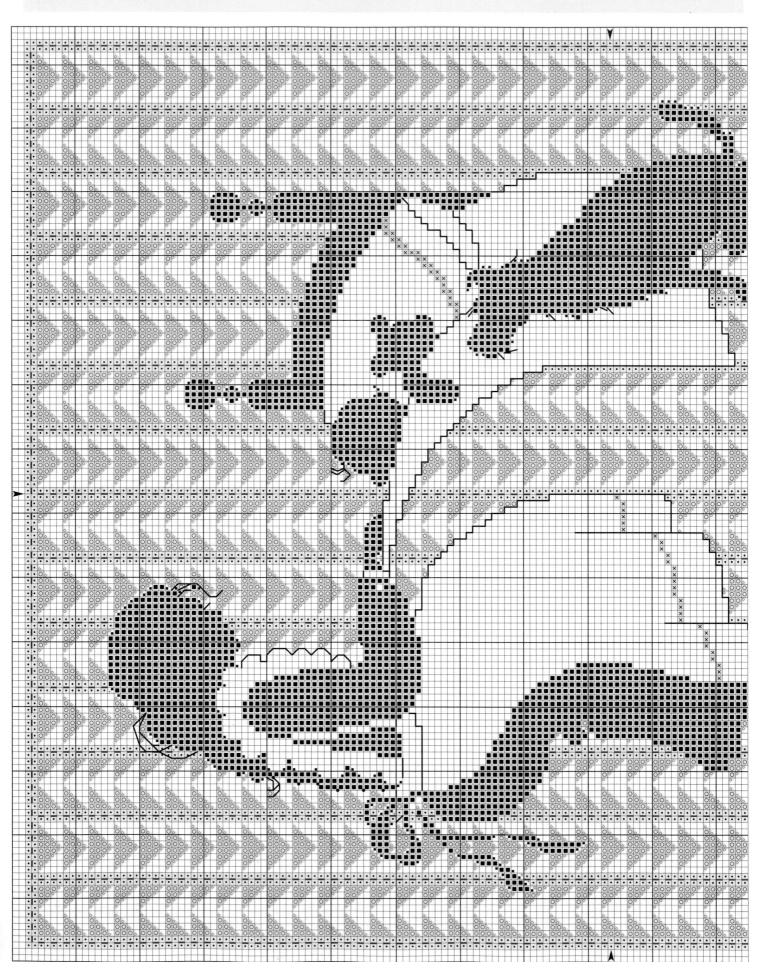

BEDTIME SILHOUETTE		
ANCHOR	DMC	
· 1026	225	Shell pink
■ 403	310	Black
✗ 1034	931	Antique blue
○ 870	3042	Antique violet

BACKSTITCH
- ╲ 403 | 310 Black – silhouettes
- ╱ 1034 | 931 Antique blue – saying

FRENCH KNOT
- ● 403 | 310 Black – buttons on dress

RUNNING STITCH
- ╱ 1034 | 931 Antique blue – quilt pattern

Stitch count: 183 high x 142 wide
Finished design sizes:
15-count fabric – 12¼ x 9⅜ inches
11-count fabric – 16⅝ x 13 inches
18-count fabric – 10½ x 7⅞ inches

★★★BEDTIME SILHOUETTE

As shown on page 85.

MATERIALS

FABRIC
18x21-inch piece of 30-count pewter Murano fabric

FLOSS
Cotton embroidery floss in colors listed in key
One additional skein of medium antique blue (DMC 931)
Three additional skeins each of pale shell pink (DMC 225) and black (DMC 310)
Five additional skeins of light antique violet (DMC 3042)

SUPPLIES
Needle
Embroidery hoop
Desired frame

INSTRUCTIONS

Tape or zigzag edges of fabric to prevent fraying. Find the center of chart and the center of fabric; begin stitching there.

Use three plies of floss to work cross-stitches over two threads of fabric. Work backstitches and running stitches using two plies of floss. Work French knots using three plies of floss. Press the finished stitchery from back. Frame as desired.

BEDTIME SILHOUETTE

Christmas
TRIMS & TREASURES

The Christmas season is a wonderful time to pass along special family traditions. Begin yours by stitching these dazzling decorations and gifts. If you start now, you can complete these Christmas treasures just in time to share with those you love.

Nativity Scene

The joyous occasion of the Savior's birth is beautifully portrayed in this elegantly cross-stitched Nativity. Each figure features highlights of satiny rayon floss and sparkling metallic thread. The Three Wise Men's robes are also accented with glistening beads, while tassels embellish the shepherd's cloak and the camel's blanket and halter. Instructions and charts begin on page 103.

Religious Symbols

No other symbol is more visually recognizable than the cross. These three ornaments, stitched on 36-count white Edinborough linen, are worked with gold cord, braid, and blending filament to make them a treasured part of your yearly Christmas remembrance. Complete instructions and charts begin on page 108.

Russian Christmas Angels

These sparkly-robed Russian Christmas angels, stitched on 28-count white Jobelan, will surely brighten your holiday season this year with their joyous message. The trio of ornaments are stitched with blending filaments and accented with beads. Instructions and chart begin on page 110.

Woodland Santa

A richly robed Santa comes forth with his friendly woodland creatures. Stitched on 28-count bone Jobelan, this piece comes to life with all the brightly colored blending filaments. The couching on his robe adds an elegant touch. Complete instructions and chart begin on page 113.

Festive Hardanger Ornaments

These gorgeous holiday ornaments, stitched with variegated threads in vibrant colors, are the perfect first project if you've always wanted to learn Hardanger embroidery. Golden beads and an heirloom-style button give these dramatic ornaments visual impact. Make these for gifts or add several to your own ornament collection. Complete instructions and charts begin on page 115.

Heavenly Angel Ornaments

Cherubs and hearts are combined to make these enchanting ornaments for Christmas. Stitched on 18-count white Aida cloth, each cuddly angel has golden thread wings. These charming designs are finished into heart shapes and trimmed elegantly with satin cord, sparkling lace, and soft tassels. Complete instructions and charts begin on page 118.

Carousel Polar Bear and Reindeer Ornaments

Our wintry polar bear and reindeer, stitched on 36-count white Edinborough linen, are captured beautifully with brightly colored blending filaments. The Victorian design makes the back of the ornaments just as beautiful as the front. Complete instructions and charts begin on page 119.

Mischief-making Reindeer

Santa is in for a fun surprise! One of the members on his reindeer team, stitched using 8½-count waste canvas, is pulling all the brightly colored Christmas lights off the tree. Create this fun-loving character on a sweatshirt to wear the whole holiday season or as a whimsical gift for someone special. Complete instructions and charts begin on page 119.

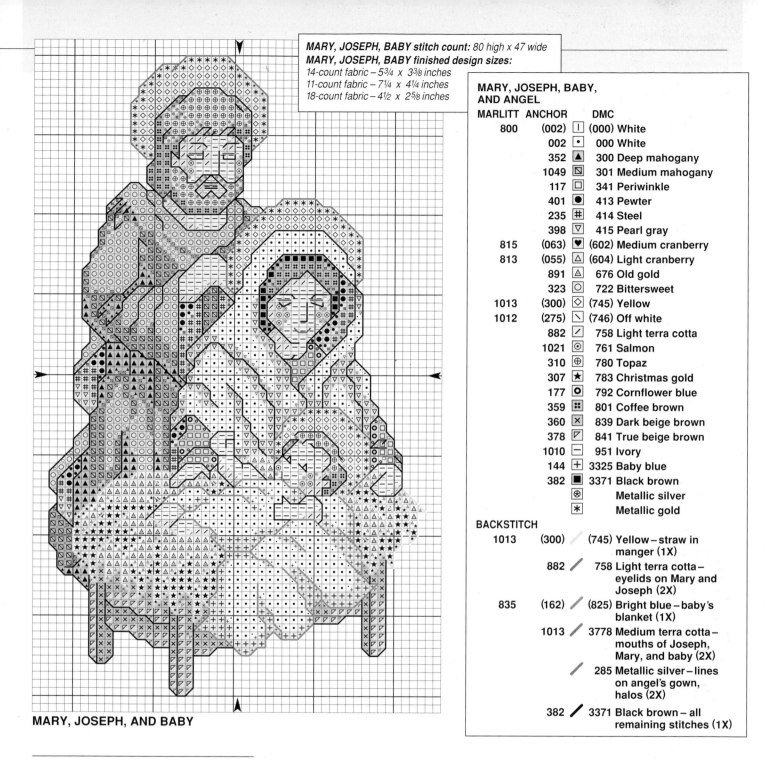

MARY, JOSEPH, BABY stitch count: 80 high x 47 wide
MARY, JOSEPH, BABY finished design sizes:
14-count fabric – 5¾ x 3⅜ inches
11-count fabric – 7¼ x 4¼ inches
18-count fabric – 4½ x 2⅝ inches

MARY, JOSEPH, BABY, AND ANGEL

MARLITT	ANCHOR		DMC	
800	(002)	⌶	(000)	White
	002	·	000	White
	352	▲	300	Deep mahogany
	1049	⊠	301	Medium mahogany
	117	▢	341	Periwinkle
	401	●	413	Pewter
	235	⊞	414	Steel
	398	▽	415	Pearl gray
815	(063)	♥	(602)	Medium cranberry
813	(055)	△	(604)	Light cranberry
	891	◬	676	Old gold
	323	◯	722	Bittersweet
1013	(300)	◇	(745)	Yellow
1012	(275)	◺	(746)	Off white
	882	∕	758	Light terra cotta
	1021	⊙	761	Salmon
	310	⊕	780	Topaz
	307	★	783	Christmas gold
	177	⦿	792	Cornflower blue
	359	⧉	801	Coffee brown
	360	✕	839	Dark beige brown
	378	▽	841	True beige brown
	1010	–	951	Ivory
	144	✛	3325	Baby blue
	382	■	3371	Black brown
		⊛		Metallic silver
		✳		Metallic gold

BACKSTITCH

1013	(300)	∕	(745)	Yellow – straw in manger (1X)
	882	∕	758	Light terra cotta – eyelids on Mary and Joseph (2X)
835	(162)	∕	(825)	Bright blue – baby's blanket (1X)
	1013	∕	3778	Medium terra cotta – mouths of Joseph, Mary, and baby (2X)
		∕	285	Metallic silver – lines on angel's gown, halos (2X)
	382	∕	3371	Black brown – all remaining stitches (1X)

MARY, JOSEPH, AND BABY

★★★NATIVITY

As shown on pages 96–97.

MATERIALS

FABRICS

18x27-inch piece of 28-count white Cashel linen
½ yard of 45-inch-wide polished cotton
Polyester fleece

THREADS

Cotton embroidery floss, Marlitt rayon floss (or cotton embroidery floss), and DMC metallic embroidery thread as listed in keys on pages 103, 105, and 107

SUPPLIES

Needle; embroidery hoop
Seed beads as listed in keys on pages 105 and 107
Sewing thread
Polyester fiberfill
4x4-inch piece of tracing paper for each figure
Cardboard; crafts glue
15-inch piece of ¼-inch-wide flat braid trim for each figure

INSTRUCTIONS

Cut linen into nine 9x6-inch pieces. Tape or zigzag edges of each piece of fabric to prevent fraying. For each figure, find the center of the chart and the center of fabric; begin stitching there.

Work all cross-stitches over two threads of fabric using three plies of cotton floss, two plies of rayon floss, or two strands of metallic embroidery thread. Work back-stitches, straight stitches, and French knots using one ply of floss

ANGEL stitch count: 65 high x 78 wide
ANGEL finished design sizes:
14-count fabric – 4⅝ x 5½ inches
11-count fabric – 6 x 7 inches
18-count fabric – 3⅝ x 4⅜ inches

Key on page 103

ANGEL

or one strand of metallic thread unless otherwise specified in key. Use one ply of floss or one strand of metallic thread to attach beads.

For tassels on shepherd and camel, thread one needle with first color of floss or metallic thread specified in key. Referring to diagrams, *page 106,* take a short stitch as indicated by dots on chart, leaving a 1-inch tail; bring thread together. Thread another needle with second color floss or metallic thread. Work three tacking stitches over tassel threads. Trim ends of first color floss or thread evenly. Sew beads to saddle as indicated on chart.

For all figures, baste fleece to stitched piece, sewing ¼ inch beyond edge of cross-stitching. Trim excess fabric ¼ inch beyond basting stitches. Using stitched piece as a pattern, cut a back from polished cotton.

For all figures except angel, sew the front to the back, right sides together, along basting line; leave bottom open. Clip curves and turn right side out. Stuff firmly with fiberfill. Turn the bottom raw edges in ¼ inch.

For each base, fold tracing paper in half; repeat, bringing the folded edges together. Matching the folds, trace the corresponding base

pattern onto tracing paper. Cut out and unfold. Transfer the oval shape onto cardboard and cut out. From the polished cotton fabric, cut an oval that is ½ inch larger than the cardboard oval. Center and glue the cardboard oval to the back of the fabric oval. Fold the raw edges to the back and glue, clipping as needed. Allow the glue to dry. Hand-stitch the base to the bottom edge of the figure. Glue the braid over the top and side seam lines.

For angel, sew front to back, right sides together along basting line, leaving an opening. Clip curves

Fold

BASE FOR MARY, JOSEPH, AND BABY
Cut 1

Fold

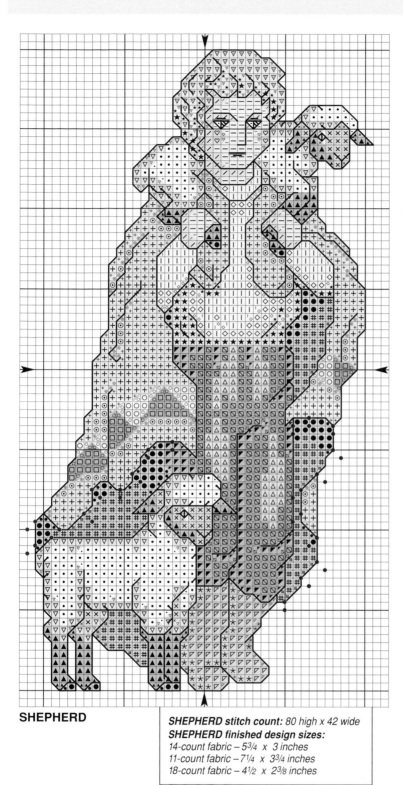

SHEPHERD

SHEPHERD stich count: 80 high x 42 wide
SHEPHERD finished design sizes:
14-count fabric – 5¾ x 3 inches
11-count fabric – 7¼ x 3¾ inches
18-count fabric – 4½ x 2⅜ inches

SHEPHERD AND CAMEL				
MARLITT	**ANCHOR**		**DMC**	
	002	·	000	White
	352	◪	300	Deep mahogany
	1049	◩	301	Medium mahogany
843	(1006)	✳	(304)	Christmas red
	403	■	310	Black
	401	●	413	Pewter
	235	⊞	414	Steel
	398	▽	415	Pearl gray
	310	✶	434	Golden brown
	1045	◹	436	Tan
1017	(046)	▫	(666)	Red
	891	▽	676	Old gold
	323	△	722	Bittersweet
820	(293)	○	(727)	Topaz
1013	(300)	◇	(745)	Yellow
1012	(275)			(746)	Off white
	882	╱	758	Light terra cotta
1021		♡	761	Salmon
	307	★	783	Christmas gold
	359	◉	801	Coffee brown
	360	▲	839	Dark beige brown
	378	✕	841	True beige brown
1010		–	951	Ivory
	187	⊙	958	True aqua
	186	✛	959	Medium aqua
		⊕	285	Silver metallic thread

BACKSTITCH

843	(1006)	╱	(304)	Christmas red – bottom edge of camel's lower blanket (2X)
	189	╱	991	Aquamarine – lines of camel's saddle, halter, collar, upper blanket, reins, and cinch
	1013	╱	3778	Medium terra cotta – shepherd's mouth and eyelids (2X)
		╱	282	Gold metallic thread – blanket stripe on shepherd (2X)
	382	╱	3371	Black brown – all remaining stitches

STRAIGHT STITCH

	002	╱	000	White – eye highlight on camel
843	(1006)	╱	(304)	Christmas red – fringe at bottom edge of camel's lower blanket (2X)

TASSELS

1017	(046)	⁝	(666)	Red (2X) tacked with DMC red (666) – shepherd's blanket
820	(293)	⁝	(727)	Topaz (3X) tacked with 282 light gold metallic thread (2X) – camel's halter and collar
		⁝	285	Silver metallic thread (5X) tacked with DMC aqua (959) – camel's saddle

SEED BEAD

		●	282	Gold metallic thread and Mill Hill 02011 gold bead

and turn right side out. Stuff figure lightly with fiberfill. Hand-stitch the opening closed. Glue the braid over the seam line all the way around the figure.

Fold

BASE FOR SHEPHERD
Cut 1

Fold

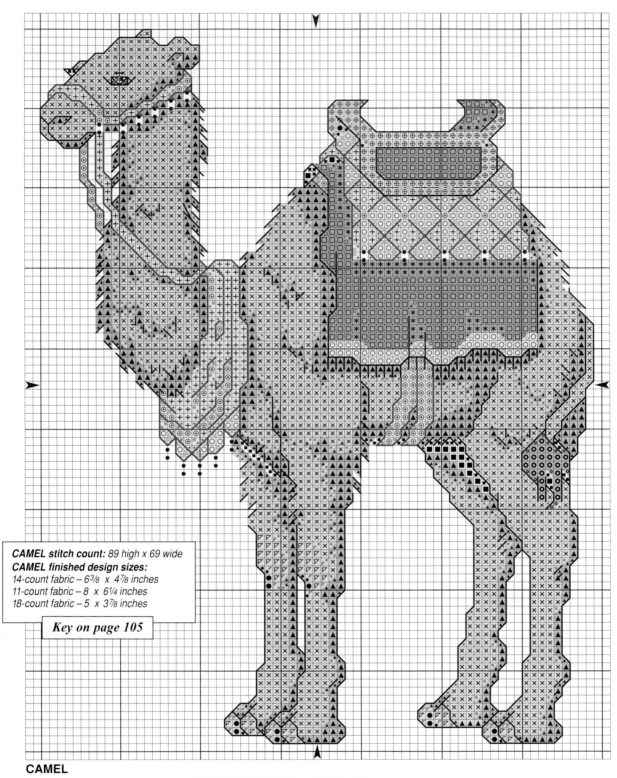

CAMEL stitch count: 89 high x 69 wide
CAMEL finished design sizes:
14-count fabric – 6³⁄₈ x 4⁷⁄₈ inches
11-count fabric – 8 x 6¹⁄₄ inches
18-count fabric – 5 x 3⁷⁄₈ inches

Key on page 105

CAMEL

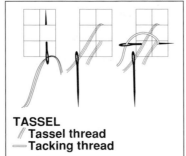

TASSEL
∥ Tassel thread
— Tacking thread

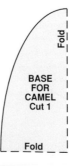

Fold

BASE
FOR
CAMEL
Cut 1

Fold

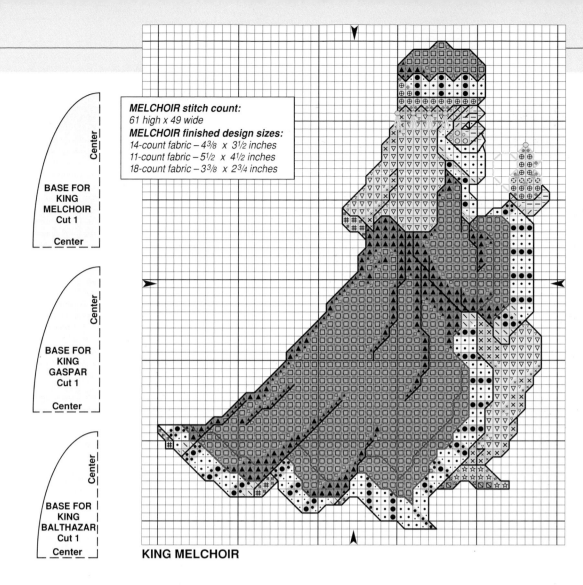

MELCHIOR stitch count:
61 high x 49 wide
MELCHIOR finished design sizes:
14-count fabric – 4⅜ x 3½ inches
11-count fabric – 5½ x 4½ inches
18-count fabric – 3⅜ x 2¾ inches

BASE FOR KING MELCHIOR Cut 1
Center

BASE FOR KING GASPAR Cut 1
Center

BASE FOR KING BALTHAZAR Cut 1
Center

KING MELCHOIR

THREE WISE MEN

MARLITT	ANCHOR		DMC	
800	(002)	·	(000)	White
819	(110)	♦	(208)	Dark lavender
819	(109)	⊞	(209)	Medium lavender
843	(1006)	▲	(304)	Christmas red
	401	⊡	413	Pewter
	235	⌗	414	Steel
	398	⟍	415	Pearl gray
	358	⊙	433	Golden brown
1017	(046)	⊡	(666)	Red
820	(293)	◇	(727)	Pale topaz
1012	(275)	│	(746)	Off white
	882	╱	758	Light terra cotta
1021		◯	761	Salmon
	309	☆	780	Deep topaz
	359	◩	801	Medium coffee brown
	360	■	898	Dark coffee brown
1067	(205)	✕	(911)	Emerald
	1010	−	951	Ivory
832	(203)	▽	(954)	Nile green
834	(189)	●	(991)	Aquamarine
	1007	△	3772	Cocoa
		✳	282	Gold metallic thread
		⊕	285	Silver metallic thread

ANCHOR   DMC

BACKSTITCH

╱ 282 Metallic gold thread – detail on sleeves, front band of King Balthazar's gown; outline of King Melchoir's urn (2X)

╱ 285 Metallic silver thread – King Balthazar's earring; outline on King Melchoir's gown (2X)

382 ╱ 3371 Black brown – all remaining stitches

STRAIGHT STITCH

1013 ╱ 3778 True terra cotta – mouth of King Balthazar

╱ 282 Metallic gold – tassels on King Melchoir's hat (2X)

╱ 285 Metallic silver thread – short stitches on King Gaspar's gown, braid on King Gaspar's gown, and design on bottle; turban on King Balthazar (2X)

ANCHOR   DMC

FRENCH KNOT

○ 282 Metallic gold thread – detail on King Melchoir's urn (2X)

SEED BEAD

● 282 Metallic gold thread and 02011 Mill Hill gold bead

● 285 Metallic silver thread and 00150 Mill Hill gray bead

● 843 Christmas red Marlitt and 00968 Mill Hill red bead

Key on page 107

BALTHAZAR stitch count:
82 high x 35 wide
BALTHAZAR finished design sizes:
14-count fabric – 5⅞ x 2½ inches
11-count fabric – 7½ x 3⅛ inches
18-count fabric – 4½ x 2 inches

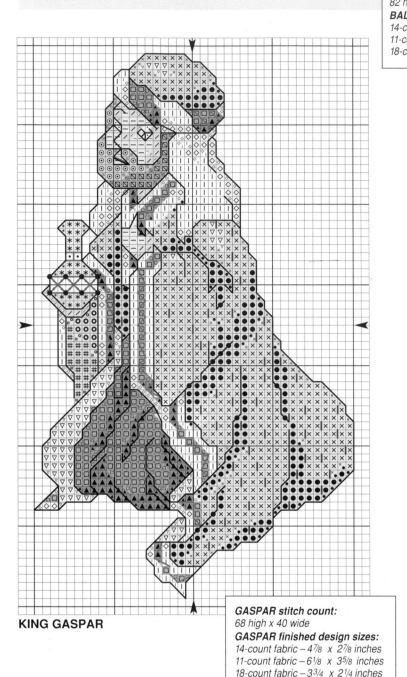

KING GASPAR

GASPAR stitch count:
68 high x 40 wide
GASPAR finished design sizes:
14-count fabric – 4⅞ x 2⅞ inches
11-count fabric – 6⅛ x 3⅝ inches
18-count fabric – 3¾ x 2¼ inches

Key on page 107

KING BALTHAZAR

✳✳RELIGIOUS SYMBOLS

As shown on page 98.

MATERIALS

For each ornament

FABRIC

6x7-inch piece of 36-count white Edinborough linen
6x7-inch piece polyester fleece
¼ yard 45-inch-wide gold lamé fabric

THREADS

Cotton embroidery floss in colors listed in key
Blending filament in color listed in key
Cord in colors listed in key
#8 braid in colors listed in key

SUPPLIES

Needle; embroidery hoop
Tracing paper; sewing thread
6x7-inch piece each of light and heavy-weight cardboard

½ yard of ⅛-inch-diameter cotton cord
3-inch piece of ¼-inch-wide metallic gold braid
2½-inch-long metallic gold tassel
Crafts glue

INSTRUCTIONS

Tape or zigzag edges of fabric to prevent fraying. Find center of chart and of fabric; begin stitching there.

Continued on page 110

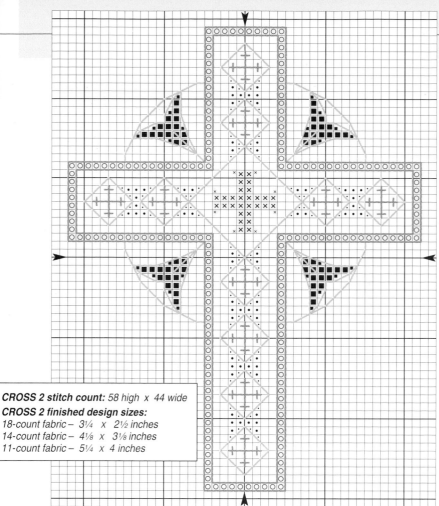

CROSS 2 stitch count: *58 high x 44 wide*
CROSS 2 finished design sizes:
18-count fabric – 3¼ x 2½ inches
14-count fabric – 4⅛ x 3⅛ inches
11-count fabric – 5¼ x 4 inches

CROSS 2

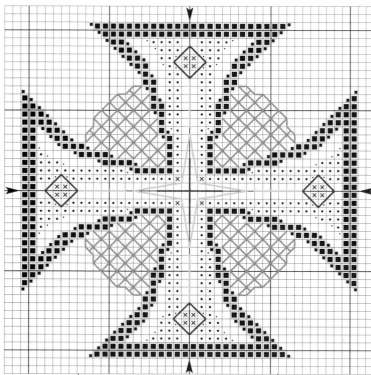

CROSS 3

CROSS 3 stitch count: *42 high x 42 wide*
CROSS 3 finished design sizes:
18-count fabric – 2⅓ x 2⅓ inches
14-count fabric – 3 x 3 inches
11-count fabric – 3⅞ x 3⅞ inches

RELIGIOUS SYMBOLS ORNAMENTS

ANCHOR		DMC	
300	•	745	Light yellow

BLENDED NEEDLE

890	■	729	Old gold (1X) and
		205C	Kreinik antique gold cord (2X)
301	☒	744	Medium yellow (1X) and
		002HL	Kreinik gold blending filament (2X)
300	◯	745	Light yellow (1X) and
		102C	Kreinik Vatican gold cord (2X)

CROSS 1

BACKSTITCH

╱ 002C Kreinik gold cord–
background (2X)

╱ 205C Kreinik antique gold #8 braid–
large cross

STRAIGHT STITCH

╱ 205C Kreinik antique gold #8 braid–
center cross

╱ 205C Kreinik antique gold cord–
corner crosses (2X)

╱ 002 Kreinik gold #8 braid–
all remaining stitches

FRENCH KNOT

● 221 Kreinik antique gold #8 braid–
center cross

CROSS 2

BACKSTITCH

╱ 205C Kreinik antique gold cord–
large cross (2X)

STRAIGHT STITCH

╱ 205C Kreinik antique gold cord–
small crosses (2X)

╱ 002 Kreinik gold #8 braid–
all remaining stitches

CROSS 3

BACKSTITCH

╱ 205C Kreinik antique gold cord–
background (2X)

STRAIGHT STITCH

╱ 205C Kreinik antique gold #8 braid–
corner diamonds, center of cross (2X)

╱ 002 Kreinik gold #8 braid–
all remaining stitches

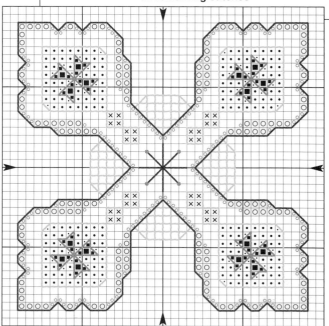

CROSS 1

CROSS 1 stitch count: *36 high x 36 wide*
CROSS 1 finished design sizes:
18-count fabric – 2 x 2 inches
14-count fabric – 2⅝ x 2⅝ inches
11-count fabric – 3¼ x 3¼ inches

109

Work all cross-stitches over two threads using two plies of floss and blended needle as specified in the key. Work the backstitches, straight stitches, and French knots using one strand of cord or braid unless otherwise specified in the key.

Trace pattern, *below,* for Cross 2; cut out. For Cross 1, trace a 3x3-inch square and for Cross 3, trace a 3½-inch diameter circle; cut out. Center pattern over stitching and draw around it; cut out 1 inch beyond line. Draw around pattern on lamé, fleece, and each piece of cardboard. Cut out lamé 1 inch beyond traced line. Cut out the fleece and cardboard pieces along line. From remaining lamé, cut a 1½x13-inch bias strip.

Glue fleece to heavy cardboard. Center design fabric, right side up, over fleece; fold edges to back and glue. Center lamé pattern shape over lightweight cardboard; fold edges to back and glue.

Fold lamé bias strip around cording, wrong sides together and raw edges even. Use a zipper foot to sew through both fabric layers close to cording. Glue seam allowance of piping to back edge of medium-weight cardboard. Trim ends as necessary and overlap at bottom.

Fold braid in half to make a loop. Glue ends to center top back edge of medium-weight cardboard. Glue tassel to center bottom back edge of medium-weight cardboard. Glue backs of cardboard pieces together.

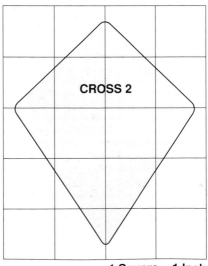

CROSS 2

1 Square = 1 Inch

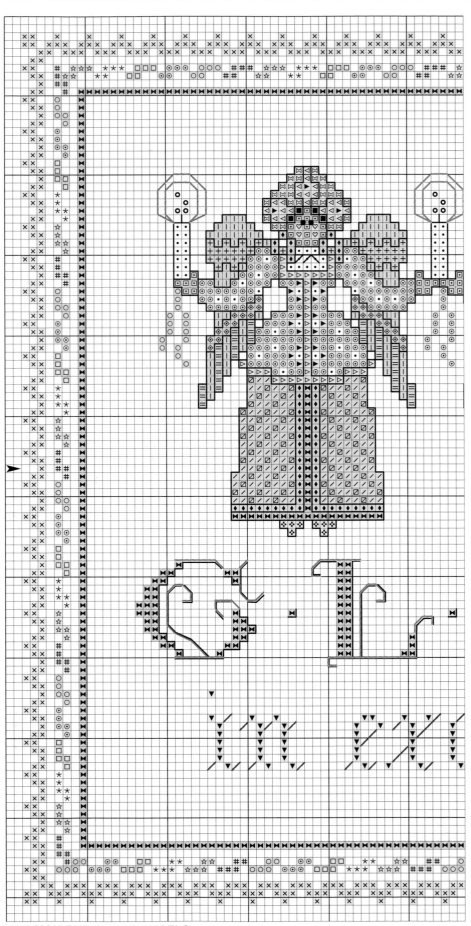

RUSSIAN CHRISTMAS ANGELS

RUSSIAN CHRISTMAS ANGELS

ANCHOR		DMC
002	·	000 White
109	⊙	209 Medium lavender
108	⊟	210 Light lavender
342	⁄	211 Pale lavender
100	◆	327 Antique violet
1025	♥	347 Deep salmon
009	⬜	352 Pale coral
008	⠒	353 Dark peach
401	▼	413 Pewter
398	✕	415 Pearl gray
305	△	725 True topaz
295	✳	726 Light topaz
300	∿	745 Yellow
1012	▣	754 Medium peach
1021	♡	761 Light salmon
128	⅂	775 Baby blue
162	◗	825 Dark bright blue
161	#	826 Medium bright blue
185	Ⓢ	964 Aqua
189	⸬	991 Dark aquamarine
187	☆	992 Medium aquamarine
186	△	993 Light aquamarine
068	⊙	3687 True mauve
049	▷	3689 Light mauve
236	■	3799 Charcoal
	⋈	102HL Kreinik Vatican gold #8 braid

BLENDED NEEDLE

109	◈	209 Medium lavender and
		012HL Kreinik purple blending filament
109	▨	209 Medium lavender and
		042 Kreinik confetti fuchsia blending filament
108	➕	210 Light lavender and
		093 Kreinik star mauve blending filament
342	⊡	211 Pale lavender and
		032 Kreinik pearl blending filament
010	★	351 Light coral and
		027 Kreinik orange blending filament
009	ⅠⅠ	352 Pale coral and
		013 Kreinik beige blending filament
009	⊕	352 Pale coral and
		095 Kreinik starburst blending filament
008	▽	353 Dark peach and
		032 Kreinik pearl blending filament

ANCHOR		DMC
926	∟	712 Cream and
		032 Kreinik pearl blending filament
305	✳	725 True topaz and
		002HL Kreinik gold blending filament
295	◇	726 Light topaz and
		091 Kreinik star yellow blending filament
300	◎	745 Yellow and
		002HL Kreinik gold blending filament
128	⊟	775 Baby blue and
		032 Kreinik pearl blending filament
160	△	813 Powder blue and
		094 Kreinik star blue blending filament
162	●	825 Dark bright blue and
		051HL Kreinik sapphire blending filament
161	⊞	826 Medium bright blue and
		044 Kreinik confetti blue blending filament
185	◹	964 Aqua and
		032 Kreinik pearl blending filament
189	▲	991 Dark aquamarine and
		044 Kreinik confetti blue blending filament
187	⸬	992 Medium aquamarine and
		029 Kreinik turquoise blending filament
186	⊠	993 Light aquamarine and
		044 Kreinik confetti blue blending filament
1028	▶	3685 Deep mauve and
		024HL Kreinik fuchsia blending filament
068	✚	3687 True mauve and
		042 Kreinik confetti fuchsia blending filament
060	⊠	3688 Medium mauve and
		042 Kreinik confetti fuchsia blending filament
049	◁	3689 Light mauve and
		007 Kreinik pink blending filament

BACKSTITCH

401	╱	413 Pewter – "in excelsis Deo!"
	╱	102HL Kreinik Vatican gold #8 braid – "gloria" and candle halos
236	╱	3799 Charcoal – all remaining stitches

FRENCH KNOT

236	●	3799 Charcoal – eyes

Stitch count: 109 high x 137 wide

Finished design sizes:
18-count fabric – 6 x 7⅝ inches
14-count fabric – 7⅞ x 9⅞ inches
11-count fabric – 10 x 12½ inches

RUSSIAN ANGEL ORNAMENT PATTERN

1 Square = 1 Inch

★★★RUSSIAN CHRISTMAS ANGEL ORNAMENTS

As shown on page 98.

MATERIALS
For each ornament
FABRICS
4x5-inch piece of 36-count white Edinborough linen
¼ yard 45-inch wide gold lamé fabric
4x5-inch piece polyester fleece
THREADS
Cotton embroidery floss and blending filament in colors listed in key
#8 braid in color listed in key
SUPPLIES
Needle; embroidery hoop
Tracing paper
⅜ yard of ⅛-inch-diameter cotton cord
4x5-inch piece each of medium and lightweight cardboard
⅜ yard white and gold metallic twisted cord
Six 8-millimeter gold beads; crafts glue

INSTRUCTIONS
Tape or zigzag edges of fabric to prevent fraying. Find center of desired angel on chart and center of fabric; begin stitching there.

Work cross-stitches over two threads of fabric using two plies of floss. Work blended needle using one ply of floss and two strands of blending filament. Work backstitches using one ply unless otherwise specified in key. Work French knots using one ply.

Fold tracing paper in half. Align fold with fold line of pattern, *left*; trace and cut out. Draw around pattern on linen and gold lamé; cut out fabrics 1 inch beyond lines. From remaining lamé, cut a 1½x14-inch bias strip. Draw around pattern on fleece and each piece of cardboard; cut out each along lines.

Glue fleece to medium-weight cardboard. Center linen, right side up over fleece; fold edges to back and glue. Center lamé arch shape over lightweight cardboard; fold edges to back and glue.

Fold bias lamé strip around cording, wrong sides together and raw edges even. Use a zipper foot to sew through both fabric layers close to cording. Glue seam allowance of piping to back edge of medium-weight cardboard overlapping ends at bottom.

Cut an 8-inch piece of twisted cord. Add 3 beads to each cord tail, tying a knot ¾ inch above ends. Fringe ends below knot. Fold cord in half. Glue fold to bottom center back edge of medium-weight cardboard.

Fold remaining twisted cord in half. Glue ends to top center back edge of medium-weight cardboard. Glue the wrong sides of cardboard pieces together.

★★★RUSSIAN CHRISTMAS ANGELS

As shown on page 98.

MATERIALS
FABRIC
16x16-inch piece of 28-count white Jobelan
THREADS
Cotton embroidery floss in colors listed in key
Blending filament in colors listed in key
#8 braid in color listed in key
SUPPLIES
Needle; embroidery hoop
Desired frame and mat

INSTRUCTIONS
Tape or zigzag the edges of the Jobelan fabric to prevent fraying. Find the center of chart and the center of fabric; begin stitching there.

Work cross-stitches over two threads of fabric using three plies of floss. Work blended needle using two plies of floss and two strands of blending filament. Work backstitches using one ply of floss unless otherwise specified in the key. Work French knots using one ply of floss.

Press finished stitchery from the back. Frame and mat as desired.

★★★WOODLAND SANTA

As shown on page 99.

MATERIALS
FABRIC
18x16-inch piece of 28-count bone Jobelan fabric
THREADS
Cotton embroidery floss in colors listed in key
Two additional skeins of white (DMC 000) and dark aquamarine (DMC 991)
Blending filament in colors listed in key
One additional spool each of gold (002), purple (012), and sapphire (051HL) Kreinik blending filament
SUPPLIES
Needle
Embroidery hoop
Desired frame and mat

INSTRUCTIONS
Tape or zigzag edges of fabric to prevent fraying. Find center of chart and of fabric; begin stitching there.

Use two plies of floss to work cross-stitches over two threads of fabric. Work blended needle as specified in key. Work straight stitches, couching, and French knots as specified in key. Use one ply of floss to work backstitches. Press finished stitchery from the back. Frame and mat as desired.

WOODLAND SANTA

***HARDANGER POINSETTIA ON RED

As shown on page 100.

MATERIALS
FABRIC
Two 6x6-inch pieces of 25-count Victorian red Lugana cloth
FLOSS
1 full skein Caron Watercolors in color specified in key
SUPPLIES
Needle
Embroidery hoop
4½x4½-inch piece of self-stick mounting board with foam
Ruler and pencil; awl
4¼x4¼-inch piece of self-stick mounting board
Scissors
Crafts glue
¾-inch-diameter poinsettia design silver button
3x3-inch piece of cardboard

INSTRUCTIONS
Tape or zigzag edges of one piece of fabric to prevent fraying. Find center of the chart and center of fabric; begin stitching there. Work all stitches over the number of threads indicated on the chart using one ply of thread. Press and set aside.

Find the center of the foam mounting board by measuring diagonally corner to corner; mark a small x. Use the awl to punch a small hole on each side of the x.

Peel protective paper from back of foam mounting board. Center the foam side on the back of the stitched design and press to stick. Peel protective paper from remaining mounting board, center on remaining piece of fabric, and press to stick. Trim each piece of fabric to within ½ inch from edge of cardboard. Fold raw edges to the back; secure with crafts glue, mitering corners as needed.

Sew button to center front of design through the holes in the cardboard;

WOODLAND SANTA

ANCHOR		DMC	
002	•	000	White
1049	☑	301	Mahogany
400	#	317	True pewter
399	○	318	Steel
398	/	415	Pearl gray
374	⊕	420	Hazel
358	◉	433	Light chestnut
1046	◢	435	Dark chestnut
362	✱	437	Medium tan
1005	✚	498	Christmas red
878	▣	501	Blue green
096	◇	554	Violet
832	∥	612	Drab brown
903	✕	640	Dark beige gray
392	▢	642	Medium beige gray
273	⊠	645	Dark beaver gray
361	⬓	738	Light tan
301	╲	744	Yellow
169	❖	806	Peacock blue
390	—	822	Pale beige gray
388	﹌	842	Beige brown
1041	▶	844	Deep beaver gray
360	◆	898	Coffee brown
338	▤	921	True copper
1003	☆	922	Light copper
850	⊘	926	Gray blue

ANCHOR		DMC	
881	│	945	Ivory
1002	▽	977	Golden brown
189	●	991	Aquamarine
905	◣	3021	Brown gray
871	◆	3041	Medium antique violet
870	◁	3042	Light antique violet
883	△	3064	Cocoa
382	■	3371	Black brown
1028	▧	3685	Dark mauve
060	◈	3688	Medium mauve

BLENDED NEEDLE

ANCHOR		DMC	
002	▢	000	White (1X) and 032 Kreinik pearl blending filament (3X)
403	✗	310	Black (2X) and 019 Kreinik pewter blending filament (2X)
148	◀	311	Navy (1X) and 051HL Kreinik sapphire blending filament (3X)
400	◈	317	True pewter (2X) and 019 Kreinik pewter blending filament (2X)
401	▦	413	Dark pewter (2X) and 019 Kreinik pewter blending filament (2X)
301	✳	744	Yellow (1X) and 002 Kreinik gold blending filament (3X)
1015	▨	918	Dark red copper (2X) and 027 Kreinik orange blending filament (2X)
1014	◉	919	True red copper (2X) and 027 Kreinik orange blending filament (2X)

ANCHOR		DMC	
BACKSTITCH			
1005	╱	498	Christmas red–church roof (3X)
382	╱	3371	Black brown– all remaining stitches
STRAIGHT STITCH			
878	╱	501	Blue green – greenery on hat (2X)
189	╱	991	Aquamarine–robe (2X)
382	╱	3371	Black brown–top of church steeple (2X)
1028	╱	3685	Dark mauve–robe (2X)
		002P	Kreinik gold cable–border and robe
		012	Kreinik purple blending filament– border (2X)
FRENCH KNOT			
1005	•	498	Christmas red–berries on hat (2X)
382	•	3371	Black brown–eyes of bird, wolf, and sable
SATIN STITCH			
382	╱	3371	Black brown–nose of sable, nose of fox
COUCHING			
		051HL	Kreinik sapphire #8 braid with
148		311	Navy–robe

Stitch count: 168 high x 140 wide
Finished design sizes:
14-count fabric–12 x 10 inches
11-count fabric–15⅜ x 12¾ inches
18-count fabric–9⅜ x 7⅞ inches

pull thread tightly, pulling shank into one hole to indent fabric.

For hanger, cut three 12-inch strands (3 plies each) of thread. Knot together at one end and braid. Knot remaining end. Fold in half and glue ends to back of stitched design at one corner.

For tassel, cut a 4-inch and a 12-inch strand (3 plies each) of thread; set aside. Wrap the rest of the skein around the 3x3-inch cardboard square. Thread 4-inch strand under wrapped thread at one edge of cardboard and tie. Cut threads at opposite edge of cardboard and remove. Wrap the 12-inch strand of thread around all the thread bundle and tie. Glue the 4-inch strands to the back of the stitched design on the corner opposite the braid. Glue the back sides of the cardboard squares together.

★★★HARDANGER POINSETTIA ON WHITE
As shown on page 100.

MATERIALS
FABRIC
Two 6x6-inch pieces of 25-count Victorian red Lugana cloth
FLOSS
1 full skein each of Caron Watercolors in colors specified in key
SUPPLIES
Needle; embroidery hoop
3½x3½-inch piece of self-stick mounting board with foam
3¼x3¼-inch piece of self-stick mounting board
Scissors; crafts glue
9 gold metallic gold pebble beads
3x3-inch piece of cardboard

INSTRUCTIONS
Tape or zigzag edges of one piece of fabric to prevent fraying. Find center of the chart and center of fabric; begin stitching there. Work all stitches over the number of threads

POINSETTIA ON RED

indicated on the chart using one ply of thread. Use one ply of thread to attach beads. Press on a padded surface and set aside.

Peel protective paper from back of foam mounting board. Center the foam side on the back of the stitched design and press to stick. Peel protective paper from remaining mounting board, center on remaining piece of fabric, and press to stick. Trim each piece of fabric to within ½ inch from edge of cardboard. Fold raw edges to the back; secure with crafts glue, mitering corners as needed.

For hanger, cut two 6-inch strands (3 plies each) of African sunset thread. Knot strands together at each end. Glue one end to back of stitched design at one corner.

For tassel, cut a 4-inch and a 12-inch strand (3 plies each) of African sunset thread; set aside. Wrap the rest of the skein around the 3x3-inch cardboard square. Thread 4-inch strand under wrapped thread at one edge of cardboard and tie. Cut thread at opposite edge of cardboard and remove cardboard. Wrap the 12-inch strand around the thread bundle and tie. Glue the 4-inch strands to corner opposite the hanger. Glue fabric-covered cardboard squares together.

POINSETTIA ON RED
SATIN STITCH
━ 055 Cerise
BUTTON
✕ ¾-inch-diameter button
Stitch count: 107 high x 107 wide
Finished design sizes:
25-count fabric – 4 ⅜ x 4 ⅜ inches
22-count fabric – 4 ⅞ x 4 ⅞ inches

POINSETTIA ON WHITE

HEAVENLY ANGEL ORNAMENTS

As shown on page 100.

MATERIALS

For each ornament

FABRICS

11x11-inch piece of 18-count white Aida cloth

6x6-inch piece of white felt

6x6-inch piece of fleece

THREADS

Cotton embroidery floss in colors listed in key

Metallic cable in color listed in key

SUPPLIES

Needle; embroidery hoop

Graph paper

6x6-inch piece of medium-weight cardboard

Crafts glue

⅞ yard of light blue or pink twisted satin cord

⅝ yard of ½-inch-wide gold flat lace

3-inch tassel to match satin cord

INSTRUCTIONS

Tape or zigzag edges of fabric to prevent fraying. Find center of chart and of fabric; begin stitching there.

Work cross-stitches using two plies of floss or one strand of metallic cable. Work backstitches using one ply of floss. If desired, work a small straight stitch highlight in center of each eye using one ply of light peach floss (DMC 948).

Enlarge heart pattern, opposite, using graph paper; cut out. Use pattern to cut one heart each from cardboard, fleece, and felt. Center and pin pattern on Aida cloth; cut out ½ inch beyond edge of pattern.

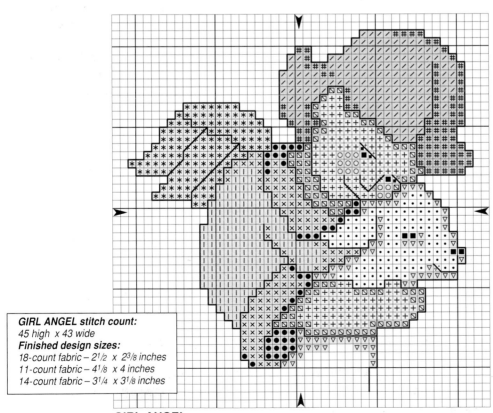

GIRL ANGEL

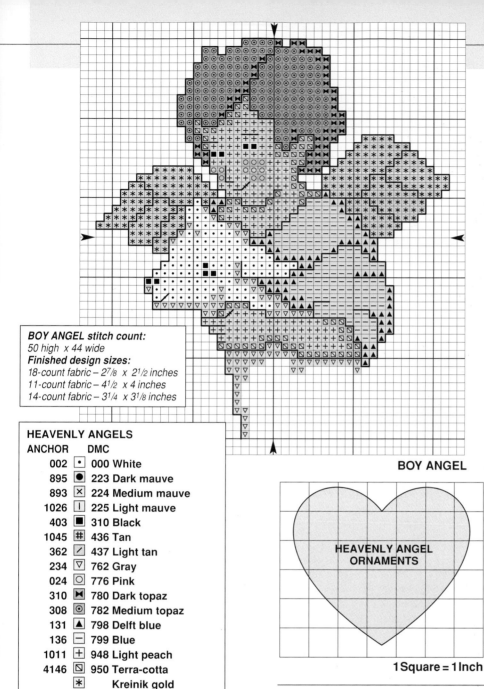

BOY ANGEL stitch count:
50 high x 44 wide
Finished design sizes:
18-count fabric – 2⁷⁄₈ x 2¹⁄₂ inches
11-count fabric – 4¹⁄₂ x 4 inches
14-count fabric – 3¹⁄₄ x 3¹⁄₈ inches

BOY ANGEL

HEAVENLY ANGELS

ANCHOR		DMC
002	·	000 White
895	●	223 Dark mauve
893	✕	224 Medium mauve
1026		225 Light mauve
403	■	310 Black
1045	#	436 Tan
362	╱	437 Light tan
234	▽	762 Gray
024	○	776 Pink
310	⋈	780 Dark topaz
308	◉	782 Medium topaz
131	▲	798 Delft blue
136	–	799 Blue
1011	+	948 Light peach
4146	◲	950 Terra-cotta
	✳	Kreinik gold 002P cable

BACKSTITCH

403	╱	310 Black – all stitches

HEAVENLY ANGEL ORNAMENTS

1 Square = 1 Inch

Glue the fleece heart to cardboard. Center Aida cloth over the fleece-covered cardboard. Fold excess Aida cloth to back and glue.

Cut enough cord to fit around edge of heart; glue, overlapping ends on back. Position and glue lace behind cord. Fold remaining cord in half and knot about 1 inch below fold. Glue ends of cord to top center of heart back. Glue tassel to bottom of heart back. Position and glue felt to back.

★★★CAROUSEL POLAR BEAR AND REINDEER ORNAMENTS

As shown on page 101.

MATERIALS
For each ornament
FABRICS
8x8-inch piece of 36-count white Edinborough linen
8x8-inch piece of fusible interfacing
THREADS
Cotton embroidery floss in colors listed in key
Blending filament in colors listed in key
#8 braid in color listed in key

★★MISCHIEF-MAKING REINDEER

As shown on page 102.

MATERIALS
FABRICS
Purchased white sweatshirt
8½x11-inch pieces of 8½-count waste canvas
Lightweight fusible interfacing
THREADS
Cotton embroidery floss and blending filament in colors listed in key
SUPPLIES
Needle; basting thread
Tweezers

SUPPLIES
Needle; embroidery hoop
White and light blue sewing thread
Polyester fiberfill
5-inch piece of ⅛-inch-wide metallic gold braid
3-inch-long metallic gold tassel

INSTRUCTIONS
Tape or zigzag edges of fabric to prevent fraying. Find center of chart and of fabric; begin stitching there.

Work all cross-stitches over two threads of fabric using two plies of floss. Work blended needle as specified in the key. Work backstitches, straight stitches, and French knots using one ply of floss.

Fuse interfacing to back of linen following manufacturer's instructions. Trim fabric to a square, ½ inch from stitching. Press top and bottom raw edges under ¼ inch. With right sides facing, fold square in half, matching pressed edges. Sew from center fold to edges along each side using a ¼-inch seam. Turn and finger press along fold lines indicated on pattern. Stuff lightly. Slipstitch top and bottom edges together.

Fold ribbon in half and tack ends to center top back edge of ornament, above pole motif. Tack tassel to center bottom back edge.

Stitch count: 62 high x 62 wide
Finished design sizes:
18-count fabric – 3½ x 3½ inches
11-count fabric – 5⅝ x 5⅝ inches
14-count fabric – 4½ x 4½ inches

CAROUSEL REINDEER

ANCHOR		DMC
118		340 Medium periwinkle
235	⊕	414 Dark steel
212	●	561 Dark seafoam
361		738 Light tan
1022	+	760 True salmon
043	◆	815 Medium garnet
360	▲	839 Dark beige brown
379	☑	840 Medium beige brown
378	✕	841 True beige brown
204	#	913 Medium Nile green
206	:	955 Pale Nile green
075	△	962 Medium rose pink
073	◪	963 Pale rose pink

ANCHOR		DMC
847	–	3072 Pale beaver gray
1024	▢	3328 Dark salmon
382	■	3371 Black brown

BLENDED NEEDLE

117	○	341 Light periwinkle (1X) and 3747 Pale periwinkle (2X)
120		
302	◇	743 True yellow (1X) and 028 Kreinik citron blending filament (2X)
301	✳	744 Medium yellow (1X) and 002 Kreinik gold blending filament (2X)
128	◁	775 Light baby blue (1X) and 095 Kreinik starburst blending filament (2X)
1023	◨	3712 Medium salmon (1X) and 003 Kreinik red blending filament (2X)

ANCHOR		DMC
BACKSTITCH		
	/	221 Kreinik antique gold #8 braid–trim on muzzle and saddle
382	/	3371 Black brown– all remaining stitches
STRAIGHT STITCH		
	/	221 Kreinik antique gold #8 braid–lines on pole
FRENCH KNOT		
302	•	743 True yellow (2X) and Kreinik citron blending filament (1X)–saddle

INSTRUCTIONS

To prevent floss from bleeding, hold floss under running water until water runs clear. Allow floss to air dry before starting project.

Wash and dry shirt. Tape or zigzag edges of waste canvas to prevent fraying. Baste waste canvas to front of sweatshirt with top edge of canvas at bottom center of neckband. Measure 3½ inches down and 2½ inches in from the right edge of canvas; begin stitching top of right antler there. Turn sweatshirt over to back side. Measure 4 inches down from the neckband and baste waste canvas so the top edge begins there. Find center of the tree on chart and center of canvas; begin stitching there. Baste pieces of waste canvas around all of sweatshirt to stitch the strand of tree lights.

Use three plies of floss to work cross-stitches. Work blended needle and half cross-stitches as specified in key. Use two plies of floss for backstitches unless otherwise specified in the key.

Remove basting threads; trim canvas close to stitching. Wet the waste canvas and using tweezers, pull the individual canvas threads from under the cross-stitches. Fuse the interfacing over the stitching on the inside of the shirt following the manufacturer's instructions.

CAROUSEL BEAR

ANCHOR		DMC	
002	·	000	White
400	◎	317	True pewter
399	△	318	Light steel
1025	◨	347	Deep salmon
212	●	561	Dark seafoam
1022	+	760	True salmon
168	⊙	807	Medium peacock blue
043	◆	815	Medium garnet
360	⋈	898	Dark coffee brown
204	#	913	Medium Nile green
206	∷	955	Pale Nile green
355	▼	975	Dark golden brown
847	—	3072	Pale beaver gray
1024	□	3328	Dark salmon
382	■	3371	Black brown
1023	◩	3712	Medium salmon
170	◆	3765	Deep peacock blue

BLENDED NEEDLE

118	✳	340 Medium periwinkle (1X) and
		023 Kreinik lilac blending filament (2X)
302	◇	743 True yellow (1X) and
		028 Kreinik citron blending filament (2X)

BLENDED NEEDLE

301	✳	744 Medium yellow (1X) and
		002 Kreinik gold blending filament (3X)
204	✛	913 Medium Nile green (1X) and
		008 Kreinik green blending filament (2X)
073	‖	963 Pale rose pink (1X) and
		008 Kreinik green blending filament (2X)

BACKSTITCH

	╱	221 Kreinik antique gold #8 braid –
		trim on muzzle and saddle
382	╱	3371 Black brown – all remaining stitches

STRAIGHT STITCH

	╱	221 Kreinik antique gold #8 braid –
		lines on pole, star on saddle

FRENCH KNOT

302	•	743 True yellow (2X) and
		Kreinik citron blending
		filament (1X) – muzzle

Stitch count: 62 high x 62 wide
Finished design sizes:
18-count fabric – 3¹/₂ x 3¹/₂ inches
11-count fabric – 5⁵/₈ x 5⁵/₈ inches
14-count fabric – 4¹/₂ x 4¹/₂ inches

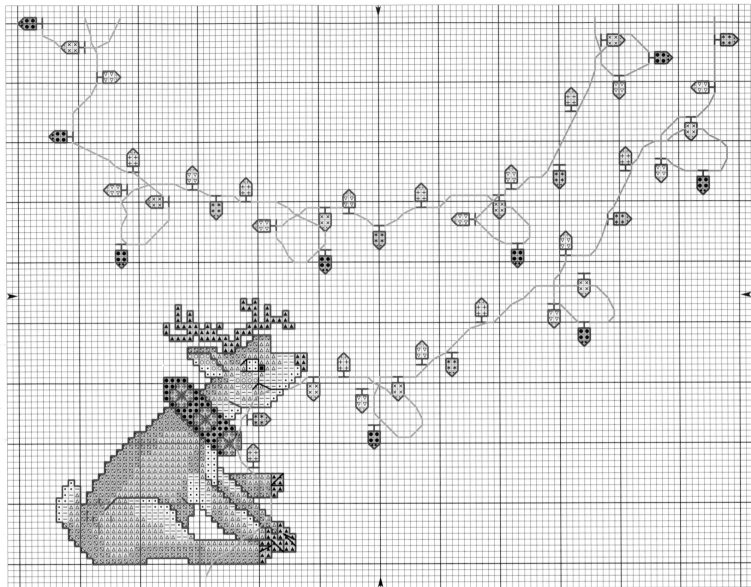

SHIRT FRONT

MISCHIEF-MAKING REINDEER SHIRT

ANCHOR		DMC	
002	·	000	White
403	■	310	Black
9046	●	321	Christmas red
310	◨	434	Chestnut
1045	△	436	Tan
334	✳	606	Orange red
226	✕	702	Christmas green
302	▽	743	Yellow
1021	○	761	Salmon
360	▲	839	Beige brown
244	⊙	987	Forest green
433	+	996	Electric blue
1009	—	3770	Ivory

BLENDED NEEDLE

847	⊕	3072 Beaver gray (3X) and 001 Kreinik silver blending filament (3X)

HALF CROSS-STITCH
(stitch in direction of symbol)

ANCHOR		DMC	
002	⧄	000	White (2X) and Kreinik pearl 032 blending filament (2X)

BACKSTITCH

403	╱	310	Black—eye, mouth, hooves
226	╱	702	Christmas green—light cords (6X)
360	╱	839	Beige brown—deer
382	╱	3371	Black brown—Christmas lights; all remaining stitches (6X)

SMYRNA CROSS

360	✳	839	Beige brown—bells on collar

FRONT stitch count: 93 high x 120 wide
FRONT finished design size:
8½-count fabric – 11 x 14 inches

BACK stitch count: 134 high x 115 wide
BACK finished design size:
8½-count fabric – 15¾ x 13½ inches

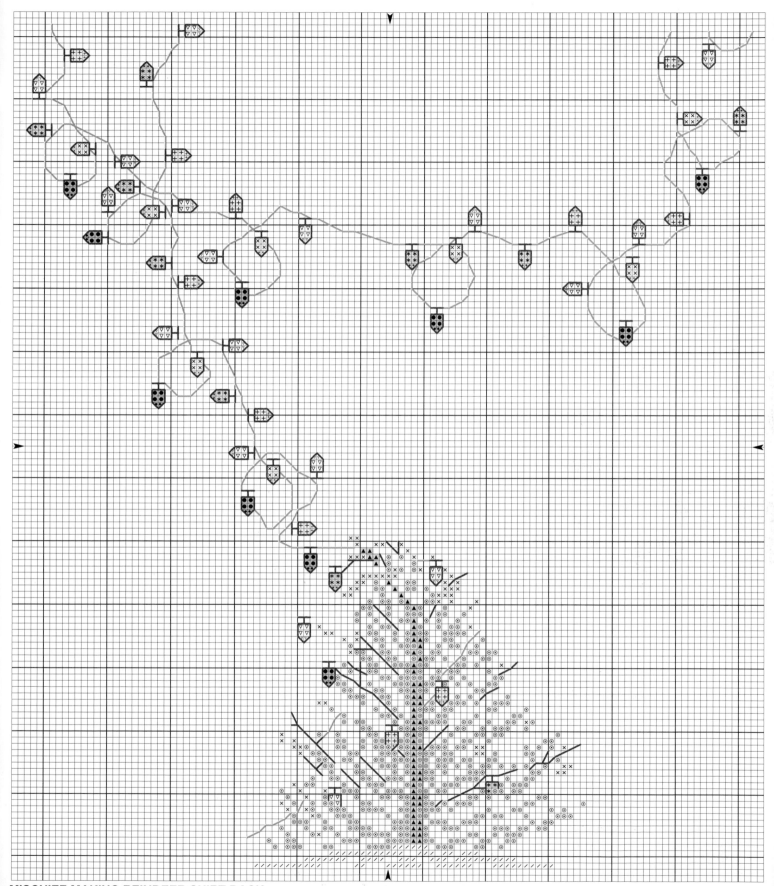

MISCHIEF-MAKING REINDEER SHIRT BACK

Floral
FANCIES

Celebrate the beauty of flowers with these fresh-as-spring designs. As you stitch your way through this glorious assortment of colorful blooms and breathtaking gardens, you'll be left with lasting floral treasures to be enjoyed a lifetime. Season after season, these radiant flowers will add a romantic touch to any room of your home.

In the Garden

Our three serene flower gardens are abloom with color on 18-count antique white Aida cloth. The colonial garden features a welcoming gate arched by climbing roses. A birdbath is placed in the center of the brightly colored country garden and is a sanctuary for any bird. A young lady will be returning for her hat in the Victorian garden. All three designs include half cross-stitches which create the subtle shading. Complete instructions and charts begin on page 130.

Victorian Tapestry

This lovely tapestry of flowers will capture the heart of any romantic when stitched on 28-count black Jobelan. Destined to become an heirloom, we have finished the work of art with elegant mats and frame. For a beautiful brooch or elegant buttons, stitch the blooms on 40-count silk gauze. Complete instructions and chart begin on page 133.

Teacup Bellpull

Enjoy all of the seasons by stitching this dainty teacup bellpull on 28-count ivory Jobelan. Let this elegant creation grace a cozy corner where you and your guests can admire it year-round. These sweet motifs could be stitched separately and used for an endless array of gift-giving projects. Complete instructions and charts begin on page 134.

Rose Garden Sampler

One can almost smell the sweet fragrance of the roses and see the flitting of the lifelike butterflies that adorn the trellis border surrounding this colorful formal garden. This exquisite sampler is stitched on 26-count natural brown linen to capture the warm, welcoming feel of a garden in full bloom. Lazy daisy stitches and French knots add texture and realism to this artistic design. Complete instructions and chart begin on page 136.

Rose Tea Linens

Set an elegant tea table with a gracious tablecloth and napkins that feature a rose-embellished teapot design cross-stitched on 28-count Jubilee fabric. The teapot's rose motif is repeated on the tea cozy, with each rose separated by a lattice of gold thread, machine-stitched over rose floss. Lace edging adds the finishing touch to these heirloom-style tea linens your family will treasure for years. Complete instructions and charts begin on page 138.

Bouquet of Sunshine

A trio of sunflowers, stitched on 28-count natural linen, reflects the warmth and simplicity of country style. Tent stitches and Smyrna cross stitches add beautiful detail, while the simple letters are repeated below for personalization. Instructions and chart begin on page 139.

COLONIAL GARDEN

✲✲✲COLONIAL GARDEN

As shown on page 124.

MATERIALS

FABRIC
8x10-inch piece of 18-count antique white Aida cloth

FLOSS
Cotton embroidery floss in colors listed in key

SUPPLIES
Needle
Embroidery hoop
Desired frame and mat

INSTRUCTIONS

Tape or zigzag edges of fabric to prevent fraying. Find center of chart and of fabric; begin stitching there. Use two plies of floss to work cross-stitches and half cross-stitches. Use one ply for backstitches. Press finished stitchery from the back. Frame and mat as desired.

COLONIAL GARDEN

ANCHOR		DMC	
002	•	000	White
110	▼	208	Dark lavender
897	‖	221	Deep shell pink
895	▣	223	Medium shell pink
1026	∧	225	Pale shell pink
218	▶	319	Dark pistachio
100	◥	327	Deep antique violet
1043	+	369	Pale pistachio
398	⊕	415	Pearl gray
358	◆	433	Dark chestnut
1046	✳	435	Light chestnut
267	⊖	470	Medium avocado
253	∿	472	Pale avocado
860	⊓	522	Olive drab
898	▦	611	Drab brown
323	◇	722	Light bittersweet
302	★	743	Medium yellow
1021	⊠	761	Light salmon
023	⦂	818	Pink
360	◎	839	Beige brown
215	✕	890	Deep pistachio
899	●	3023	Light brown gray
397	✕	3024	Pale brown gray

ANCHOR		DMC	
036	♡	3326	Rose
1024	⊞	3328	Dark salmon
268	★	3346	Hunter green
262	△	3363	Medium loden
260	◀	3364	Light loden
382	▪	3371	Black brown

HALF CROSS-STITCH

895	╱	223	Medium shell pink
1026	╱	225	Pale shell pink
1043	╱	369	Pale pistachio
1021	╱	761	Light salmon
397	╱	3024	Pale brown gray

BACKSTITCH

235	╱	414	Steel–gate
360	╱	839	Beige brown– branches, house
215	╱	890	Deep pistachio– flower stems
382	╱	3371	Black brown– gate latch, basket

Stitch count: 69 high x 102 wide
Finished design sizes:
18-count fabric – 3⅞ x 5¾ inches
11-count fabric – 6⅜ x 9⅜ inches
14-count fabric – 5 x 7⅜ inches

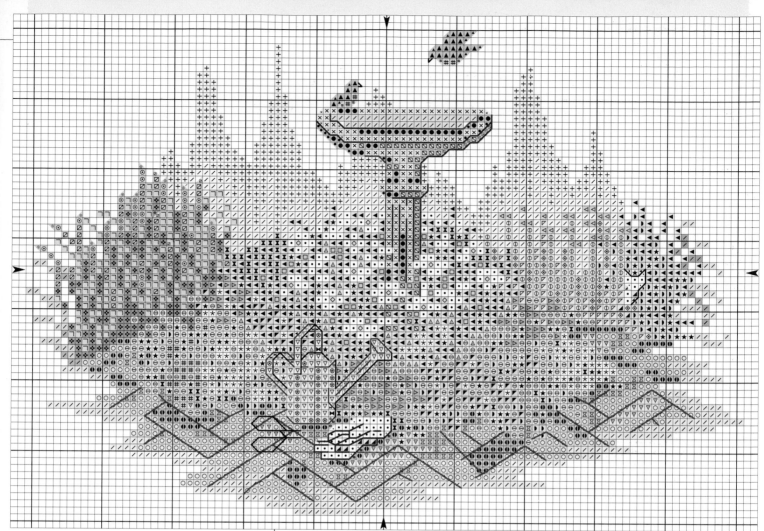

COUNTRY GARDEN

✦✦✦COUNTRY GARDEN

As shown on page 124.

MATERIALS

Fabric
8x10-inch piece of 18-count antique white Aida cloth

Floss
Cotton embroidery floss in colors listed in key

Supplies
Needle

Embroidery hoop

Desired frame and mat

INSTRUCTIONS

Tape or zigzag edges of fabric to prevent fraying. Find center of chart and of fabric; begin stitching there. Use two plies of floss to work cross-stitches. Use two plies to work backstitches, straight stitches, and half cross-stitches. Press finished stitchery from back. Frame and mat as desired.

COUNTRY GARDEN

ANCHOR		DMC	
002	⊡	000	White
109	☑	209	Medium lavender
399	◪	318	Steel
218	▶	319	Dark pistachio
5975	◑	356	Terra cotta
1043	+	369	Pale pistachio
914	⊠	407	Cocoa
267	⊖	470	Medium avocado
1005	▷	498	Christmas red
877	◈	502	Medium blue green
1042	◐	504	Pale blue green
860	�	522	Olive drab
206	▽	564	Seafoam
273	◩	645	Dark beaver gray
326	◤	720	Dark bittersweet
323	◇	722	Light bittersweet
302	✳	743	Medium yellow
1012	◯	754	Peach
1022	▽	760	True salmon
128	▽	775	Light baby blue
359	▲	801	Coffee brown
215	⊠	890	Deep pistachio
1034	⋈	931	Medium antique blue
1033	⊛	932	True antique blue
076	◁	961	Rose pink
899	●	3023	Light brown gray
397	✕	3024	Pale brown gray
870	◎	3042	Light antique violet
681	✤	3051	Gray green
1024	#	3328	Dark salmon

ANCHOR		DMC	
268	★	3346	Hunter green
262	△	3363	Medium loden
260	◀	3364	Light loden
087	▢	3607	Fuchsia

HALF CROSS-STITCH

218	╱	319	Dark pistachio
1043	╱	369	Pale pistachio
860	╱	522	Olive drab
1012	╱	754	Peach
144	╱	800	Delft blue
681	╱	3051	Gray green
260	╱	3364	Light loden

BACKSTITCH

273	╱	645	Dark beaver gray— birdbath
1041	╱	844	Deep beaver gray— birdbath, gloves
1035	╱	930	Dark antique blue— watering can
382	╱	3371	Black brown— cat, watering can

STRAIGHT STITCH

273	╱	645	Dark beaver gray— bricks
382	╱	3371	Black brown— shears, birds

Stitch count: 69 high x 102 wide

Finished design sizes:
18-count fabric – 3⅞ x 5¾ inches
11-count fabric – 6⅜ x 9⅜ inches
14-count fabric – 5 x 7⅜ inches

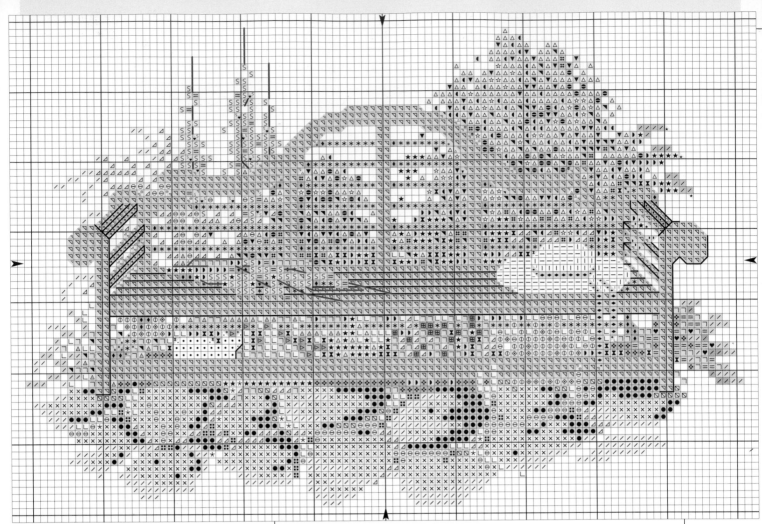

VICTORIAN GARDEN

★★★VICTORIAN GARDEN

As shown on page 125.

MATERIALS

FABRIC
8x10-inch piece of 18-count antique white Aida cloth

FLOSS
Cotton embroidery floss in colors listed in key

SUPPLIES
Needle
Embroidery hoop
Desired frame and mat

INSTRUCTIONS

Tape or zigzag edges of fabric to prevent fraying. Find center of chart and of fabric; begin stitching there. Use two plies of floss to work cross-stitches and half cross-stitches. Use one ply for backstitches and straight stitches. Press stitchery from back. Frame and mat as desired.

VICTORIAN GARDEN

ANCHOR		DMC	
002	•	000	White
110	▼	208	Dark lavender
342	△	211	Pale lavender
218	◗	319	Dark pistachio
100	◣	327	Deep antique violet
119	⊞	333	Deep periwinkle
977	◆	334	Dark baby blue
117	☆	341	Light periwinkle
358	◆	433	Dark chestnut
1046	✳	435	Light chestnut
362	◥	437	Tan
267	⊖	470	Medium avocado
266	◿	471	Light avocado
1005	▷	498	Christmas red
877	◈	502	Medium blue green
1042	⊙	504	Pale blue green
860	⊓	522	Olive drab
096	◖	554	Violet
898	⠿	611	Drab brown
273	◩	645	Dark beaver gray
302	★	743	True yellow
300	Ⅰ	745	Light yellow
275	—	746	Off white
045	⊞	814	Garnet
215	⊠	890	Deep pistachio
089	⊜	917	Plum
899	●	3023	Light brown gray
397	✕	3024	Pale brown gray

ANCHOR		DMC	
681	⊞	3051	Gray green
268	★	3346	Hunter green
264	∟	3348	Yellow green
059	♥	3350	Dusty rose
262	△	3363	Medium loden
060	═	3688	Medium mauve
049	S	3689	Light mauve

HALF CROSS-STITCH

266	╱	471	Light avocado
860	╱	522	Olive drab
899	╱	3023	Light brown gray
397	╱	3024	Pale brown gray
681	╱	3051	Gray green
268	╱	3346	Hunter green
264	╱	3348	Yellow green

BACKSTITCH

218	╱	319	Dark pistachio— stems
359	╱	801	Coffee brown— bench, cat

STRAIGHT STITCH

218	╱	319	Dark pistachio— stems of flowers on bench

Stitch count: 68 high x 102 wide
Finished design sizes:
18-count fabric – 3⅞ x 5¾ inches
11-count fabric – 6¼ x 9⅜ inches
14-count fabric – 5 x 7⅜ inches

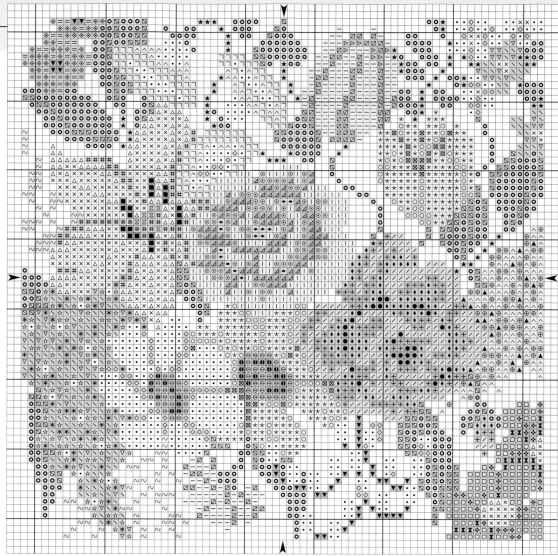

VICTORIAN TAPESTRY

★★VICTORIAN TAPESTRY

As shown on page 126.

MATERIALS

FABRIC
9x9-inch piece of 28-count black Jobelan

FLOSS
Cotton embroidery floss in colors listed in key

SUPPLIES
Needle; embroidery hoop
Desired frame and mat

INSTRUCTIONS

Tape or zigzag edges of fabric to prevent fraying. Find center of chart and center of fabric; begin stitching there. Use two plies of floss to work cross-stitches over two threads of fabric. Press finished stitchery from the back. Frame and mat as desired.

VICTORIAN TAPESTRY

ANCHOR		DMC		ANCHOR		DMC
002	⊡	000 White		890	◯	729 Medium old gold
342	◣	211 Lavender		300	✕	745 Yellow
895	▷	223 Medium shell pink		1021	⧄	761 Salmon
1026	—	225 Pale shell pink		128	∧	775 Light baby blue
1019	●	315 Dark antique mauve		1016	◿	778 Pale antique mauve
1017	＋	316 Medium antique mauve		307	⌗	783 Christmas gold
010	◆	351 Light coral		176	▲	793 Medium cornflower blue
009	◿	352 Pale coral		175	⊕	794 Light cornflower blue
008	⊙	353 Dark peach		1014	✕	919 Red copper
217	◺	367 Pistachio		1011	▯	948 Light peach
1047	◈	402 Mahogany		355	■	975 Dark golden brown
374	◉	420 Hazel		246	★	986 Dark forest green
310	▼	434 Medium golden brown		242	◯	989 Pale forest green
1046	⊠	435 True golden brown		899	◇	3023 Brown gray
1042	~	504 Blue green		888	⊖	3045 Yellow beige
098	✳	553 Medium violet		144	⌐	3325 True baby blue
096	▽	554 Light violet		068	◆	3687 True mauve
886	✦	677 Pale old gold		049	☆	3689 Light mauve
901	⊠	680 Dark old gold				
326	✧	720 Dark bittersweet				
324	＝	721 Medium bittersweet				
323	▢	722 Light bittersweet				
305	△	725 Topaz				

Stitch count: 75 high x 75 wide

Finished design sizes:
14-count fabric – 5³⁄₈ x 5³⁄₈ inches
11-count fabric – 6⁷⁄₈ x 6⁷⁄₈ inches
18-count fabric – 4¹⁄₄ x 4¹⁄₄ inches

★★★★VICTORIAN TAPESTRY BUTTONS

As shown on page 126, finished buttons are ⅝ inches diameter.

MATERIALS *for four buttons*
FABRIC
4x4-inch piece of 40-count silk gauze mounted in cardboard frame
FLOSS
Cotton embroidery floss in colors listed in key on page 133
SUPPLIES
Basting thread; needle; magnifier
Four ⅝-inch-diameter button forms
Button cover; all-purpose cement

INSTRUCTIONS

Using basting thread, divide gauze in half horizontally and vertically to form four 1x1-inch squares. Find the center of desired motif and center of one quarter of fabric; begin stitching there. Work half cross-stitches over one thread, using one ply of floss.

Remove silk gauze from frame and press on wrong side. Center design over button form; trim fabric leaving as much fabric around each button as possible. Run gathering thread ⅛ inch from cut edge. Pull thread to smooth fabric around top of form. Assemble button following manufacturer's instructions. Remove button shank; attach button cover with cement.

★★★★VICTORIAN TAPESTRY BROOCH

As shown on page 126, finished brooch, including lace, measures 1¾ inches diameter.

MATERIALS
FABRIC
4x4-inch piece of 40-count silk gauze mounted in cardboard frame
FLOSS
Cotton embroidery floss in colors listed in key on page 133

SUPPLIES
Needle; magnifier (optional)
1-inch-diameter button form
4-inch piece of ½-inch-wide ivory lace
3½-inch piece of 2-millimeter pearls-by-the-yard
Crafts glue; wire cutters
1-inch pin back; all-purpose cement

INSTRUCTIONS

Find center of desired motif and center of fabric; begin stitching there. Work half cross-stitches over one thread, using one ply of floss.

Remove silk gauze from frame and press on wrong side. Center design over button form; trim fabric ½ inch beyond edge. Run gathering thread ¼ inch from cut edge. Pull thread to smooth fabric around top of form.

Assemble button following manufacturer's instructions. Use one ply of white to sew lace to edge of design then glue pearls around edge. Use wire cutters to remove button shank. Attach pin back with cement.

★★★TEACUP BELLPULL

As shown on page 126.

MATERIALS
FABRICS
20x12-inch piece of 28-count ivory Jobelan
16x6-inch piece of lightweight fusible interfacing
⅓ yard of 45-inch-wide blue taffeta
FLOSS
Cotton embroidery floss in colors listed in keys
SUPPLIES
Needle
Embroidery hoop
Sewing thread
Two 16-inch pieces of ⅛-inch-diameter cording
5-inch-wide brass bellpull hardware

INSTRUCTIONS

Tape or zigzag edges of fabric to prevent fraying. Measure 4½ inches from top of fabric. Using three plies

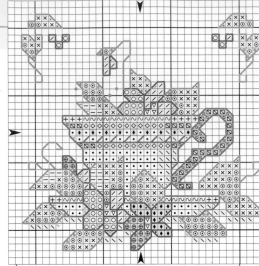

SPRING TEACUP FOR BELLPULL

ANCHOR		DMC
002	⊡	000 White
342	⧄	211 Pale lavender
215	⊙	320 True pistachio
118	⊡	340 Medium periwinkle
117	◇	341 Light periwinkle
214	✕	368 Light pistachio
398	◣	415 Pearl gray
098	◆	553 Medium violet
096	⊕	554 Light violet
293	▽	727 Pale topaz
259	—	772 Loden
128	⁓	775 Light baby blue
023	○	818 Pink
144	⊞	3325 True baby blue
BACKSTITCH		
119	╱	333 Deep periwinkle– cup and saucer
217	╱	367 Medium pistachio– leaves, vines
098	╱	553 Medium violet– violets, corner motifs
FRENCH KNOT		
217	●	367 Medium pistachio – dots (2X)

Stitch count: 35 high x 35 wide
Finished design sizes:
14-count fabric – 2½ x 2½ inches
11-count fabric – 3¼ x 3¼ inches
18-count fabric – 2 x 2 inches

of DMC 739, stitch a horizontal running stitch there, going over three threads, then under one thread of fabric. Leaving one thread below row, repeat running stitch, shifting first stitch two threads to right. Repeat the two rows of running stitches four more times, each 2⅞ inches apart. Measure 4½ inches from left edge of fabric. Stitch two vertical rows of running stitches as for horizontal rows. Repeat on right side.

Find center of desired chart and center of one square; begin stitching there.

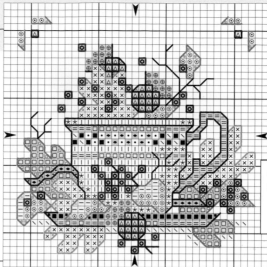

Stitch count: 35 high x 35 wide
Finished design sizes:
14-count fabric – 2½ x 2½ inches
11-count fabric – 3¼ x 3¼ inches
18-count fabric – 2 x 2 inches

SUMMER TEACUP FOR BELLPULL

ANCHOR		DMC	
002	•	000	White
009	▢	352	Coral
398	◥	415	Pearl gray
885	S	739	Tan
300	▯	745	Yellow
1021	○	761	Salmon
132	●	797	Royal blue
136	+	799	Delft blue
076	✳	961	Rose pink
246	▲	986	Dark forest green
242	◉	989	Pale forest green
059	♥	3350	Dusty rose
086	⊕	3608	Fuchsia

BACKSTITCH

132	╱	797	Royal blue – cup and saucer
246	╱	986	Dark forest green – leaves; flower stems (2X)
059	╱	3350	Dusty rose – flowers, corner motifs

STRAIGHT STITCH

136	╱	799	Delft blue – cup decoration (2X)

FRENCH KNOT

136	●	799	Delft blue – cup (3X)
242	●	989	Pale forest green – dots above cup (2X)

Stitch count: 35 high x 35 wide
Finished design sizes:
14-count fabric – 2½ x 2½ inches
11-count fabric – 3¼ x 3¼ inches
18-count fabric – 2 x 2 inches

AUTUMN TEACUP FOR BELLPULL

ANCHOR		DMC	
002	•	000	White
109	⊕	209	Medium lavender
1049	=	301	Mahogany
398	◥	415	Pearl gray
1046	△	435	True golden brown
877	◉	502	Medium blue green
875	⊟	503	True blue green
300	▯	745	Yellow
359	◆	801	Medium coffee brown
333	◉	900	Burnt orange
1003	▢	922	Copper
381	■	938	Deep coffee brown
260	☒	3364	Light loden

ANCHOR		DMC	
BLENDED NEEDLE			
1002	✳	977	Pale golden brown (2X) and
303		742	Tangerine (1X)
BACKSTITCH			
1049	╱	301	Mahogany – mahogany leaves
878	╱	501	Dark blue green – blue green leaves
359	╱	801	Medium coffee brown – branches (2X)
359	╱	801	Medium coffee brown – cup and saucer, thistles, stems, some berries and leaves
333	╱	900	Burnt orange – rest of berries
262	╱	3363	Medium loden – leaf green leaves

Stitch count: 35 high x 35 wide
Finished design sizes:
14-count fabric – 2½ x 2½ inches
11-count fabric – 3¼ x 3¼ inches
18-count fabric – 2 x 2 inches

Use three plies of floss to work cross-stitches over two threads of fabric. Work backstitches, straight stitches, and French knots using one ply unless otherwise specified in keys. Work blended needle as specified in the key.

Trim stitched fabric to 16x6 inches; fuse interfacing to wrong side following manufacturer's instructions.

WINTER TEACUP FOR BELLPULL

ANCHOR		DMC	
002	•	000	White
1006	♥	304	Christmas red
979	●	312	Navy
398	◥	415	Pearl gray
374	★	420	Medium hazel
212	▲	561	Dark seafoam
210	◉	562	Medium seafoam
208	⊟	563	True seafoam
046	✳	666	Red

ANCHOR		DMC	
295	▽	726	Topaz
890	⊖	729	Old gold
BACKSTITCH			
979	╱	312	Navy
212	╱	561	Dark seafoam
890	╱	729	Old gold
043	╱	815	Garnet
944	╱	869	Dark hazel

From blue taffeta, cut one 16x6-inch bellpull back, and two 1x16-inch bias piping strips. Center cording lengthwise on wrong side of piping strips. Fold fabric around cording, raw edges together. Use a zipper foot to sew through both layers close to stitching. Sew one piece of covered cording to each long side of bellpull, raw edges even.

Sew front to back with right sides facing, leaving an opening at top for turning. Trim seams, turn, sew opening closed, and press. Insert ends of bellpull through bellpull hardware from front. Fold 1 inch to the back and whipstitch the fabric ends to the back of the bellpull.

★★★ROSE GARDEN SAMPLER

As shown on page 127.

MATERIALS
FABRIC
17x20-inch piece of 26-count
  natural brown linen
FLOSS
Cotton embroidery floss in colors
  listed in key on page 138
Three additional skeins of white
  (DMC 000)
One additional skein of pale gray
  blue (DMC 928)
SUPPLIES
Needle; embroidery hoop
Desired frame and mat

INSTRUCTIONS
Tape or zigzag edges of fabric to prevent fraying. Find center of chart and of fabric; begin stitching there.

Use two plies of floss to work cross-stitches over two threads of fabric. Use two plies to work lazy daisy stitches. Work backstitches using one ply and French knots using two plies unless otherwise specified in key. Press the finished stitchery from the back. Frame and mat as desired.

ROSE GARDEN SAMPLER

ROSE GARDEN SAMPLER

ANCHOR	DMC	Color
002	000	White
110	208	Dark lavender
108	210	Light lavender
9046	321	Christmas red
059	326	Deep rose
038	335	Medium rose
010	351	Coral
5975	356	Terra cotta
914	407	Cocoa
310	434	Chestnut
1045	436	Tan
231	453	Shell gray
266	471	Avocado
683	500	Deep blue green
878	501	Dark blue green
877	502	Medium blue green
1042	504	Pale blue green
1041	535	Ash gray
212	561	Dark seafoam
210	562	Medium seafoam
208	563	True seafoam
206	564	Light seafoam
293	727	Pale topaz
890	729	Old gold
024	776	Pink
308	782	Medium topaz
177	792	Dark cornflower blue
176	793	Medium cornflower blue
175	794	Light cornflower blue
043	815	Medium garnet
360	839	Beige brown
052	899	Light rose
897	902	Deep garnet
204	913	Nile green
274	928	Gray blue
861	935	Pine green
4146	950	Rose beige
681	3051	Gray green
268	3345	Medium hunter green
267	3346	Light hunter green
266	3347	Medium yellow green
264	3348	Light yellow green
382	3371	Black brown
1028	3685	Deep mauve
068	3687	True mauve
060	3688	Medium mauve
049	3689	Light mauve

BACKSTITCH

ANCHOR	DMC	Color – Notes
002	000	White – lattice lines in border (3X)
212	561	Dark seafoam – flourish lines, rose stems around saying (2X); rosebud sepals around saying
210	562	Medium seafoam – leaf flourishes around saying
293	727	Pale topaz – wings of butterfly near gazebo
176	793	Medium cornflower blue – wings of butterflies near gazebo
897	902	Deep garnet – rose stems, thorns (2X)
382	3371	Black brown – butterflies (2X)
360	898	Dark coffee brown – flourishes on saying and Bible verse (1X); stems, bodies of butterflies near gazebo (2X); all remaining stitches

FRENCH KNOT

ANCHOR	DMC	Color – Notes
002	000	White – flowers of bush roses in the center (4X)
110	208	Dark lavender – flourish around the saying (4X)
010	351	Light coral – centers of pink and white roses at bottom
293	727	Pale topaz – flowers of bush roses in center (4X); centers of yellow roses at top
360	898	Dark coffee brown – rose hips, center of large pink rose, and saying
382	3371	Black brown – ends of butterfly antennae

Stitch count: 180 high x 140 wide
Finished design sizes:
13-count fabric – 13¾ x 10¾ inches
11-count fabric – 16⅜ x 12¾ inches
18-count fabric – 10 x 7⅞ inches

**ROSE TEAPOT COZY

As shown on page 128, finished teapot cozy measures 8x10 inches.

MATERIALS

FABRICS
Two 9x11-inch pieces of 28-count white Jubilee fabric
Two 9x11-inch pieces of polyester fleece; two 9x11-inch pieces white lining fabric

THREADS
Cotton embroidery floss in colors listed in key; one additional skein of medium dusty rose (DMC 3733)
Gold metallic and white sewing threads

SUPPLIES
Erasable marker; needle
Embroidery hoop; two purchased 2¾-inch-long white tassels
¼ yard of 1-inch-wide flat white lace
1 yard of ¼-inch-wide light pink picot-edged satin ribbon
1 yard of ¼-inch-wide rose picot-edged satin ribbon
20-inch piece of ¼-inch-wide elastic

INSTRUCTIONS

Zigzag or serge edges of Jubilee fabric pieces to prevent fraying. Using erasable marker, draw a 2-inch-wide grid of diagonal squares that is centered on each piece of fabric.

For front, with a long edge at top, find center of one square and center of chart; begin stitching a rose motif there.

Work all cross-stitches using two plies of floss over two threads of fabric. Work backstitches using one ply. Repeat rose motif in center of each complete square on grid.

For back, with a long edge at top, stitch one rose motif in only the center square. Baste a piece of fleece to wrong side of each piece of Jubilee fabric. Lay a six-ply length of DMC 3733 floss over each line of grid; machine zigzag over floss using gold sewing thread. Repeat for each line of marked grid. Erase marker lines.

For side seams, on wrong side of front, measure and mark the point 2 inches from bottom on both sides. Measure and mark the point 2 inches from top edge on left side only. With right sides facing, sew front and back together using ½-inch seams and stitching from marked point to top or bottom edge. Press seams open; turn.

Sew lining pieces in same manner. Press seams open, but do not turn.

Baste straight edge of lace ⅜ inch from top edge of Jubilee fabric with right sides facing. With right sides facing, sew Jubilee fabric and lining together along top edge, catching in edge of lace. Sew bottom edge and both sides of slit (handle opening) on right side. Turn and press.

For bottom casing, stitch around bottom edge ½-inch from seam line. Open one lining seam between bottom seam and casing stitching. Insert elastic into bottom casing.

Slip cozy over teapot. Adjust fit of elastic, remove cozy, and secure ends. Sew lining opening closed.

For top casing, stitch around top edge, ½ inch from seam line. Hand sew lining to Jubilee fabric along side (spout) opening below casing stitching.

Insert both ribbons through top casing. Place cozy on teapot; pull ribbons to tighten and tie into a bow. Adjust gathers evenly. Tack tassels just below ribbon ties.

★★★ROSE TEA LINENS

As shown on page 128, finished tablecloth is 46x46 inches; napkins are 16x16 inches.

MATERIALS
FABRIC
1¾ yards of 55-inch-wide 28-count white Jubilee fabric
THREADS
Cotton embroidery floss in colors listed in key
Two additional skeins of medium dusty rose (DMC 3733)
Two spools of gold metallic sewing thread
White sewing thread
SUPPLIES
Needle; embroidery hoop
10 yards of 1-inch-wide white lace

INSTRUCTIONS
Cut a 46½x46½-inch tablecloth and two 16½x16½-inch napkins from fabric. Zigzag or serge edges of fabric to prevent fraying. On one corner of napkin or tablecloth, measure 5 inches from each edge. Begin stitching center of motif there. Work cross-stitches over two threads of fabric using two plies of floss. Work backstitches using one ply. Repeat teapot motif in each corner of tablecloth.

Fold zigzagged edges under ¼ inch, mitering corners; topstitch. Sew flat lace to wrong side of stitched hem, mitering lace at corners. Position a six-ply length of DMC 3733 floss over stitching; zigzag over floss using gold sewing thread.

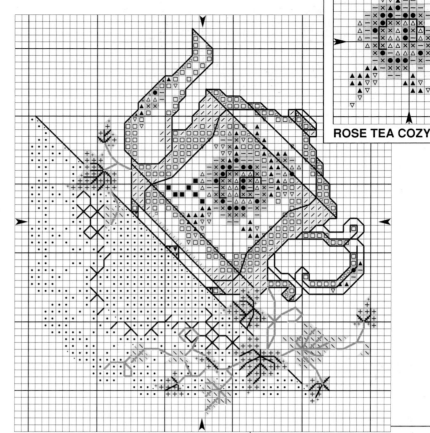

ROSE TEA COZY

ROSE TEA LINENS

★★★★BOUQUET OF SUNSHINE

As shown on page 129.

MATERIALS
FABRIC
15x17-inch piece of 28-count natural linen
FLOSS
Cotton embroidery floss in colors listed in key on page 141
One additional skein each of true golden brown (DMC 435), true yellow (DMC 743), dark hazel (DMC 869), and dark antique violet (DMC 3740)
SUPPLIES
Needle; embroidery hoop; frame

INSTRUCTIONS
Tape edges of fabric. Find center of chart and fabric; begin stitching there.

Use three plies to work cross-stitches over two threads. Work all other stitches as specified in key. Chart initials and date using alphabet; stitch in spaces provided. Press and frame.

ROSE TEA LINENS AND COZY		
ANCHOR		**DMC**
399	/	318 Steel
217	▲	367 Medium pistachio
214	▽	368 Light pistachio
398	▢	415 Pearl gray
860	+	522 Dark olive drab
858	◣	524 Light olive drab
392	■	642 Beige gray
885	•	739 Tan
073	△	963 Pale rose pink
059	●	3350 Deep dusty rose
076	✕	3731 Dark dusty rose
075	—	3733 Medium dusty rose
236	▼	3799 Dark charcoal
BACKSTITCH		
218	/	319 Dark pistachio – veins of dark leaves
217	/	367 Medium pistachio – veins of light leaves, vines
401	/	413 Pewter – rose, teapot detail
885	/	739 Tan (2X) – doily
236	/	3799 Dark charcoal – teapot outline, table edge

TEA LINENS stitch count: 57 high x 51 wide
TEA LINENS finished design sizes:
14-count fabric – 4 x 3⅝ inches
11-count fabric – 5⅛ x 4⅝ inches
18-count fabric – 3⅛ x 2⅞ inches
TEA COZY stitch count: 18 high x 16 wide
TEA COZY finished design sizes:
14-count fabric – 1¼ x 1⅛ inches
11-count fabric – 1⅝ x 1½ inches
18-count fabric – 1 x ⅞ inches

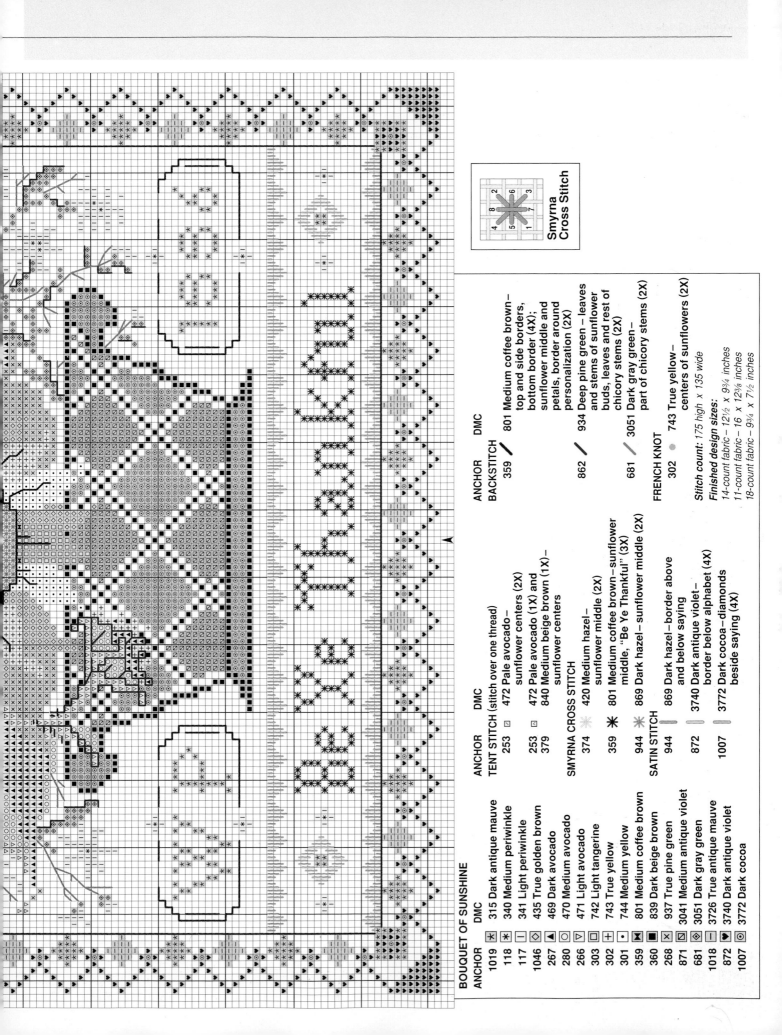

BOUQUET OF SUNSHINE

ANCHOR		DMC	
1019	✳	315	Dark antique mauve
118	✱	340	Medium periwinkle
117	I	341	Light periwinkle
1046	◇	435	True golden brown
267	◀	469	Dark avocado
280	○	470	Medium avocado
266	▷	471	Light avocado
303	□	742	Light tangerine
302	+	743	True yellow
301	·	744	Medium yellow
359	⊠	801	Medium coffee brown
360	■	839	Dark beige brown
268	✕	937	True pine green
871	⊡	3041	Medium antique violet
681	◈	3051	Dark gray green
1018	—	3726	True antique mauve
872	▶	3740	Dark antique violet
1007	⊙	3772	Dark cocoa

ANCHOR		DMC	
TENT STITCH (stitch over one thread)			
253	☑	472	Pale avocado— sunflower centers (2X)
253	☒	472	Pale avocado (1X) and
379		840	Medium beige brown (1X)— sunflower centers

SMYRNA CROSS STITCH

374	✳	420	Medium hazel— sunflower middle (2X)
359	✳	801	Medium coffee brown—sunflower middle, "Be Ye Thankful" (3X)
944	✳	869	Dark hazel—sunflower middle (2X)

SATIN STITCH

944	—	869	Dark hazel—border above and below saying
872	—	3740	Dark antique violet— border below alphabet (4X)
1007	—	3772	Dark cocoa—diamonds beside saying (4X)

ANCHOR		DMC	
BACKSTITCH			
359	╱	801	Medium coffee brown— top and side borders, bottom border (4X); sunflower middle and petals, border around personalization (2X)
862	╱	934	Deep pine green — leaves and stems of sunflower buds, leaves and rest of chicory stems (2X)
681	╱	3051	Dark gray green— part of chicory stems (2X)

FRENCH KNOT

302	●	743	True yellow— centers of sunflowers (2X)

Stitch count: 175 high x 135 wide

Finished design sizes:
14-count fabric – 12½ x 9¾ inches
11-count fabric – 16 x 12⅜ inches
18-count fabric – 9¾ x 7½ inches

Smyrna Cross Stitch

Holiday T R E A T S

*I*n this festive chapter, we celebrate an array of holidays with special projects to get you in gear for memorable days. From the spine-tingling Halloween house shown here, to a delightful box of Valentine chocolates, a special stitching treat is sure to be found on the next few pages.

Halloween Hauntings

Treat yourself to this spooky mansion, stitched with eerie glow-in-the-dark threads on hand-dyed Aida cloth. Cross-stitched bats float with button ghosts, while cats and jack-o'-lanterns stand guard. Waste canvas is the secret to the "spooktacular" shirt and the ghostly earrings are stitched on plastic canvas. Complete instructions and chart begin on page 148.

Jolly Finger Puppets

Santa, joined by Mrs. Claus, a cheery elf, and skating reindeer, are ready to come out and play. These fun-loving finger puppets stitch up easily on 14-count perforated plastic. Stitch up several sets to provide the children hours of entertainment at pre-Christmas gatherings. These small holiday charmers will also make great tree trims or stocking stuffers for Christmas morning. Complete instructions and charts begin on page 150.

Christmas Joy Bellpull

Spread Christmas cheer by displaying this slender banner from a doorknob, on a hutch or cupboard door, or drape it in a basket with holiday evergreens. This tiny yet elegant piece is just over nine inches long and is stitched on 16-count white Aida cloth using only a handful of colors. Gold blending filament and jingle bells add a touch of sparkle to make this design a real attention grabber. Complete instructions and chart begin on page 152.

144

Candy Heart

Stitch your special valentine this box of dreamy quilt-free chocolates on 28-count carnation pink Jubilee fabric. The creamy caramels, chewy nougats, and crunchy nuts are framed in a satin-covered heart-shaped candy box. For more sweet-tooth fun, stitch some of the candies as button covers to wear all year long. Instructions and chart begin on page 153.

Christmas Napkins and Place Mats

Dress up your Christmas table with these quaint Santa place mats and napkins. Stitched here on white?? 14-count Aida cloth, you can select the color fabric that looks best with your dishes and decor. This festive set is sure to make Christmas dining more memorable than ever before. Complete instructions and charts begin on page 156.

Spring Napkins and Place Mats

When Easter time draws near, set a table that is as fresh as spring itself. Start with these table linens that are abloom with dainty pink clover and soft white rabbits. Lazy daisy and straight stitches add lovely detail to this sweet design. Complete instructions and charts begin on page 156.

Summer Napkins and Place Mats

Add even more "flare" to your Fourth of July celebration with red, white, and blue place mat and napkin sets on the picnic table. Created using mostly whole stitches, this patriotic pair is a great project for a beginner. Complete instructions and charts begin on page 156.

Harvest Napkins and Place Mats

Bordered with plump golden pumpkins, this bountiful Thanksgiving set can grace the table during the entire fall season. To finish these spectacular linens, simply topstitch near the raw edges and remove threads to create the fringe. Complete instructions and chart begin on page 156.

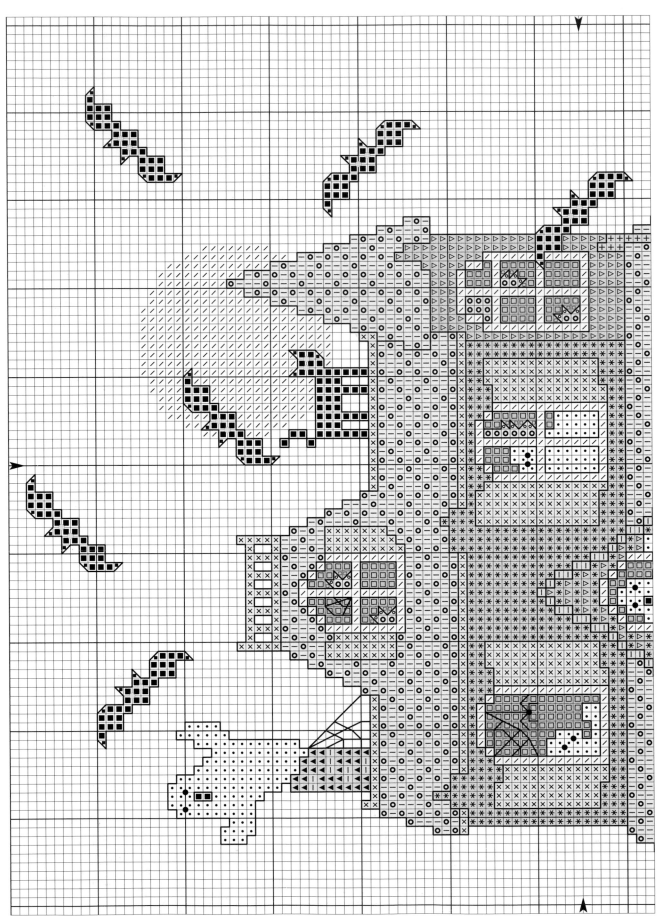

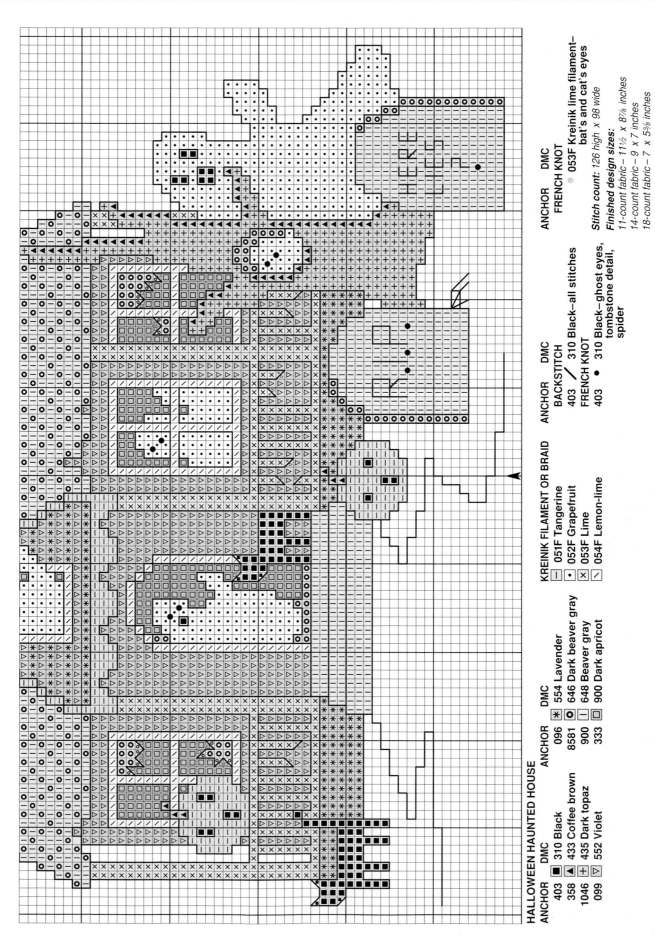

HALLOWEEN HAUNTED HOUSE

ANCHOR		DMC	
403	■	310	Black
358	◀	433	Coffee brown
1046	+	435	Dark topaz
099	▷	552	Violet

ANCHOR		DMC	
096	✳	554	Lavender
8581	○	646	Dark beaver gray
900			648	Beaver gray
333	□	900	Dark apricot

KREINIK FILAMENT OR BRAID

—		051F	Tangerine
•		052F	Grapefruit
✕		053F	Lime
/		054F	Lemon-lime

ANCHOR		DMC	
BACKSTITCH			
403	/	310	Black–all stitches
FRENCH KNOT			
403	•	310	Black–ghost eyes, tombstone detail, spider

ANCHOR		DMC	
FRENCH KNOT			
●		053F	Kreinik lime filament– bat's and cat's eyes

Stitch count: 126 high x 98 wide

Finished design sizes:
11-count fabric – 11½ x 8⅞ inches
14-count fabric – 9 x 7 inches
18-count fabric – 7 x 5⅝ inches

*BOO EARRINGS

As shown on page 142.

MATERIALS
FABRIC
Two 2x2-inch pieces of 14-count perforated plastic
THREADS
Cotton embroidery floss and #8 fine braid in colors listed in key on page 149
SUPPLIES
Needle; beading wire
2 6-mm black beads
Gold fish hook earrings

INSTRUCTIONS
Find center of ghost motif in upper left-hand corner of chart and center of one piece of plastic; begin stitching there. Use two plies of floss or one strand of braid for cross-stitches. Work backstitches and French knots using one ply. Repeat using second piece of plastic. Trim one square beyond stitched area.

Tie a 6-inch piece of beading wire to each fish hook earring and slip a single black bead over both ends of wire. Tie two ends to top of plastic design. Baste extra ends of wire to back of stitched design. Trim excess wire.

**HALLOWEEN SWEATSHIRT

As shown on page 142.

MATERIALS
FABRICS
Purchased purple sweatshirt
12x12-inch piece of 14-count waste canvas
12x12-inch piece of lightweight fusible interfacing
THREADS
Cotton embroidery floss and #8 fine braid in colors listed in key on page 149
SUPPLIES
Needle; basting thread; tweezers

INSTRUCTIONS
Wash and dry shirt. Tape or zigzag edges of waste canvas to prevent fraying. Baste waste canvas to front of sweatshirt, centering left to right with top edge of canvas at bottom of neck band. Using the photograph on page 142 as a guide, find the center of motifs on chart and the center of canvas; begin stitching there.

Work cross-stitches using three plies of floss or one strand of braid. Work backstitches using one ply of floss. Work the French knots using one strand of braid.

Remove basting threads; trim canvas close to stitching. Wet the canvas; using tweezers, pull individual canvas threads from under the cross-stitches. Fuse interfacing over the stitching on the inside of the shirt following manufacturer's instructions.

***HALLOWEEN HAUNTINGS

As shown on page 143.

MATERIALS
FABRIC
19x17-inch piece of 11-count white Aida cloth
THREADS
Cotton embroidery floss in colors listed in key on page 149
Two spools each of #8 fine braid in colors listed in key on page 149
One additional spool of lime (053F) #8 fine braid
SUPPLIES
Orange fabric dye
Needle; embroidery hoop
Ceramic buttons: 3 ghosts, 1 cat, 1 pumpkin
Desired frame and mat

INSTRUCTIONS
Dye the Aida cloth following directions on dye package. Allow to dry and press fabric well.

Tape or zigzag the edges of fabric to prevent fraying. Find the center of chart and the center of fabric; begin stitching there.

Work cross-stitches using five plies of floss or two strands of braid. Work backstitches using two plies of floss. Work the French knots using two plies of floss or one strand of braid.

Press lightly on the back using a pressing cloth. Sew the buttons to finished stitchery referring to the photograph, *page 143.* Frame and mat as desired.

**JOLLY FINGER PUPPETS

As shown on page 144.

MATERIALS *for each puppet*
FABRICS
5x6-inch piece of 14-count clear perforated plastic
5x6-inch piece of white felt
THREADS
Cotton embroidery floss in colors listed in key
Blending filament in color listed in key
SUPPLIES
Needle
White or clear sewing thread

INSTRUCTIONS
Find the center of the chart and the center of the perforated plastic; begin stitching there. Use six plies of floss for half cross-stitches except blended needle. Work blended needle as specified in the key. Work backstitches, straight stitches, and lazy daisy stitches using two plies of floss unless otherwise specified in the key. Work French knots using one ply of floss unless otherwise specified in the key.

Cut out finished design one square beyond stitching. Draw around the perforated plastic on the felt; cut out. Whipstitch the felt onto the back of the perforated plastic, leaving the bottom open.

SANTA PUPPET

MRS. CLAUS PUPPET

CHRISTMAS CHARACTER FINGER PUPPETS

ANCHOR		DMC	
HALF CROSS-STITCH			
002	•	000	White
1006	◆	304	Medium Christmas red
403	■	310	Black
979	#	312	Light navy
9046	✕	321	True Christmas red
150	⋈	336	Medium navy
011	□	350	Coral
310	⊙	434	Chestnut
1045	△	436	Tan
238	▽	703	Chartreuse
088	◉	718	Plum
1012	╱	754	Peach
1022	○	760	Salmon
307	◨	783	Christmas gold
359	◆	801	Coffee brown
043	♥	815	Garnet
229	●	910	Emerald
204	∼	913	Nile green
1010	—	951	Ivory
189	▲	991	Dark aquamarine
187	+	992	Medium aquamarine
410	★	995	Electric blue
086	◺	3608	Fuchsia
1031	◇	3753	Antique blue
1037	I	3756	Baby blue
BLENDED NEEDLE			
307	✳	783	Christmas gold (1X) and 021 Kreinik copper blending filament (2X)

ANCHOR		DMC	
BACKSTITCH			
403	╱	310	Black – Santa's boots and belt
310	╱	434	Chestnut – Santa's and Mrs. Claus' noses
229	╱	910	Emerald – Mrs. Claus' bonnet and apron
382	╱	3371	Black brown – stitching on elf's boots and buttonholes; all remaining stitches
STRAIGHT STITCH			
002	╱	000	White – Santa's hair strands
403	╱	310	Black – Santa's and Mrs. Claus' glasses
310	╱	434	Chestnut – reindeer's antlers (6X)
229	╱	910	Emerald – reindeer's scarf fringe
382	╱	3371	Black brown – Mrs. Claus' eyebrows and reindeer's buttonholes
BLENDED STRAIGHT STITCH			
307	╱	783	Christmas gold (1X) and 021 Kreinik copper blending filament (2X) – Santa's buckles
FRENCH KNOT			
002	·	000	White – Mrs. Claus' bonnet
9046	●	321	True Christmas red – Mrs. Claus' buttons and apron
410	•	995	Electric blue – Santa's eyes
382	●	3371	Black brown – Mrs. Claus' eyes (2X) and Mrs. Claus' cookie (1X)
LAZY DAISY			
382	⟩	3371	Black brown – reindeer's skate laces

SANTA stitch count: 60 high x 37 wide
SANTA finished design sizes:
14-count fabric – 4⅜ x 2¾ inches
11-count fabric – 5½ x 3⅜ inches
18-count fabric – 3⅓ x 2⅛ inches

ELF stitch count: 60 high x 44 wide
ELF finished design sizes:
14-count fabric – 4⅜ x 3¼ inches
11-count fabric – 5½ x 4 inches
18-count fabric – 3⅓ x 2½ inches

MRS. CLAUS stitch count: 60 high x 38 wide
MRS. CLAUS finished design sizes:
14-count fabric – 4⅜ x 2¾ inches
11-count fabric – 5½ x 3½ inches
18-count fabric – 3⅓ x 2⅛ inches

REINDEER stitch count: 60 high x 40 wide
REINDEER finished design sizes:
14-count fabric – 4⅜ x 2⅞ inches
11-count fabric – 5½ x 3⅝ inches
18-count fabric – 3⅓ x 2¼ inches

ELF PUPPET

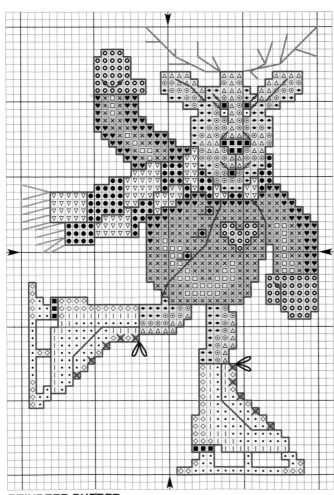

REINDEER PUPPET

CHRISTMAS JOY BELLPULL

***CHRISTMAS JOY BELLPULL

As shown on page 144.

MATERIALS

FABRICS
6x15-inch piece of 16-count white Aida cloth

6x15-inch piece of heavy fusible interfacing

6x15-inch piece of white fabric

⅛ yard of 45-inch-wide red cotton fabric

THREADS
Cotton embroidery floss in colors listed in key

Blending filament in color listed in key

SUPPLIES
Needle; embroidery hoop

⅔ yard of ⅛-inch-wide red satin ribbon

Two 3-millimeter gold jingle bells

One 3-millimeter silver jingle bell

Red sewing thread

CHRISTMAS JOY BELLPULL

ANCHOR		DMC	
9046	◙	321	Christmas red
010	⊟	351	Coral
923	⬤	699	Christmas green
043	▲	815	Garnet
209	⊞	912	Emerald

BLENDED NEEDLE

890	✳	729 Old gold (1X) and 002HL Kreinik gold Balger blending filament (4X)

BACKSTITCH

360	╱	898 Coffee brown–joy (1X); leaves and berries (2X)

STRAIGHT STITCH

923	╱	699 Christmas green–pine needles (2X)
360	╱	898 Coffee brown–pine branches (2X)

FRENCH KNOT

209	●	912 Emerald–background

BELLPULL stitch count: 134 high x 20 wide

BELLPULL finished design sizes:
14-count fabric – 9⅝ x 1½ inches
16-count fabric – 8⅜ x 1¼ inches
11-count fabric – 12¼ x 2 inches

INSTRUCTIONS

Tape or zigzag the edges of the Aida fabric to prevent it from fraying. Find the center of the chart and the center of the Aida fabric; begin stitching there.

Use three plies of cotton embroidery floss to work the cross-stitches. Work the blended needle, straight stitches, and the backstitches as specified in the key. Work the French knots using two plies of embroidery floss.

Fuse the interfacing to the back of the Aida cloth following the manufacturer's instructions.

Trim the fabric ¾ inch beyond the stitching at the top and the sides and 2¼ inches beyond the stitching at the bottom. Trim the bottom of the bellpull to a point.

Use the trimmed fabric as a pattern to cut one from the white fabric. Baste together with the wrong sides facing.

Cut a 1¼x30-inch strip from the red cotton fabric. Press one long edge of the red fabric strip under ¼ inch. With the right sides and the raw edges together, pin the long unpressed edge of the strip to the back of the Aida cloth, mitering the corners and pressing the short end under ¼ inch. Machine-stitch ¼-inch from the raw edge. Fold the pressed edge of the red fabric strip to the right side of the Aida cloth and topstitch close to the pressed edge.

Cut the ribbon into two 2-inch lengths and one 3-inch length. Thread the 3-inch length of ribbon through the top of each jingle bell. Fold the ribbons in half and tack the ends to the front of the bellpull, ½ inch from the bottom of the holly leaf. Cut two 5-inch lengths and tie into a 1½-inch-wide bow.

Tack the bow to the top of the ribbons with the jingle bells.

For the hanger, cut a 6-inch length of ribbon. Tack one end of the ribbon to each top corner of the bellpull.

****CANDY HEART

As shown on page 145.

MATERIALS

FABRICS
14x14-inch piece of 28-count carnation pink Jubilee fabric

¾ yard of 45-inch-wide red satin

Two 12x12-inch pieces of ½-inch-thick foam

Two 12x12-inch pieces of fleece

THREADS
Cotton embroidery floss in colors listed in key on page 154

Blending filament in colors listed in key on page 154

Metallic embroidery thread in colors listed in key on page 154

#5 pearl cotton in colors listed in key on page 154

SUPPLIES
Needle

Embroidery hoop

Beads in colors listed in key

Purchased 1-pound heart-shaped chocolate box with extended top and bottom

12x12-inch piece of foam-covered mounting board

1 yard of 1¾-inch-wide white pre-gathered lace

1 yard of ⅛-inch-diameter pearls by the yard

Pink sewing thread

Crafts glue

INSTRUCTIONS

Tape or zigzag the edges of the Jubilee fabric to prevent fraying. Find the center of the chart and the center of the fabric; begin stitching there. Use three plies of floss or two strands of metallic thread to work the cross-stitches over two threads of Jubilee fabric. Work the blended needle as specified in the key. Work backstitches and attach beads using one ply of floss. Referring to the diagrams, *page 155,* work the spider web and the interlaced cross-stitches using one strand of #5 pearl cotton. Press the finished stitchery from the back.

Remove the cardboard extensions from the top and the bottom of the heart-shaped box. Trace around the box bottom on the back of the mounting board. Cut out ⅛ inch inside the tracing line. Test fit by inserting into the box bottom; trim as necessary. Cut two heart shapes from the foam using the mounting board as pattern; set aside.

From the red satin, cut two 3x32-inch strips and two 12x12-inch squares. Glue one satin strip to the sides of the box top; clip as necessary and fold the excess fabric to the inside. Fold the raw edge under and overlap at the seam; glue. Repeat for the bottom of the box.

Glue both thicknesses of foam to the box top extension, one atop the other. Trim the foam that extends beyond the edges. Position one piece of the fleece over the foam. Fold the excess fleece to the back, clipping as necessary, and glue. Position and glue the satin square in the same manner. Glue the lace to the edge of the extension on the back side; pearls on the top side. Position and glue the box top to the top extension; set aside.

Cover the bottom extension with the remaining satin square, clipping as necessary and folding the excess fabric to the back. Position and glue the box bottom to the bottom extension.

Position the remaining fleece on the mounting board. Clip as necessary and fold the excess fabric to the back; glue. Center the stitchery on the covered mounting board. Use a double length of thread to run gathering stitches ¼ inch from the edge of the mounting board. Pull up the gathers to smooth the fabric. Lace the edges of the fabric together, stitching from side to side at the back to secure. If desired, tape over the threads at the back of the mounting board. Insert the mounted stitchery into the heart-shaped box.

★★★★CANDY BUTTON COVERS

As shown on page 145.

MATERIALS
for each button cover
FABRICS
5x5-inch piece of 28-count carnation pink Jubilee fabric
3x3-inch piece of lightweight fusible interfacing
THREADS
Cotton embroidery floss in colors listed in key
Blending filament as listed in key (optional)
Metallic embroidery thread as listed in key (optional)
#5 pearl cotton as listed in key (optional)
SUPPLIES
Needle
Embroidery hoop
Beads in colors listed in key (optional)
1⅝-inch-diameter button form
Button cover finding
Sewing thread
Wire cutters
All-purpose cement

INSTRUCTIONS
Tape or zigzag the edges of the Jubilee fabric to prevent fraying. Find the center of the desired candy motif and the center of the Jubilee fabric; begin stitching there.

Work all of the stitches and attach the beads as directed for the Candy Heart, *pages 153–155.*

Fuse the interfacing to the back of the fabric following manufacturer's instructions. Center the design over the button form. Trim fabric ½ inch beyond the edge. Run a gathering thread ¼ inch from the cut edge. Pull up the gathers to smooth the fabric. Assemble the button following the manufacturer's instructions.

Remove the button shank using wire cutters. Cement button to button cover finding.

CANDY HEART AND BUTTON COVERS

ANCHOR		DMC	
002	⊡	000	White
352	▼	300	Mahogany
1006	△	304	Christmas red
400	♡	317	Pewter
1043	○	369	Pistachio
914	⊠	407	Medium cocoa
358	▯	433	Deep golden brown
310	✕	434	Medium golden brown
1045	●	436	Dark tan
050	✳	605	Pale cranberry
891	⊕	676	Old gold
361	◲	738	Light tan
309	◁	781	Topaz
359	╱	801	Medium coffee brown
390	◥	822	Beige gray
380	◇	838	Beige brown
360	✛	898	Dark coffee brown
381	■	938	Deep coffee brown
881	⊙	945	Ivory
203	⊞	954	Light Nile green
206	▽	955	Pale Nile green
355	▲	975	Dark golden brown
1050	★	3031	Mocha
382	⊟	3371	Black brown
025	⊡	3716	Rose pink
1007	♥	3772	Dark cocoa
1008	☐	3773	Rose beige
	▽	285	Metallic silver

BLENDED NEEDLE			
1006	◩	304	Christmas red (1X) and 003HL Kreinik red filament (2X)
059	◪	600	Deep cranberry (1X) and 092 Kreinik star pink filament (2X)
062	▶	603	Deep cranberry (1X) and 092 Kreinik star pink filament (2X)
050	⊗	605	Pale cranberry (1X) and 032 Kreinik pearl filament (2X)
023	⊛	818	Pink (1X) and 032 Kreinik pearl filament (2X)
897	⋈	902	Garnet (1X) and 031 Kreinik crimson filament (2X)

BACKSTITCH			
310	╱	434	Medium golden brown – two candies at top
210	╱	562	Seafoam – mint leaf
382	╱	3371	Black brown – all remaining stitches

MILL HILL SEED BEADS		
○	00148	Peach
○	00431	Jade
○	00968	Red
○	02003	Peach creme
○	02012	Royal plum

MILL HILL SMALL BUGLE BEADS		
▭	70161	Crystal
▭	72053	Nutmeg

RIBBED SPIDER'S WEB STITCH		
⊛	869	Hazel #5 pearl cotton

INTERLACED CROSS-STITCH		
◇	869	Hazel #5 pearl cotton – base
◇	745	Yellow #5 pearl cotton – interlacing

Stitch count: *118 high x 114 wide*
Finished design sizes:
14-count fabric – 8⅜ x 8⅛ inches
16-count fabric – 7⅜ x 7⅛ inches
18-count fabric – 6½ x 6⅜ inches

CANDY HEART AND BUTTON COVERS

RIBBED SPIDER'S WEB

INTERLACED CROSS-STITCH

CHRISTMAS PLACE MAT

★★★ TABLE LINENS

As shown on pages 146 and 147.

MATERIALS *for one setting*
FABRICS
12x18½-inch piece of 14-count Aida
15x15-inch piece of 14-count Aida
FLOSS
**Cotton embroidery floss in colors
listed in keys on pages 156–159**
SUPPLIES
**Needle; embroidery hoop
Sewing thread to match Aida cloth**

INSTRUCTIONS

Topstitch around napkin or place mat ½-inch from raw edges of desired color fabric. Measure 1½ inches from topstitching at lower left corner of napkin or upper left corner of place mat; begin stitching center of desired

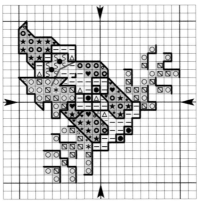

CHRISTMAS NAPKIN NAPKIN

motif there. Use two plies to work cross-stitches. Work straight stitches, French knots, lazy daisy stitches, and backstitches using one ply unless otherwise specified in keys.

For fringe, remove the threads between topstitching and cut edges. Press piece from the back.

CHRISTMAS PLACE MAT AND NAPKIN

ANCHOR		DMC	
387	⊟		Ecru
9046	◉	321	True Christmas red
358	◆	433	Dark chestnut
1046	▦	435	Light chestnut
362	+	437	Tan
1005	◉	498	Dark Christmas red
392	△	642	Beige gray
8581	⋈	646	Medium beaver gray
293	◇	727	Topaz
890	☆	729	Old gold
161	▢	813	Powder blue
043	★	815	Medium garnet
160	✕	826	Bright blue
1041	●	844	Deep beaver gray
218	✳	890	Pistachio
897	♥	902	Deep garnet
881	⑤	945	Ivory
266	◎	3347	Yellow green
262	⊠	3363	Loden

BACKSTITCH

382	╱	3371	Black brown—letters on blocks (2X); all remaining stitches

STRAIGHT STITCH

387	╱		Ecru—Santa's eyebrows and mustache (6X)
358	╱	433	Dark chestnut – doll's hair (2X)
1046	╱	435	Light chestnut – basket handle (3X)
8581	╱	646	Medium beaver gray—Christmas balls (3X)
382	╱	3371	Black brown—apple stems

FRENCH KNOT

382	●	3371	Black brown—eyes (2X)

PLACE MAT stitch count: 67 high x 77 wide

PLACE MAT finished design sizes:
14-count fabric – 5 x 5½ inches
11-count fabric – 6 x 7 inches
18-count fabric – 3¾ x 4¼ inches

NAPKIN stitch count: 21 high x 22 wide

NAPKIN finished design sizes:
14-count fabric –1½ x 1¾ inches
11-count fabric – 2 x 2 inches
18-count fabric –1¼ x 1¼ inches

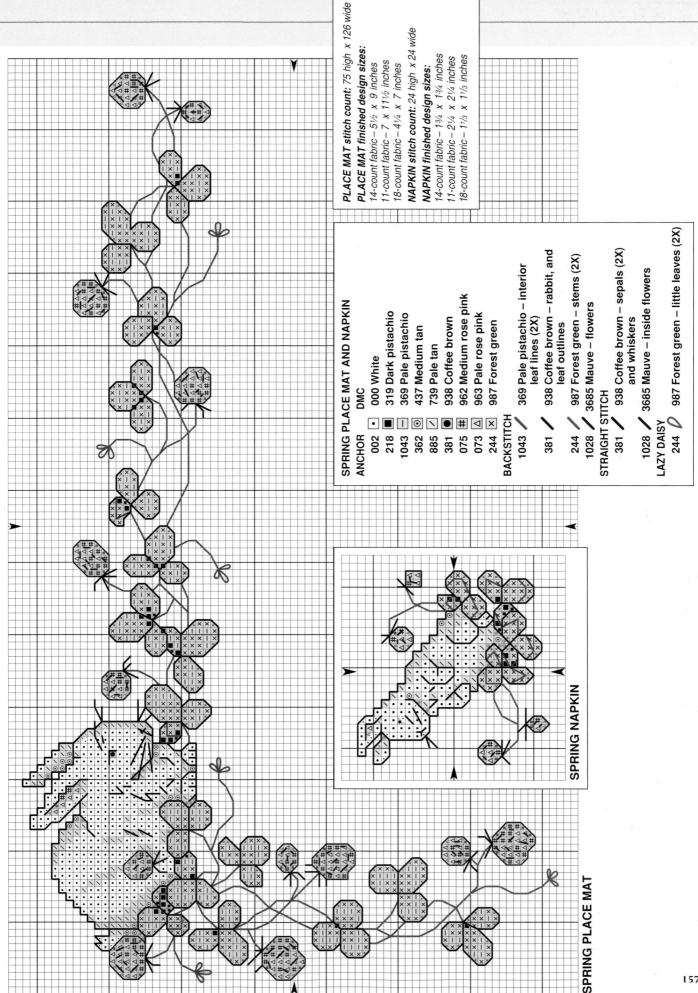

SPRING PLACE MAT AND NAPKIN

ANCHOR		DMC	
002	·	000	White
218	■	319	Dark pistachio
1043	I	369	Pale pistachio
362	⊙	437	Medium tan
885	╲	739	Pale tan
381	●	938	Coffee brown
075	#	962	Medium rose pink
073	△	963	Pale rose pink
244	✕	987	Forest green

BACKSTITCH

1043	╱	369	Pale pistachio – interior leaf lines (2X)
381	╱	938	Coffee brown – rabbit, and leaf outlines
244	╱	987	Forest green – stems (2X)
1028	╱	3685	Mauve – flowers

STRAIGHT STITCH

381	╱	938	Coffee brown – sepals (2X) and whiskers
1028	╱	3685	Mauve – inside flowers

LAZY DAISY

244	⬮	987	Forest green – little leaves (2X)

PLACE MAT stitch count: 75 high x 126 wide
PLACE MAT finished design sizes:
14-count fabric – 5½ x 9 inches
11-count fabric – 7 x 11½ inches
18-count fabric – 4¼ x 7 inches

NAPKIN stitch count: 24 high x 24 wide
NAPKIN finished design sizes:
14-count fabric – 1¾ x 1¾ inches
11-count fabric – 2¼ x 2¼ inches
18-count fabric – 1⅓ x 1⅓ inches

SPRING NAPKIN

SPRING PLACE MAT

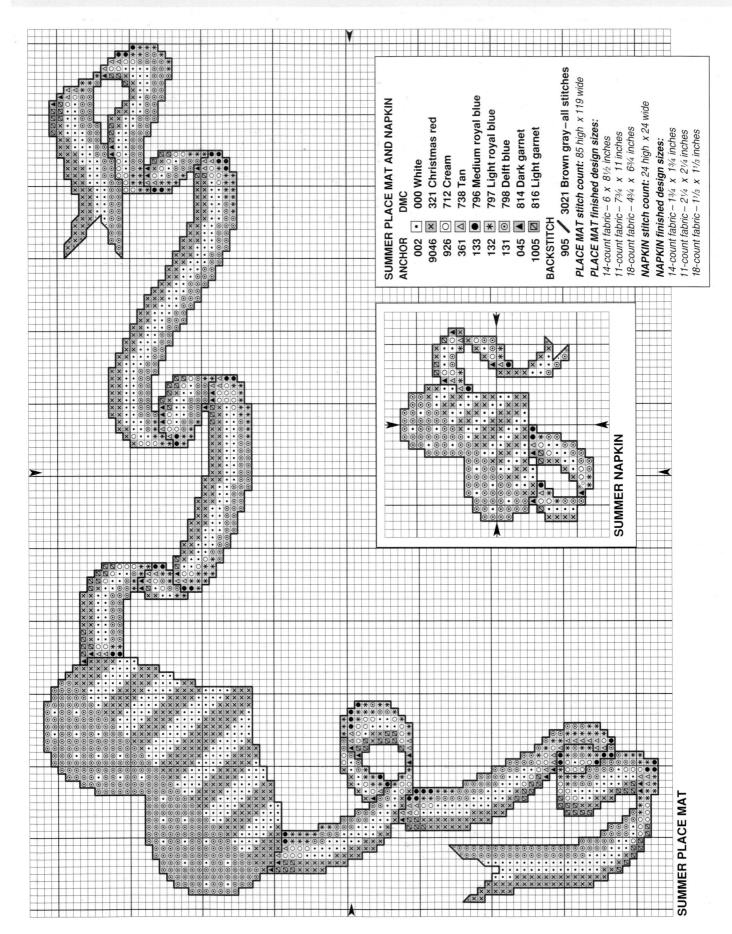

SUMMER PLACE MAT AND NAPKIN

ANCHOR		DMC	
002	•	000	White
9046	✕	321	Christmas red
926	○	712	Cream
361	△	738	Tan
133	●	796	Medium royal blue
132	✳	797	Light royal blue
131	⊙	798	Delft blue
045	◤	814	Dark garnet
1005	◪	816	Light garnet

BACKSTITCH

905 ╱ 3021 Brown gray—all stitches

PLACE MAT stitch count: 85 high x 119 wide

PLACE MAT finished design sizes:
14-count fabric – 6 x 8½ inches
11-count fabric – 7¾ x 11 inches
18-count fabric – 4¾ x 6¾ inches

NAPKIN stitch count: 24 high x 24 wide

NAPKIN finished design sizes:
14-count fabric – 1¾ x 1¾ inches
11-count fabric – 2¼ x 2¼ inches
18-count fabric – 1⅓ x 1⅓ inches

SUMMER NAPKIN

SUMMER PLACE MAT

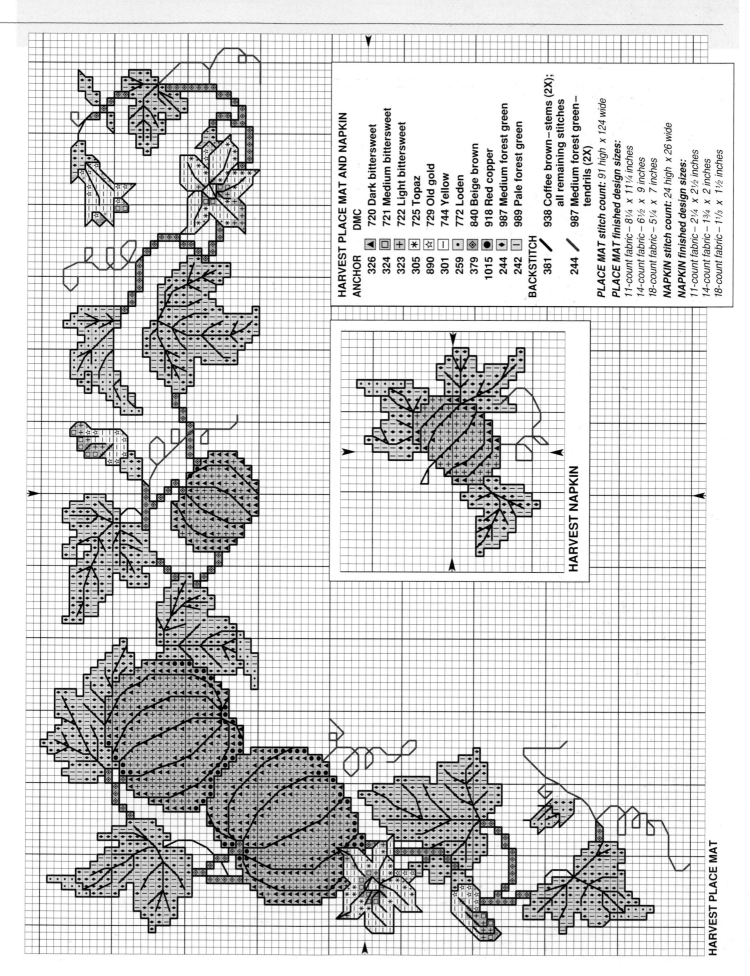

HARVEST PLACE MAT AND NAPKIN

ANCHOR		DMC	
326	▲	720	Dark bittersweet
324	▢	721	Medium bittersweet
323	+	722	Light bittersweet
305	✱	725	Topaz
890	☆	729	Old gold
301			744	Yellow
259	•	772	Loden
379	◈	840	Beige brown
1015	●	918	Red copper
244	◆	987	Medium forest green
242	―	989	Pale forest green

BACKSTITCH

| 381 | ╱ | 938 | Coffee brown–stems (2X); all remaining stitches |
| 244 | ╱ | 987 | Medium forest green–tendrils (2X) |

PLACE MAT stitch count: 91 high x 124 wide

PLACE MAT finished design sizes:
11-count fabric – 8¼ x 11¼ inches
14-count fabric – 6½ x 9 inches
18-count fabric – 5¼ x 7 inches

NAPKIN stitch count: 24 high x 26 wide

NAPKIN finished design sizes:
11-count fabric – 2¼ x 2½ inches
14-count fabric – 1¾ x 2 inches
18-count fabric – 1⅓ x 1½ inches

HARVEST NAPKIN

HARVEST PLACE MAT

Sensational SAMPLERS

Creating a sampler is a great joy for many stitchers. We have chosen a variety to celebrate everything from the beautiful sights in nature to heartwarming weddings. Each sampler is a unique work of art, sure to become a cherished family keepsake.

Wedding Sampler

Make a romantic momento for a bride and groom to cherish for a lifetime. This exquisite wedding sampler, stitched on 27-count natural linen, is accompanied by a beautiful trio of accessories. The garter, rice bag, and ring pillow will surely make the bride's day extra special. Complete instructions and chart begin on page 166.

Gathering Honey Sampler

This harmonious piece, stitched on 26-count golden flax linen, depicts a beautiful scenery of honeybees flying effortlessly in an orderly garden of flowers. Honeycombs and sprigs of colorful springtime flowers border the fragrant garden. Complete instructions and chart begin on page 171.

Anniversary Sampler

Honor a special anniversary of loved ones by stitching this personalized sampler on 28-count ivory Jobelan. Add glimmering touches of silver or gold for a 25th or 50th anniversary celebration. Complete instructions and chart begin on page 173.

Quaker Sampler

Stitch this nineteenth-century sampler on 28-count mushroom Brittney cloth. This piece features traditional Quaker designs such as the large block letters, medallions, and floral sprays. For a personal touch, try stitching it in a different palette of colors. Complete instructions and chart begin on page 175.

Dutch Sampler

This tribute of pictorial motifs, stitched on 28-count cream Glasgow linen, reflects the golden age of the Dutch culture. Small animals and flowers fill any empty space giving it a very uplifting appearance. It features three distinct alphabets, one plain, one simple, and one created using Algerian eyelets. Complete instructions and chart begin on page 175.

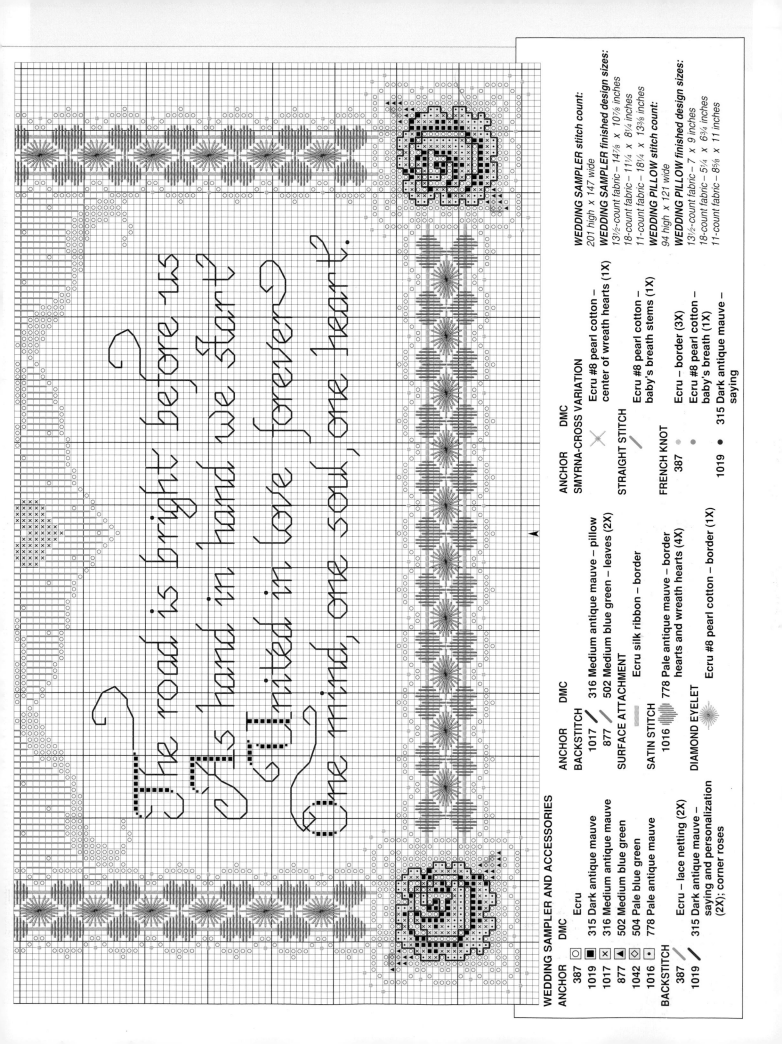

The road is bright before us

As hand in hand we start

United in love forever,

One mind, one soul, one heart.

WEDDING SAMPLER AND ACCESSORIES

ANCHOR	DMC	
387	○	Ecru
1019	■	315 Dark antique mauve
1017	×	316 Medium antique mauve
877	▲	502 Medium blue green
1042	◇	504 Pale blue green
1016	•	778 Pale antique mauve

BACKSTITCH

387	⁄	Ecru – lace netting (2X)
1019	⁄	315 Dark antique mauve – saying and personalization (2X); corner roses

ANCHOR	DMC	
BACKSTITCH		
1017	⁄	316 Medium antique mauve – pillow
877	⁄	502 Medium blue green – leaves (2X)

SURFACE ATTACHMENT

Ecru silk ribbon – border

SATIN STITCH

1016   778 Pale antique mauve – border hearts and wreath hearts (4X)

DIAMOND EYELET

Ecru #8 pearl cotton – border (1X)

ANCHOR	DMC	
SMYRNA-CROSS VARIATION		
	✕	Ecru #8 pearl cotton – center of wreath hearts (1X)

STRAIGHT STITCH

Ecru #8 pearl cotton – baby's breath stems (1X)

FRENCH KNOT

387	•	Ecru – border (3X)
	•	Ecru #8 pearl cotton – baby's breath (1X)
1019	•	315 Dark antique mauve – saying

WEDDING SAMPLER stitch count:
201 high x 147 wide
WEDDING SAMPLER finished design sizes:
13½-count fabric – 14⅞ x 10⅞ inches
18-count fabric – 11¼ x 8¼ inches
11-count fabric – 18¼ x 13⅜ inches
WEDDING PILLOW stitch count:
94 high x 121 wide
WEDDING PILLOW finished design sizes:
13½-count fabric – 7 x 9 inches
18-count fabric – 5¼ x 6¾ inches
11-count fabric – 8⅝ x 11 inches

★★★★WEDDING SAMPLER

As shown on page 160.

MATERIALS

FABRIC
24x18-inch piece of 27-count
    natural linen
FLOSS
Cotton embroidery floss in colors
    listed in key on page 167
SUPPLIES
Needle
Embroidery hoop
2¾ yards of ¹⁄₁₆-inch-wide cream
    satin ribbon
Desired frame and mat

INSTRUCTIONS

Tape or zigzag edges of fabric to
prevent fraying. Find the center of
chart and the center of the fabric;
begin stitching there.

Use two plies of floss to work all
cross-stitches over two threads of
fabric. Work diamond eyelets,
Smyrna-cross variations, satin
stitches, straight stitches, and
French knots as specified in the key.
Diagrams for diamond eyelet and
Smyrna-cross variation stitches are
below. Work the backstitches using
one ply unless otherwise specified
in the key. For surface attachment,
thread ecru silk ribbon in needle
and run under satin stitches as
indicated on chart; secure ends on
back. Press finished stitchery from
the back. Frame and mat as desired.

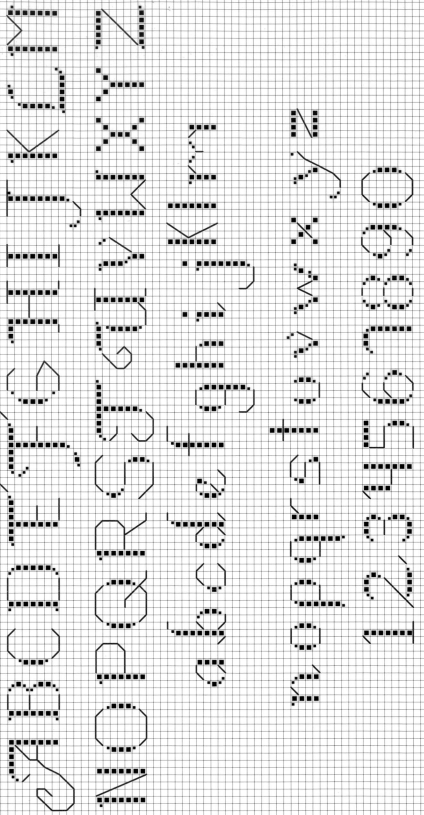

WEDDING ALPHABET

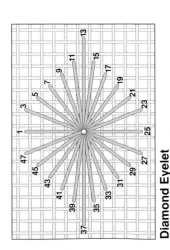

Diamond Eyelet

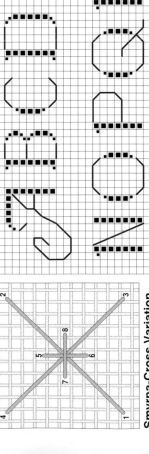

Smyrna-Cross Variation

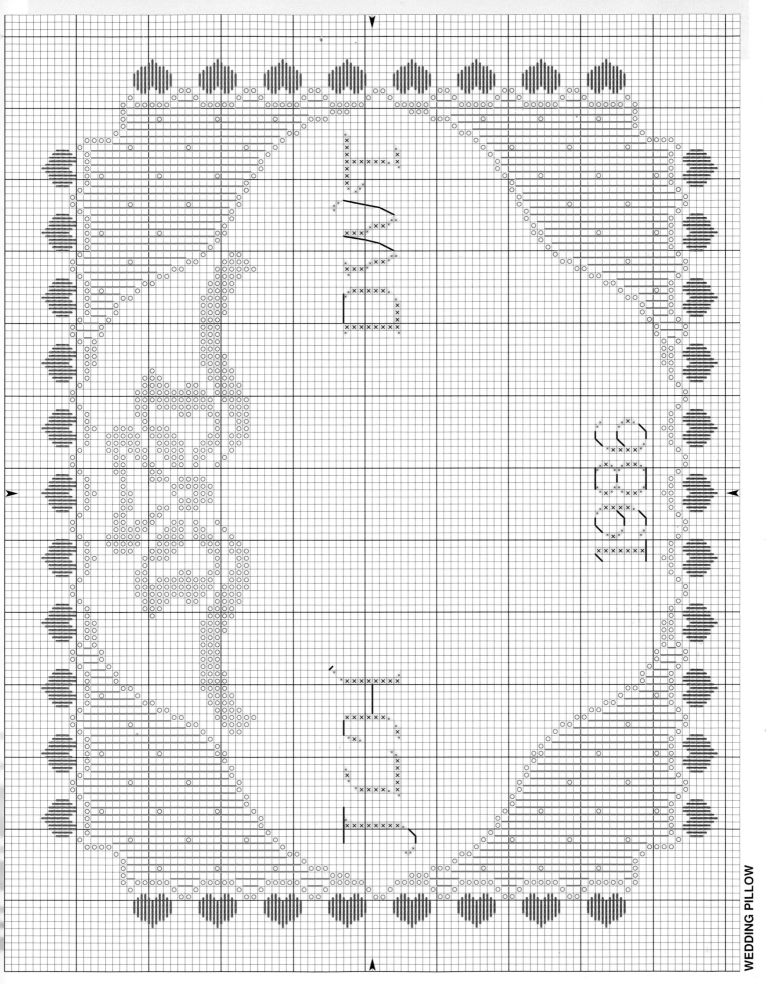

**PILLOW

As shown on page 161.

MATERIALS
FABRICS
11x13-inch piece of 27-count natural linen
½ yard 45-inch-wide ecru broadcloth
FLOSS
Cotton embroidery floss in colors listed in key on page 167
SUPPLIES
Needle; embroidery hoop
1¾ yard of 2-inch-wide mauve pre-gathered lace
1¾ yard of 2½-inch-wide ecru pre-gathered lace
Sewing thread; polyester fiberfill
1½ yards of ⅛-inch-wide mauve and gold twist braid
6 yards of ⅛-inch-wide mauve satin ribbon
1 yard of ⅛-inch-wide ecru satin ribbon; metallic gold thread
Two 20-millimeter crafting rings

INSTRUCTIONS
Tape or zigzag the edges of the linen to prevent fraying. Find the center of the chart and the center of fabric; begin stitching there. Use two plies of floss to work cross-stitches over two threads of fabric. Work satin stitches as specified in the key. Work backstitches using one ply unless otherwise specified in key.

Trim linen to measure 13x10½ inches. With right sides up, baste straight edges of mauve and ecru lace together. Pin straight edge of laces even with raw edges of linen, with right sides together. Sew, using ½-inch seam.

Cut a 13x10½-inch back piece from the broadcloth. Pin the broadcloth to linen, right sides together, and stitch leaving a 4-inch opening. Turn the pillow right side out. Stuff the pillow with polyester fiberfill and slip-stitch the opening closed. Tack the braid around the pillow edge.

Cut four 1-yard pieces of mauve satin ribbon. Tie a small bow in center of each and tack one bow to each corner of pillow. Tie knots in ribbon ends to prevent fraying.

Cut four more 12-inch-long mauve ribbons, two 12-inch-long ecru ribbons, and two 12-inch-long gold metallic threads. Align the eight strands and fold in the middle. Use one of the mauve ribbons to tie a firm knot, then small bow, around the center of the remaining ribbons and thread. Tack ribbons and gold thread just below the bow motif on the pillow. Tie gold metallic thread around the two crafting rings.

**GARTER

As shown on page 160.

MATERIALS *for each garter*
FABRIC
3x3-inch piece of 27-count natural linen
3x3-inch piece of lightweight fusible interfacing
FLOSS
Antique mauve (DMC 3727) and ecru cotton embroidery floss
SUPPLIES
Needle; 1-inch-diameter button form
Matching sewing thread
5½-inch piece of ½-inch-wide pre-gathered ivory lace
Two 16½-inch pieces of ⅝-inch-wide mauve satin ribbon
Two 16½-inch pieces of ½-inch-wide pre-gathered ivory lace
1 yard of 2-inch-wide ivory lace
12-inch piece of ½-inch-wide elastic
Two 14-inch pieces of ⅛-inch-wide mauve satin ribbon
Two 14-inch pieces of ⅛-inch-wide ivory satin ribbon; crafts glue

INSTRUCTIONS
Tape or zigzag edges of linen to prevent fraying. Find center of one heart motif on pillow chart, *page 169*, and center of fabric. Work the satin stitches using two plies of antique mauve (DMC 3727) floss. Work vertical stripes behind heart motif by backstitching with ecru floss over two threads; separate each stripe with two threads.

Fuse interfacing to back of fabric following manufacturer's instructions. Center design over button form; trim fabric ½ inch beyond edge. Run a gathering thread ¼ inch from cut edge. Pull up gathers to smooth fabric. Assemble button following manufacturer's instructions.

For twisted cord, cut three 18-inch strands of light antique mauve (DMC 3727) floss. Combine into a single strand. Twist until tightly wound; fold in half. Hold ends while two halves twist around each other. Knot unfinished end.

Position and glue cord around front edges of button, overlapping ends at bottom. Gather 5½-inch piece of lace to fit perimeter of button; glue lace around button behind cord. Set aside.

Sandwich straight edge of one piece of ½-inch-wide lace between both pieces of ½-inch satin ribbon, with wrong sides of ribbon together; stitch close to edge of ribbon. Gather 2-inch-wide lace; baste to remaining piece of ½-inch lace, adjusting gathers. Sew joined laces between opposite long edges of satin ribbons, stitching close to edge of ribbons.

Insert elastic through casing formed by ribbons; stitch ends to secure. Sew ends of ribbon together to form garter. Sew button to center of garter. Tie two pieces each of mauve and ecru satin ribbon into a bow. Attach bow with sewing thread to center bottom of button.

***RICE BAG

As shown on page 161.

MATERIALS
FABRIC
5x5-inch piece of 27-count natural linen
4½x4½-inch piece of ecru satin

FLOSS
Dark antique mauve (DMC 315) cotton embroidery floss and ecru #8 pearl cotton

SUPPLIES
Needle
½ yard of ⅛-inch-wide burgundy satin ribbon
6-inch piece of ½-inch-wide lace

INSTRUCTIONS

Tape or zigzag edges of linen to prevent fraying. Find center of 4-heart motif to right of year on sampler chart, *page 166*, and center of fabric; begin stitching there. Use two plies of floss to work satin stitches and one strand of pearl cotton for the Smyrna-cross variation stitch in the center.

Trim linen to measure 4½x4½. Fold in half lengthwise with right sides together. Machine-stitch across bottom and up the open side, using a ¼-inch seam and leaving top open; turn.

Fold ecru satin square in half lengthwise with right sides together. Sew up open side, using a ⅜-inch seam and leaving top and bottom open. Do not turn right side out.

Slide linen bag into lining, right sides together, aligning top edges. Machine-stitch around top of bag. Turn right side out through hole in bottom of lining. Turn raw edges of lining bottom under ⅜ inch and slip stitch together. Tuck lining into bag. Press bag carefully. Carefully fold top edge down twice, exposing satin, and tack edges down to bag in several places. Sew ecru lace to edge of bag.

Cut a 5-inch long piece of burgundy satin ribbon. Wrap ribbon around bottom outside of bag and tack in place. With the remaining ribbon, determine a center point and tack to the back of the bag. Wrap ribbons around the bag and tie into a bow in front.

GATHERING HONEY

ANCHOR	DMC	Name
002	000	White
110	208	Dark lavender
108	210	Light lavender
342	211	Pale lavender
010	351	Light coral
878	501	Dark blue green
877	502	Medium blue green
875	503	True blue green
098	553	Medium violet
096	554	Light violet
212	561	Dark seafoam
210	562	Medium seafoam
208	563	True seafoam
889	610	Deep drab brown
898	611	Dark drab brown
832	612	Medium drab brown
273	645	Dark beaver gray
1040	647	True beaver gray
900	648	Light beaver gray
886	677	Pale old gold
326	720	Dark bittersweet
324	721	Medium bittersweet
293	727	Pale topaz
890	729	Medium old gold
1012	754	Peach
308	782	Medium topaz
177	792	Dark cornflower blue
176	793	Medium cornflower blue
175	794	Light cornflower blue
013	817	Deep coral
1044	895	Hunter green
360	898	Coffee brown
204	913	Medium Nile green
848	927	Light gray green
274	928	Pale gray blue
206	955	Pale Nile green
244	987	Medium forest green
243	988	Light forest green
242	989	Pale forest green
681	3051	Dark gray green
261	3053	Light gray green
264	3348	Yellow green
382	3371	Black brown
087	3607	Dark fuchsia
086	3608	Medium fuchsia
085	3609	Light fuchsia

BACKSTITCH

ANCHOR	DMC	Description
877	502	Medium blue green – berry leaves (3X)
212	561	Dark seafoam – flourish lines around saying (2X)
210	562	Medium seafoam – ends of flourish (2X)
890	729	Medium old gold – honeycomb (3X)
1041	844	Deep beaver gray – frame corner bracket and flag stones
242	989	Pale forest green – periwinkle leaves (3X)
360	898	Coffee brown – saying except Proverbs (2X); all remaining backstitches

STRAIGHT STITCH

ANCHOR	DMC	Description
002	000	White – periwinkle centers (2X)
110	208	Dark lavender – violet
208	563	True seafoam – strawberry stems (2X)
886	677	Pale old gold – right side of bee hive weave (2X)
308	782	Medium topaz – yellow creeping jenny stamen (3X); left side of bee hive weave (2X)
360	898	Coffee brown – berries, tops of bee legs, strawberry seeds (2X)
851	924	Deep gray blue – large bee wings
264	3348	Yellow green – creeping jenny stems (2X)
382	3371	Black brown – center bee bodies (2X)

LAZY DAISY

ANCHOR	DMC	Description
850	926	Medium gray blue – center bee wings (2X)

FRENCH KNOT

ANCHOR	DMC	Description
110	208	Dark lavender – saying (3X)
293	727	Pale topaz – dill in lower right square of garden (2X)
890	729	Medium old gold – dill in lower right square of garden (2X)
308	782	Medium topaz – strawberry flowers (2X)
360	898	Coffee brown – saying (2X)

Stitch count: 180 high x 140 wide

Finished design sizes:
13-count fabric – 13⅞ x 10¾ inches
18-count fabric – 10 x 7⅞ inches
11-count fabric – 16⅜ x 12¾ inches

Pleasant words are like a honeycomb,

PROVERBS 16:24

Pleasantness to the soul

and health to the body.

★★★GATHERING HONEY

As shown on page 162.

MATERIALS
FABRIC
21x18-inch piece of 26-count golden flax linen
FLOSS
Cotton embroidery floss in colors listed in key on page 171
SUPPLIES
Needle; embroidery hoop
Desired frame and mat

INSTRUCTIONS
Tape or zigzag edges of fabric to prevent fraying. Find center of chart and of fabric; begin stitching there. Use two plies to work cross-stitches over two threads of fabric. Work backstitches and straight stitches using one ply unless otherwise specified in key. Work lazy daisies and French knots as specified. Press stitchery from back. Frame and mat.

★★★★ANNIVERSARY SAMPLER

As shown on page 163.

MATERIALS
FABRIC
18x16-inch piece of 28-count ivory Jobelan
FLOSS
Cotton embroidery floss in colors listed in key on page 175
SUPPLIES
Needle
Embroidery hoop
Desired frame and mat

INSTRUCTIONS
Tape or zigzag edges of fabric to prevent fraying. Find center of chart and of fabric; begin stitching there. Use three plies to work cross-stitches over two threads of fabric. Work backstitches using one ply unless otherwise specified in key. Work French knots as specified. Press stitchery from back. Frame and mat.

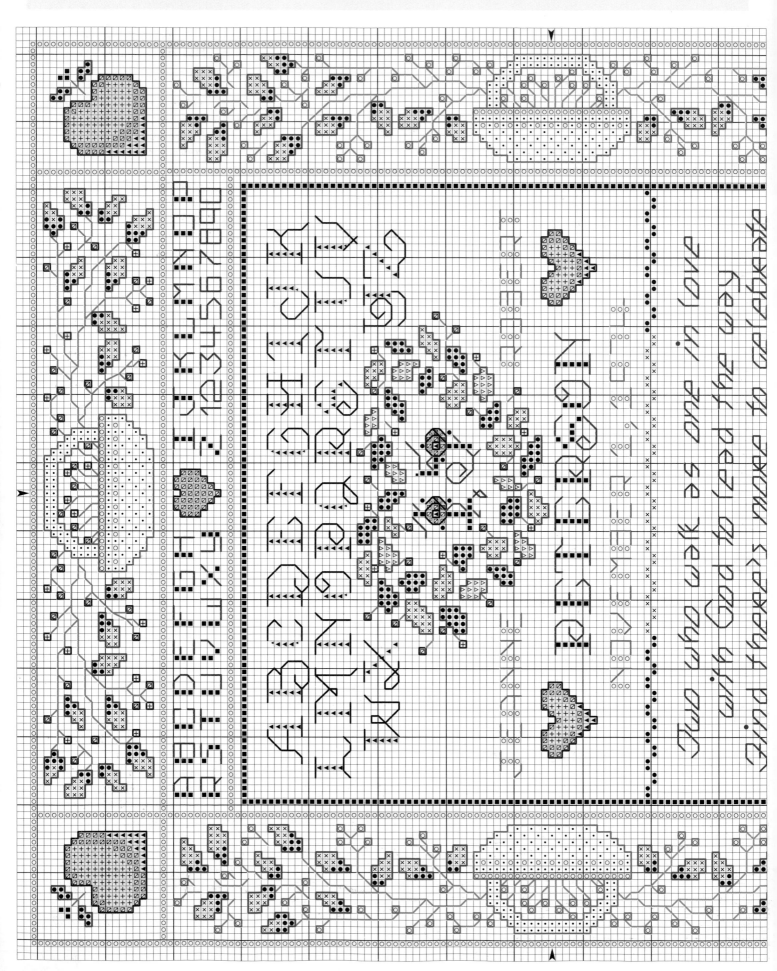

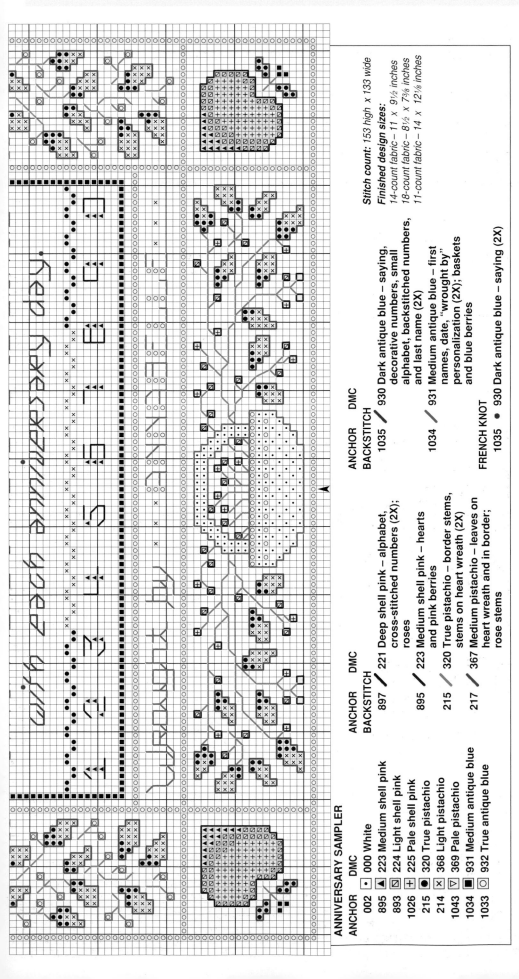

ANNIVERSARY SAMPLER

ANCHOR	DMC	
002	•	000 White
895	◀	223 Medium shell pink
893	▨	224 Light shell pink
1026	➕	225 Pale shell pink
215	●	320 True pistachio
214	✕	368 Light pistachio
1043	▷	369 Pale pistachio
1034	■	931 Medium antique blue
1033	○	932 True antique blue

ANCHOR DMC

BACKSTITCH

897 ╱ 221 Deep shell pink – alphabet, cross-stitched numbers (2X); roses

895 ╱ 223 Medium shell pink – hearts and pink berries

215 ╱ 320 True pistachio – border stems, stems on heart wreath (2X)

217 ╱ 367 Medium pistachio – leaves on heart wreath and in border; rose stems

ANCHOR DMC

BACKSTITCH

1035 ╱ 930 Dark antique blue – saying, decorative numbers, small alphabet, backstitched numbers, and last name (2X)

1034 ╱ 931 Medium antique blue – first names, date, "wrought by" personalization (2X); baskets and blue berries

FRENCH KNOT

1035 ● 930 Dark antique blue – saying (2X)

Stitch count: 153 high x 133 wide

Finished design sizes:
14-count fabric – 11 x 9½ inches
18-count fabric – 8½ x 7⅜ inches
11-count fabric – 14 x 12⅛ inches

✶✶QUAKER SAMPLER

As shown on page 164.

MATERIALS

FABRIC

17x12-inch piece of 28-count mushroom Brittney fabric

FLOSS

Cotton embroidery floss in colors listed in key on page 177

SUPPLIES

Needle; embroidery hoop

Desired frame and mat

INSTRUCTIONS

Tape or zigzag edges of fabric to prevent fraying. Find center of fabric and of chart; begin stitching there. Use two plies of floss to work cross-stitches over two threads of fabric, *except* alphabet. Use one ply to work alphabet over one thread (see enlarged chart, *page 177*). Work backstitches using two plies. Press finished stitchery from the back. Frame and mat as desired.

✶✶✶✶DUTCH SAMPLER

As shown on page 165.

MATERIALS

FABRIC

15x19-inch piece of 28-count cream Glasgow linen

FLOSS

Cotton embroidery floss in colors listed in key on page 177

One additional skein each of deep cocoa (DMC 632), dark beige gray (DMC 640), medium antique blue (DMC 931), mocha (DMC 3031), dark gray green (DMC 3051), and deep antique blue (DMC 3750)

SUPPLIES

Needle; embroidery hoop

Desired frame and mat

Continued on page 177

176

QUAKER SAMPLER

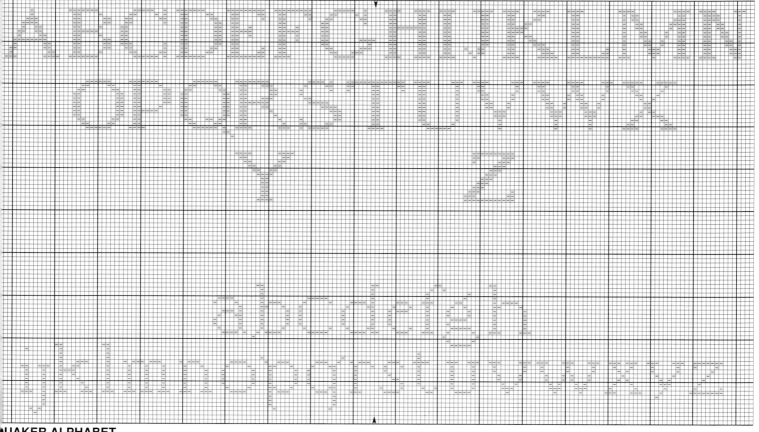

QUAKER ALPHABET

QUAKER SAMPLER

ANCHOR		DMC	
878	●	501	Blue green
860	▽	522	Olive drab
379	✕	840	Beige brown
871	⊞	3041	Antique violet
883	⊡	3064	Cocoa

PETITE CROSS

878	⊟	501	Blue green – alphabet (1X)

BACKSTITCH

379	╱	840	Beige brown – all backstitches (2X)

Stitch count: 159 high x 91 wide

Finished design sizes:
14-count fabric – 11⅜ x 6½ inches
11-count fabric – 14½ x 8⅜ inches
18-count fabric – 8⅞ x 5⅛ inches

INSTRUCTIONS

Tape or zigzag edges of fabric to prevent fraying. Find center of chart, *pages 178–179*, and of fabric; begin stitching there. Use two plies of floss to work cross-stitches over two threads of fabric. Work double running stitch using two plies and small and large Algerian eyelets with three plies. Press stitchery from back. Frame and mat as desired.

DUTCH SAMPLER

ANCHOR		DMC	
5975	✕	356	Terra cotta
374	▽	420	Medium hazel
373	−	422	Light hazel
936	◆	632	Deep cocoa
903	◩	640	Beige gray
1034	⊞	931	Medium antique blue
360	■	3031	Mocha
681	▲	3051	Dark gray green
261	❘	3053	Light gray green
1036	●	3750	Deep antique blue
1032	◇	3752	Light antique blue
1007	⌗	3772	Dark cocoa
1008	▢	3773	Rose beige

SMALL ALGERIAN EYELETS

914	✳	407	Medium cocoa
936	✳	632	Deep cocoa
903	✳	640	Beige gray
1034	✳	931	Medium antique blue
1036	✳	3750	Deep antique blue

LARGE ALGERIAN EYELETS

1036	✸	3750	Deep antique blue

DOUBLE RUNNING STITCH

914	╱	407	Medium cocoa – eyelet letters D, H, and M, filagree hearts (2X)
374	╱	420	Medium hazel – filagree letters D, H, M, R, and V (2X)
373	╱	422	Light hazel – filagree letters B, F, K, O, T, and X (2X)

DOUBLE RUNNING STITCH

936	╱	632	Deep cocoa – eyelet letters C, G, and L, filagree heart (2X)
1034	╱	931	Medium antique blue – eyelet letters B, F, and K (2X)
360	╱	3031	Mocha – tree of life (2X)
681	╱	3051	Dark gray green – medallion, filagree letters C, G, L, P, U, and Z (2X)
262	╱	3052	Medium gray green – filagree letters A, E, I, N, S, and W (2X)
1036	╱	3750	Deep antique blue – eyelet letters A, E, and I (2X)

Stitch count: 136 high x 211 wide

Finished design sizes:
14-count fabric – 9¾ x 15⅛ inches
11-count fabric – 12⅜ x 19¼ inches
18-count fabric – 7⅝ x 11¾ inches

Medium Algerian Eyelet

Small Algerian Eyelet

DUTCH SAMPLER

178

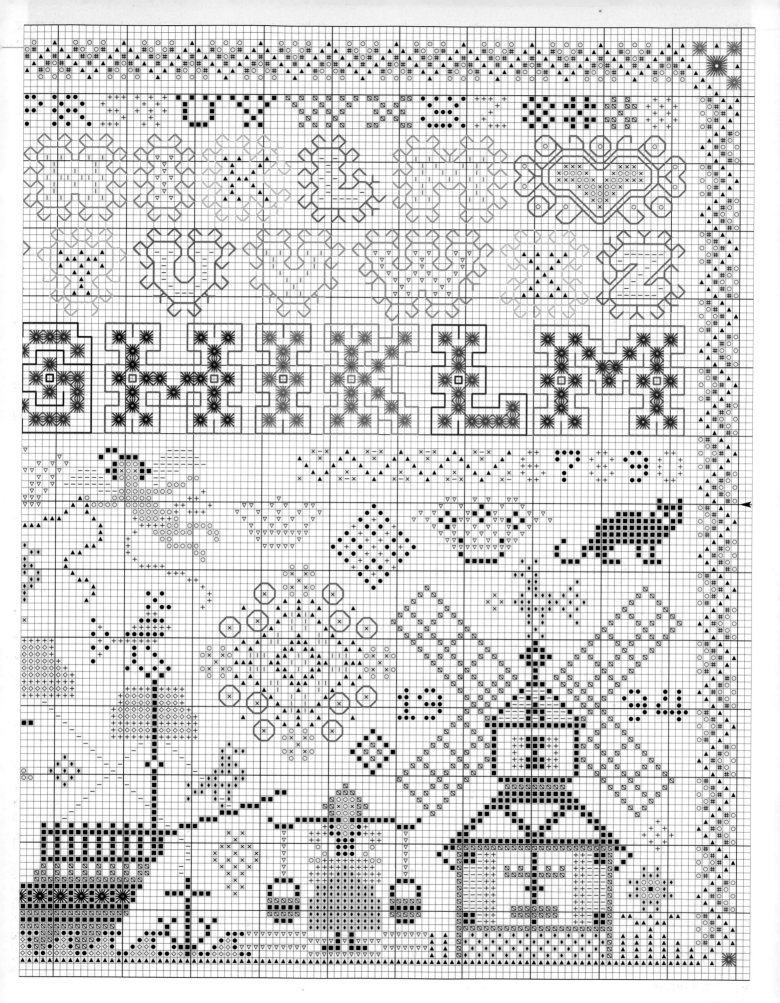

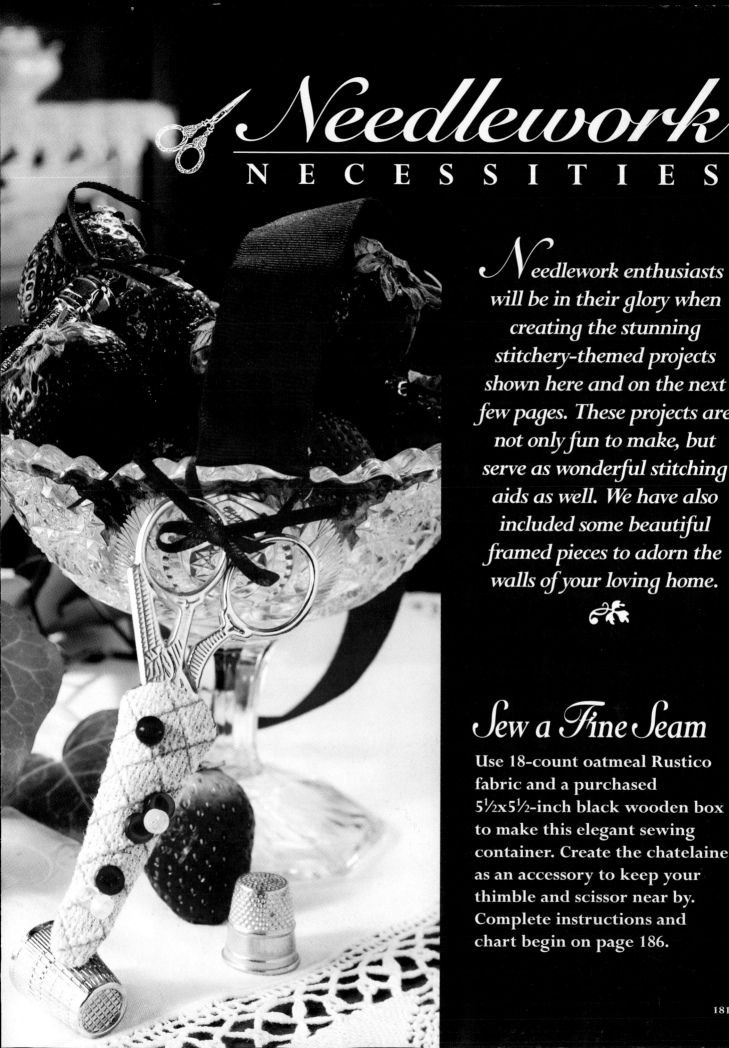

Needlework
N E C E S S I T I E S

N eedlework enthusiasts will be in their glory when creating the stunning stitchery-themed projects shown here and on the next few pages. These projects are not only fun to make, but serve as wonderful stitching aids as well. We have also included some beautiful framed pieces to adorn the walls of your loving home.

Sew a Fine Seam

Use 18-count oatmeal Rustico fabric and a purchased 5½x5½-inch black wooden box to make this elegant sewing container. Create the chatelaine as an accessory to keep your thimble and scissor near by. Complete instructions and chart begin on page 186.

Handmade Labels

Add an extra-special personal touch to all your handmade projects by adding these tiny cross-stitched labels. The motifs are stitched on 32-count Belfast linen and work up easily. Use the various motifs and alphabets to create a stack of labels as a gift for a crafty friend. Complete instructions and charts begin on page 187.

Antique Needlework Tools

Old-fashioned findings can be fascinating, especially when coming across obsolete crafting and sewing tools. Stitching this sampler on 32-count cream Irish linen is a lovely tribute to antique needlework tool collections. Hang this piece close to your own collection or make it for a fellow stitchery lover. Complete instructions and chart begin on page 188.

As Ye Sew

Any crafter or seamstress would love to have this lighthearted verse on display in their home. Stitched on 14-count white Aida cloth, this whimsical design reminds us of what a tedious task removing all those unwanted stitches can be. Complete instructions and chart begin on page 189.

Collector's Cabinet

This mini collector's cabinet works wonderfully for storing spools of thread, thimbles, bobbins, or any other small crafting necessity. Stitch this brightly colored treasure on 18-count ivory Aida cloth and save space in your sewing basket by placing several items in the compartments. This detailed design could also be framed or mounted in the lid of a sewing box. Complete instructions and chart begin on page 190.

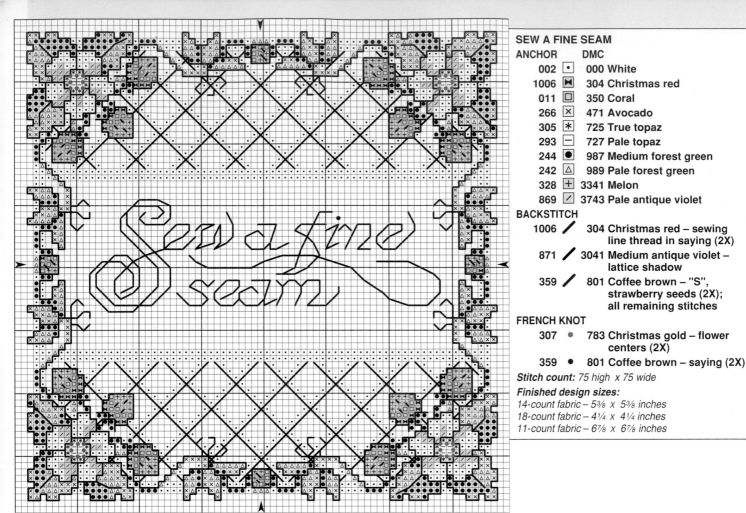

SEW A FINE SEAM

ANCHOR		DMC
002	·	000 White
1006	⋈	304 Christmas red
011	□	350 Coral
266	×	471 Avocado
305	✳	725 True topaz
293	−	727 Pale topaz
244	●	987 Medium forest green
242	△	989 Pale forest green
328	+	3341 Melon
869	⟋	3743 Pale antique violet

BACKSTITCH

1006	╱	304 Christmas red – sewing line thread in saying (2X)
871	╱	3041 Medium antique violet – lattice shadow
359	╱	801 Coffee brown – "S", strawberry seeds (2X); all remaining stitches

FRENCH KNOT

307	●	783 Christmas gold – flower centers (2X)
359	●	801 Coffee brown – saying (2X)

Stitch count: 75 high x 75 wide

Finished design sizes:
14-count fabric – 5⅜ x 5⅜ inches
18-count fabric – 4¼ x 4¼ inches
11-count fabric – 6⅞ x 6⅞ inches

SEW A FINE SEAM

**SEW A FINE SEAM BOX

As shown on page 180.

MATERIALS
FABRIC
9x9-inch piece of 18-count oatmeal Rustico fabric
FLOSS
Cotton embroidery floss in colors listed in key
SUPPLIES
Needle
Embroidery hoop
5½x5½-inch black wooden box with framed lid for stitchery insertion

INSTRUCTIONS
Tape or zigzag edges of fabric to prevent fraying. Find center of chart and of fabric; begin stitching there.

Use two plies of floss to work cross-stitches and French knots. Work backstitches using one ply unless otherwise specified in key. Assemble box following manufacturer's instructions.

**CHATELAINE

As shown on pages 180–181.

MATERIALS
FABRICS *for thimble holder:*
Two 5x5-inch pieces of 18-count oatmeal Rustico fabric; two 4x4-inch pieces of red cotton fabric
FABRICS *for scissors case:*
Two 5x3-inch pieces of 18-count oatmeal Rustico fabric
Two 5x3-inch pieces of red cotton fabric
FLOSS
Cotton embroidery floss in colors listed in key
SUPPLIES
Needle; embroidery hoop
2 yards of 1-inch-wide red grosgrain ribbon
Two ¾-inch-wide vest buckles
Red sewing thread
Four ¼-inch-diameter red buttons
Three ⅜-inch-diameter white buttons
Small red strawberry needle emery

2½ yards of ⅛-inch-wide red satin ribbon
Scissors; other desired accessories

INSTRUCTIONS
For thimble holder, zigzag edges of fabric to prevent fraying. Find lower left-hand corner of chart. On bottom of Rustico fabric, measure 1½ inches in from left edge and 1½ inches from bottom; begin stitching leaf/flower/strawberry motif there.

Use two plies of floss to work cross-stitches. Work backstitches using one ply of floss. Using white floss, cross-stitch two rows at bottom and left edge, positioning one row up and one row in from outermost stitches. Stitch these rows until stitched area reaches a count of 36 high x 36 wide. As desired, fill in square using grid motif from chart. Trim ½ inch from stitching. Use stitched piece as a pattern to cut one back from remaining Rustico fabric and two lining pieces from red fabric.

HANDMADE LABELS

Sew thimble holder front to back, using ¼-inch seams; leave top edge open. Sew lining pieces together in the same manner, except, leave an opening at bottom; *do not* turn.

Cut a 7-inch piece of ribbon; slip-stitch ends of ribbon to top of holder at sides. Stitch holder to lining at top edge. Turn right side out. Slip-stitch opening closed; press. Set aside.

For scissors case, zigzag edges of fabric. Find grid motif on chart and center of one piece of Rustico fabric; stitch a 1x3-inch area of grid pattern.

Work stitches as directed for thimble holder. With one short stitched end at left, use erasable marker to draw from left corners to center of right end. Cut out ½ inch from lines. Attach buttons as desired. Use stitched piece as a pattern to cut one back from the remaining Rustico fabric and two lining pieces from the red fabric.

Sew case front to back, leaving top edge open. Sew lining pieces together in same manner, except, leave an opening at bottom; *do not* turn.

Stitch case to lining at top edge. Turn right side out. Slip-stitch opening closed and press.

To assemble chatelaine, fold grosgrain ribbon in half and sew together along long edges. Slip vest buckles onto ribbon, stopping 7 inches from ribbon ends.

Fold a 7-inch piece of satin ribbon in half and sew to the top of strawberry emery. Cut four 12-inch pieces of satin ribbon. With ends even, tie two ribbons into a bow. Repeat with remaining ribbons; trim ends. Tack bows to top of strawberry emery.

Press ends of grosgrain ribbon under ¼ inch; fold under ½ inch. Place hanging ribbons of thimble holder and strawberry emery at fold; hand stitch grosgrain ribbon together. Repeat for opposite end, placing remaining satin ribbon at fold; tie scissors onto ribbon.

**HANDMADE LABELS

As shown on page 182.

MATERIALS
FABRIC *for all labels*
12x6-inch piece of desired cross-stitch fabric
12x6-inch piece of fusible interfacing
FLOSS
Cotton embroidery floss in desired colors, using key as a guide
SUPPLIES
Graph paper
Needle
Embroidery hoop
#8 pearl cotton to coordinate with design

INSTRUCTIONS
Tape or zigzag edges of fabric to prevent fraying. Chart desired motif, referring to chart, *above.* Find center of chart and center of fabric; begin stitching there.

Use two plies of floss for all cross-stitches. Work backstitches, straight stitches, lazy daisy stitches, and French knots as specified in key.

Cut fabric ¼-inch beyond each side of design. Use this as a pattern to cut interfacing. Fuse interfacing to back of design following the manufacturer's directions.

To finish, use the buttonhole stitch to complete the edges of the design using #8 pearl cotton in a desired coordinating color.

HANDMADE LABELS

◎	Color 1
✕	Color 2
▲	Color 3
▽	Color 4

BACKSTITCH
╱ Color A
╱ Color B

STRAIGHT STITCH
╱ Color A
╱ Color B

LAZY DAISY
Color A – lamb (2X)
Color B – heart with needle (2X)

FRENCH KNOT
● Color A (2X)

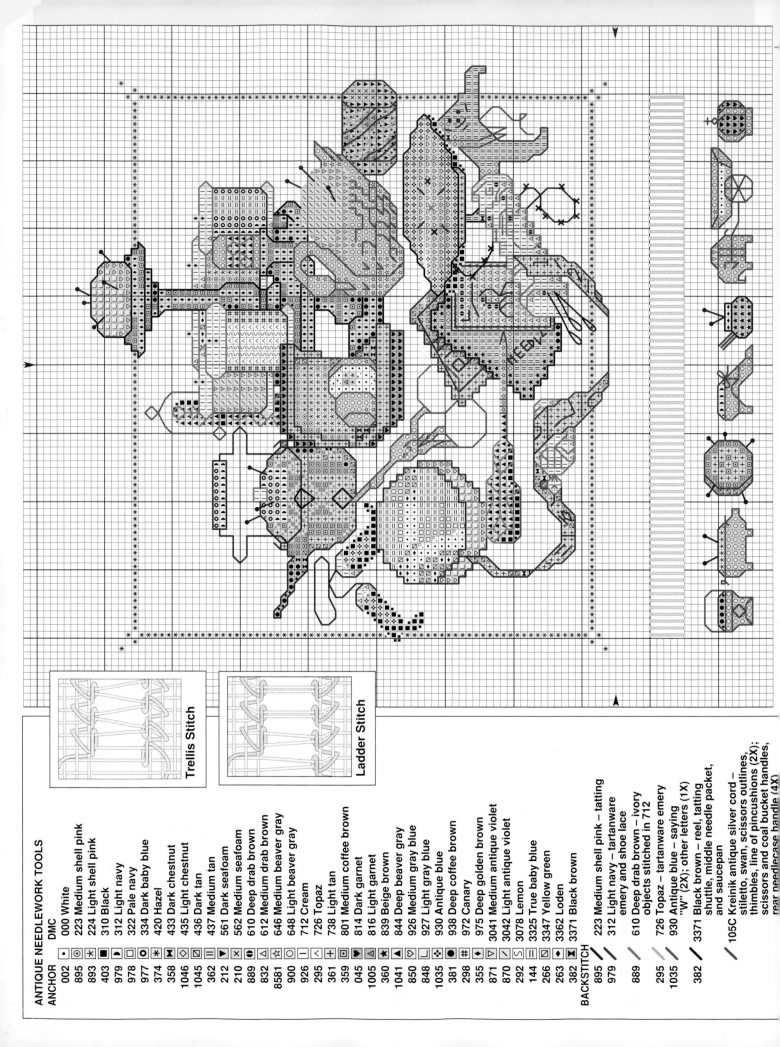

Trellis Stitch

Ladder Stitch

ANTIQUE NEEDLEWORK TOOLS

ANCHOR		DMC	
002	·	000	White
895	⊙	223	Medium shell pink
893	✦	224	Light shell pink
403	■	310	Black
979	▲	312	Light navy
978	□	322	Pale navy
977	◉	334	Dark baby blue
374	✱	420	Hazel
358	⬙	433	Dark chestnut
1046	◇	435	Light chestnut
1045	⊟	436	Dark tan
362	═	437	Medium tan
212	▶	561	Dark seafoam
210	⊠	562	Medium seafoam
889	◈	610	Deep drab brown
832	◁	612	Medium drab brown
8581	☆	646	Medium beaver gray
900	○	648	Light beaver gray
926	—	712	Cream
295	⊾	726	Topaz
361	+	738	Light tan
359	⊡	801	Medium coffee brown
045	▶	814	Dark garnet
1005	◀	816	Light garnet
360	★	839	Beige brown
1041	◀	844	Deep beaver gray
850	▷	926	Medium gray blue
848	⌐	927	Light gray blue
1035	❖	930	Antique blue
381	●	938	Deep coffee brown
298	#	972	Canary
355	◆	975	Deep golden brown
871	▷	3041	Medium antique violet
870	⊘	3042	Light antique violet
292	⊿	3078	Lemon
144	═	3325	True baby blue
266	◫	3347	Yellow green
263	◆	3362	Loden
382	⊠	3371	Black brown

BACKSTITCH

895	╱	223	Medium shell pink – tatting
979	╱	312	Light navy – tartanware emery and shoe lace
889	╱	610	Deep drab brown – ivory objects stitched in 712
295	╱	726	Topaz – tartanware emery
1035	╱	930	Antique blue – saying "W" (2X); other letters (1X)
382	╱	3371	Black brown – reel, tatting shuttle, middle needle packet, and saucepan
	╱	105C	Kreinik antique silver cord – stiletto, swan, scissors outlines, thimbles, line of pincushions (2X); scissors and coal bucket handles, rear needlecase handle (4X)

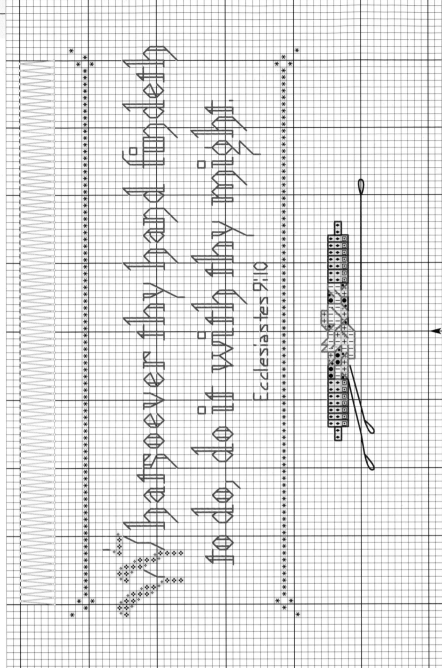

Whatsoever thy hand findeth

to do, do it with thy might.

Ecclesiastes 9:10

KEY

STRAIGHT STITCH

001	Kreinik silver blending filament – decorations on rear needlecase, thimble on stand, and stiletto (2X)
381	938 Deep coffee brown – boot string, kettle handle, narrow section of tape measure, leaves on tatting shuttle (2X); other objects
210	562 Medium seafoam – thread on bear
359	801 Medium coffee brown – kettle, bottom needlecase (2X)
1041	844 Deep beaver gray – pins and needles

SATIN STITCH

| 360 | 839 Beige brown – sauce pan handle |

FRENCH KNOT

| 1041 | 844 Deep beaver gray – pins |
| 381 | 938 Deep coffee brown – bear eyes and nose |

LAZY DAISY

002	000 White – tatting shuttle flower (2X)
895	223 Medium shell pink – tatting
893	224 Light shell pink – tatting shuttle flowers (2X)
979	312 Light navy – shoe lace
1041	844 Deep beaver gray – needle eyes

LADDER STITCH

TRELLIS STITCH

Stitch count: 169 high x 96 wide
Finished design sizes:
14-count fabric – 12⅛ x 6⅞ inches
11-count fabric – 15⅝ x 8¾ inches
18-count fabric – 9½ x 5⅜ inches

ANTIQUE NEEDLEWORK TOOLS

***ANTIQUE NEEDLEWORK TOOLS

As shown on page 183.

MATERIALS
FABRIC
14x9-inch piece of 32-count cream Irish linen
FLOSS
Cotton embroidery floss in colors listed in key; cream sewing thread
SUPPLIES
Needle; embroidery hoop; frame

INSTRUCTIONS
Tape or zigzag the edges of the Irish linen to prevent fraying. Find the center of the chart and the center of the Irish linen; begin stitching there.

Use two plies of floss for all cross-stitches over two threads of linen. Work straight stitches, satin stitches, French knots, lazy daisy stitches, and backstitches using one ply of floss unless otherwise specified in the key.

Refer to chart and carefully clip *horizontal* threads in *center* of ladder- and trellis-stitched areas. Carefully withdraw cut threads to where stitching starts and ends; tack threads to back. Use sewing thread to work ladder and trellis stitches, referring to diagrams, *left*.

Press the finished stitchery from the back and frame as desired.

***AS YE SEW

As shown on page 184.

MATERIALS
FABRIC
10x12-inch piece of 14-count white Aida cloth
FLOSS
Cotton embroidery floss in colors listed in key on page 190
SUPPLIES
Needle; embroidery hoop
Desired frame and mat

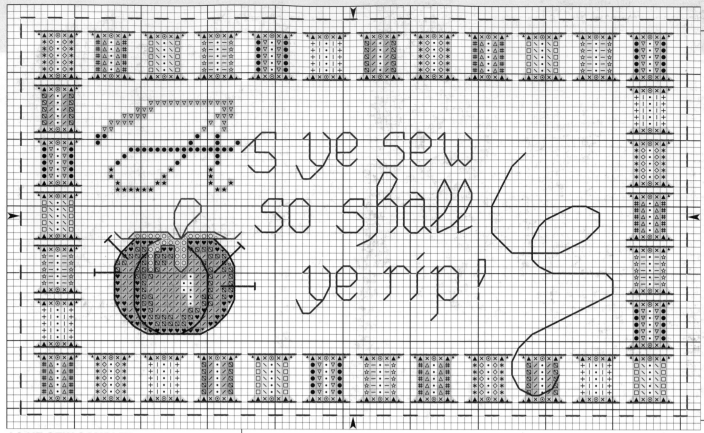

AS YE SEW SAMPLER

INSTRUCTIONS

Tape or zigzag edges of fabric to prevent fraying. Find center of chart and of fabric; begin stitching there.

Use three plies of floss to work cross-stitches. Work running stitches and straight stitches using two plies and backstitches using one ply unless otherwise specified in key. Press stitchery from back. Frame and mat.

★★★COLLECTOR'S CABINET

As shown on page 185.

MATERIALS

FABRIC
7x7-inch piece of 18-count ivory Aida cloth
FLOSS
Cotton embroidery floss in colors listed in key
SUPPLIES
Needle; embroidery hoop
Small collector's cabinet with 3½x3½-inch opening
3⅝x3⅝-inch piece each of heavy cardboard and polyester fleece
3¼x3¼-inch piece of ½-inch-deep piece of plastic foam; crafts glue

AS YE SEW

ANCHOR		DMC	
002	·	000	White
109	#	209	Medium lavender
342	△	211	Pale lavender
011	◨	350	Medium coral
010	◿	351	Light coral
295	+	726	Topaz
300	ı	745	Yellow
259	◩	772	Pale loden
177	★	792	Dark cornflower blue
176	●	793	Medium cornflower blue
175	▽	794	Light cornflower blue
013	♥	817	Deep coral
4146	⊙	950	Light rose beige
186	✳	959	Medium aqua
185	◇	964	Light aqua
266	▢	3347	Yellow green
260	○	3364	Light loden
060	☆	3688	Medium mauve
049	−	3689	Light mauve
1007	▲	3772	Dark cocoa
1008	⊠	3773	Medium rose beige

ANCHOR		DMC	
BACKSTITCH			
936	╱	632	Deep cocoa – tops and bottoms of spools
177	╱	792	Dark cornflower blue – saying (2X)
013	╱	817	Deep coral – thread in needle (2X)
681	╱	3051	Gray green – pincushion loop (2X); pincushion top
382	╱	3371	Black brown – pincushion
STRAIGHT STITCH			
382	╱	3371	Black brown – pins (2X)
RUNNING STITCH			
177	╱	792	Dark cornflower blue – border (2X)

Stitch count: 59 high x 99 wide
Finished design sizes:
18-count fabric – 3⅜ x 5½ inches
11-count fabric – 5⅜ x 9 inches
14-count fabric – 4¼ x 7⅛ inches

INSTRUCTIONS

Tape or zigzag the edges of the Aida fabric to prevent fraying. Find the center of the chart and the center of the Aida fabric; begin stitching there.

Use two plies of floss to work cross-stitches. Work backstitches, straight stitches, French knots, and lazy daisy stitches using one ply unless otherwise specified in the key.

Trim the stitched fabric to measure 5x5 inches, making sure the design is centered. Lightly glue the fleece to the cardboard. Center the fleece unit to the back of the stitched design. Pull the fabric edges to back of the cardboard; glue it in place.

Insert the plastic foam into the design area of the collector's cabinet and glue in place. Insert the finished design unit.

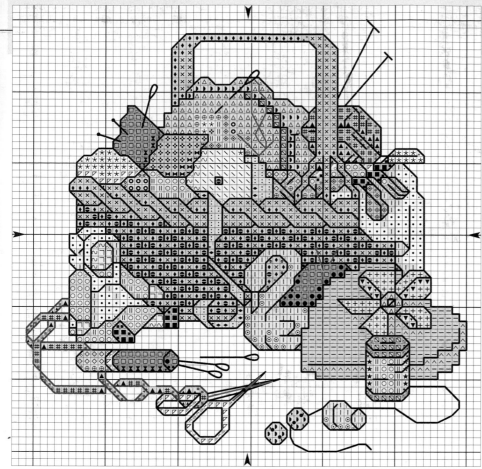

COLLECTOR'S CABINET

ANCHOR		DMC	
002	·	000	White
109	△	209	Medium lavender
342	−	211	Pale lavender
979	★	312	Navy
100	⋈	327	Antique violet
977	‖	334	Dark baby blue
118	#	340	Periwinkle
217	▼	367	Medium pistachio
214	+	368	Light pistachio
235	◉	414	Steel
398			415	Pearl gray
310	◆	434	Chestnut
1045	✕	436	Dark tan
1005	▢	498	Christmas red
098	✢	553	Violet
212	◕	561	Dark seafoam
206	◇	564	Light seafoam
088	◈	718	Plum
361	◩	738	Light tan
885	◨	739	Pale tan
302	▽	743	True yellow
301	⋆	744	Medium yellow
177	▲	792	Cornflower blue
359	◲	801	Coffee brown
045	●	814	Dark garnet
043	⊠	815	Medium garnet
209	⊕	912	Emerald
881	∼	945	Dark ivory
1010	▱	951	Medium ivory

ANCHOR		DMC	
144	◯	3325	True baby blue
382	■	3371	Black brown
068	◆	3687	True mauve
060	⫶	3688	Medium mauve
1018	◗	3726	True antique mauve
1016	△	3727	Light antique mauve

BACKSTITCH

979	╱	312	Navy – thread from spool
177	╱	792	Cornflower blue – ribbon tied to scissors (2X)
382	╱	3371	Black brown – top of spool (2X); all remaining stitches

STRAIGHT STITCH

002	╱	000	White – blades of scissors (2X); pins in swan pincushion
212	╱	561	Dark seafoam – floss on needle
382	╱	3371	Black brown – hoop clamp, knitting needles (2X); most pins and needles, blades of scissors

FRENCH KNOT

002	●	000	White – pins in swan pincushion
382	●	3371	Black brown – remaining pins, scissors, and buttons

LAZY DAISY

382	◊	3371	Black brown – needles

Stitch count: 60 high x 61 wide

Finished design sizes:
14-count fabric – 4⅜ x 4⅜ inches
18-count fabric – 3⅜ x 3⅜ inches
11-count fabric – 5½ x 5⅝ inches

COLLECTOR'S CABINET

SOURCES/SUPPLIERS

Many of the materials and items used in this book are available at craft and needlework stores. For more information, write or call the manufacturers below.

Chapter One
Flies and Lures: Glass paperweight kit—The Yarn Tree, P.O. Box 724, Ames, IA 50010, 515/232-3121.

Chapter Four
Cool Penguin and Polar Bear: Plastic cup holders—Daniel Enterprises, P.O. Box 1105, Laurinburg, NC 28352.

Chapter Six
Victorian Tapestry: Silk gauze—Kreinik Manufacturing, 800/537-2166.

Chapter Seven
Halloween Hauntings: Beading wire, beads, fish hook earrings—Darice, Inc., 2160 Drake Rd., Strongville, OH 44136.

Chapter Nine
Sew A Fine Seam: Black wooden box —Just Nan, 2602 E. 74th Place, Tulsa, OK 74136, 918/494-0361; Collector's Cabinet—Sudberry House, Box 895, Old Lyme, CT 06371, 800/243-2607.

FABRICS
Charles Craft, P.O. Box 1049, Laurinberg, NC 28353, 800/277-0980; Wichelt Imports, Inc., R.R. 1, Stoddard, WI 54658; Zweigart, 2 Riverview Dr., Somerset, NJ 08873-1139, 908/271-1949.

PERFORATED PLASTIC
Darice, Inc., 2160 Drake Rd., Strongville, OH 44136.

THREADS
Anchor, Consumer Sevice Dept., P.O. Box 27067, Greenville, SC 29616; DMC, Port Kearney Bldg. 10, South Kearney, NJ 07032-0650; Kreinik Manufacturing, 800/537-2166.

TRIMS AND BEADS
Cord: Heritage Trimming, Parade Hill Road, Barnstead, NH 03218, 603/435-6795; Piping: Hollywood Trims, 42005 Cook Street, Suite 106, Palm Desert, CA 92260, 619/773-1027; Ribbon: C.M. Offray & Sons, Inc., Route 24, Box 601, Chester, NJ 07930-0601; Seed beads: Mill Hill beads, 800/447-1332.

Flowers: Boesen the Florist, 3801 Ingersoll, Des Moines, IA 50312. Framing: Dot's Frame Shop, 4223 Fleur Drive, Des Moines, IA 50321.

DESIGNERS

Many of the wonderful designs in this book were created by designers on the Cross Stitch & Country Crafts staff. In addition, we thank the following designers:

INDEX